Enjoying Maine

Other books by Bill Caldwell

Maine Magic, 1979

Islands of Maine, 1981

Rivers of Fortune, 1983

BILL CALDWELL

Enjoying Maine

LIVELY STORIES ABOUT PEOPLE & PLACES

FROM THE SEACOAST TO THE NORTH COUNTRY,

TO THE MOUNTAINS, FROM FISHERMEN TO LOGGERS,

AS ENJOYED BY MAINE'S FAVORITE

NEWSPAPER COLUMNIST

Guy Gannett Publishing Co.

 PORTLAND / MAINE

Printed by Gannett Graphics, Augusta, Maine

First Printing June 1977
Second Printing December 1977
Third Printing October 1978
Fourth Printing September 1983

Library of Congress Number 77-78126

ISBN 0-930096-50-9

To my wife Barbara and our children John and Susan

for deciding that Maine was the place to live;

and to Jean Gannett Hawley,

publisher of Guy Gannett Publishing Co.,

and my valued friend, who suggested this book;

and to the editors of the Portland Press Herald

and the Maine Sunday Telegram during the years

these columns were written — Bob Beith, Ernie Chard, Steve Riley

and John K. Murphy. They gave me the freedom to roam and

write about Enjoying Maine.

CONTENTS

DRAWINGS BY KIM MURPHY

The short columns originally appeared in the Portland Press Herald. The longer pieces ran in the Maine Sunday Telegram. Drawings are by my friend and newsroom colleague Kimberly Clifford Murphy.

Most pictures are from the files of Guy Gannett Publishing Co. They were taken mostly by my photographer colleagues on the Press Herald and Sunday Telegram. My special thanks go to Don Johnson, Tom Jones and Alice Brown with whom I enjoyed so many Maine assignments on which so many of these pictures were made by them. A few pictures originated outside the Gannett newspapers photographers. Ivan Flye of Newcastle made the picture of Adelaide Byers. Vern Warren made the action shot of Darrell Lamb harpooning a tuna. Roger P. Jordan made the portrait of Chief Justice Williamson. The picture of Victory Chimes with Mrs. Guild at the helm supplied by Mrs. Guild. A few pictures were made by Bill and John Caldwell; a few are from the Inland Fish and Game Department. The picture of my hometown of Damariscotta is by Richard Sturges, my friend and neighbor. Jake Day's sketches illustrate the story we did together on the north woods wardens.

Guy Fleming, who lives nearby at Alna, Maine, designed the book; drew the maps which are the endpapers; and designed the book jacket.

Enjoying Maine

I /

Small Town Living
in Maine

W<small>E HAD NEVER LIVED</small> in a small town until 1964 when we came to Damariscotta, Maine. Population was 1,000—give or take a few, depending on whether there were births or deaths in our hospital last night. Now we're up to about 1,400 people. In summer that number grows to almost 5,000 in the region.

The core of our town is Main street, about 200 yards long; and the people you meet there year-round.

Malcolm Hunter, a hulk of a man with a gentle, patient voice, has been First Selectman for years. He used to drive a bakery truck. Now he is manager of the Parts at Bob Strong's garage.

Taking a drive with Malcolm is like riding with an encyclopedia of Lincoln County. As you pass each house on any country road, Malcolm can tell you who lives inside, what they do and all about the family.

Malcolm's son is a Rhodes Scholar at Oxford, England. A big strapping athlete, he is perhaps the first environmentalist from the University of Maine to be named a Rhodes Scholar. His specialty? The dialects of song birds. This son of Damariscotta's First Selectman travels throughout Europe, Africa and Asia tracking down the changing dialects of the same strain of song birds.

Chester Rice is at this writing, our Second Selectman. Thin and *coming close to 40 now, Chester is in the road business. He is a hometown boy who stayed and has made good. His big fleet of gravel trucks and heavy road equipment gets bigger every year.*

But the road man who puts sand on our street is Oliver Wendell Holmes. That name looks good on the door of his dump trucks.

The post office is the hub of town. This is where we meet mornings to get the mail and afternoons to catch the 4 p.m. collection. Jake Day, the most loved painter in town, hangs a few of his paintings here. Not many post offices have original art on their walls. Al Slocum is the oldest hand beyond the counter. Al used to command destroyers in World War II. Dig a little and you find spies, pilots, infantrymen and paratroopers, submarine men and chopper pilots disguised as lobstermen, furnace men, merchants in Damariscotta.

We've got two drugstores. Perley Waltz and Winty Jacobs run the store by the post office. What with its soda fountain and a massive array of stock from almonds to zippers, you have to turn sideways to get through the aisle to the prescription counter at the back. Briggs' Pharmacy is bigger and brighter, but less crowded. Briggsy is the smallest guy on Main Street, physically, but he was a basketball star at Lincoln Academy and is still playing. The Greyhound buses stop at Briggs' so you can see who is leaving town from here. Mostly, the passengers are birdwatchers—the people who come to the Audubon camp down the peninsula on Hog Island.

I think Damariscotta may have been the only town with three banks and one full-time policeman. George Hutchings is our Chief. His young daughter joins the force when summer traffic is heavy on Main Street. She stopped it cold for a bit when she first directed traffic in a mini skirt. George's wife is often working as matron in the County jail 10 miles down the road in Wiscasset. Our town doesn't pay much to its Chief, but he likes the job and stretches the pay by putting others in the family to work in law enforcement. We added a full time lady policeman, Mary Genthner, who packs a gun and is a graduate of the Maine Police Academy.

In town, business is on a first name basis. In Maine, almost

*everybody uses first names. It is a good practice. To see how good,
figure how it might change relationships in cities if you knew
everybody with whom you did business, by their first name.*

*Two big grocery stores, a fine town library, three clothing stores,
two gift shops, a very good bookstore, three hardware stores, a state
liquor store, barber and beauty shops, a department store with
its spin-off bargain basement, plus a passel of business offices of
insurancemen, lawyers, oil dealers, doctors and dentists and real
estate agents make up Main Street.*

*"Down street" is the place to go for a visit anytime you want a
bit of company or news. Shopping is more than buying stuff. It is
visiting.*

*We have a movie house, upstairs, over the Yellowfront grocery
in the old Opera House. The walls are covered still with silk
damask and the stage is cavernous. We have movies on Friday,
Saturday and Sunday nights. Sometimes there are 50 people,
sometimes 15; and the noisy kids night is Saturday.*

*On a storming night our first winter, Barbara and I bundled up
and walked through a snowstorm to the movie house, a quarter
mile away. We bought two tickets for, I think, 75 cents each from
Don Burnham and went into our seats in the almost empty theater
and sat and sat. Then Don came in and told the five of us in the
audience that because of small attendance the show would be
cancelled. Then Don, whom we barely knew, took Barbara and
me aside: "Sorry to spoil your night out" he said, refunding our
money, "But I've got some good hard cider and some new cards
in the kitchen. So the night won't be a waste for you, come back
and drink a little, play a little cards." Did you ever go to a movie
house like that?*

*This winter our night time policeman, Charlie Bowers, who
doubles with a daytime job stocking grocery store shelves, showed
me what living in a small town means even when you are asleep at
2 a.m. A newspaper truck was delivering two of the very heavy
page make-up tables that were used in our composing room before
we went electronic. I was sentimental about the old composing
room and these tables were to be dropped off on Main Street with*

a few hundred copies of the morning Press Herald. I did not know the delivery truck got to town about 2 a.m. I did not know the tables weighed 250 pounds; and once dumped off the truck—how to lift them up again?

Well, night policeman Charlie Bowers, was on the scene. When he heard that the tables were for Bill, he fetched his pick-up. The newspaper driver and Charlie then slid the tables from truck to pick-up. At six in the morning after he was relieved from duty, Charlie drove the 250 pound tables down to my place and he helped me stow them in the garage. "Keep your money" said Charlie, when I tried to give him something.

Dana worked in Waltz's drugstore for years. Everybody in town knew and liked Dana. She went to California. Out there she got very sick with cancer and lonely. So Winty and Perley put a jar on the counter at the drugstore labeled "To bring Dana home". Soon there was money enough in it to buy Dana a round trip air ticket from California to Maine. The day she arrived, a big home-made banner spanned Main Street. Everybody coming to town had to see it. The banner said "Welcome Home, Dana. Glad to see you." I ran a couple of paragraphs about Dana in a column, before she came home, told about her cancer and gave her address in the California hospital. Out in California, postmen carried three big bags of mail, all for Dana, all from her small town Maine friends. In California, they could not believe that a small town girl who worked in a Damariscotta drug store could get more mail than any celebrity who had ever been a patient in that big city hospital in California. Dana got better.

Every store on Main street closes when an old timer dies and there is a funeral or memorial service for him or her. For a couple of hours, the town shuts down. Store owners and helpers go to service, come back and open up. Often they toll the church bells.

If the good in a small town warms your heart, then the bad damn near breaks it. Both happen right under your nose, to and by people you know. A doctor got shot in the gut in his Main Street office by a kid trying to get drugs. We have teenagers killed in accidents where booze and speed are involved. We get bullies. We get fights and assaults and some damn stupid burglaries. *There is more crime than ever. And we can't get a handle on it any better than the big cities can.*

The difference is in knowing the people. Small town law breakers can be bad. But there is seldom a vicious killer. Most small town living is good, very good indeed. But it is not any paradise, without crime. Nor is small town Maine a cheap place to live, especially along the coast. Property taxes in small coastal towns—and inland by the lakes and ski mountains—are skyrocketing. Land values have tripled between 1967 and 1977 and the State has increased many small town taxes by 25-30 percent yearly. You get few bargains in the stores. Where you can save is on frills, entertainment, clothes, tips and keeping up with the Joneses. But for middle income living, Maine is probably more expensive than most states.

Is it worth it? Yes, a thousand times yes. Not only is there so much beauty in Maine, but there is a sense of values, a give and take among people, a respect between people and local government that most of America has lost.

In small town Maine, we are holding on tight.

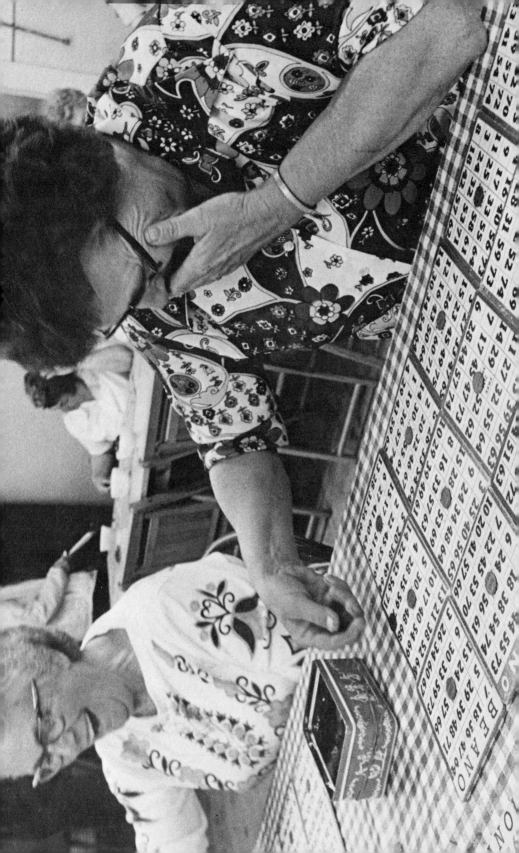

SMILE, WHEN YOUR SEPTIC TANK BACKS UP

DAMARISCOTTA — If you can smile when your septic tank backs up, that is proof positive you are enjoying life in Maine.

Ours backed up last week. Now that the panic is past, we are smiling—thanks to expert aid from Steve Prentice, Chester Rice, Louis French and Keith Burns. When a septic tank is backing up on you in Maine, you need plenty of group action fast to handle the emergency.

Our warning was a ghostly gurgling in the kitchen sinks. I inspected them. No sign of any back-up. But a weird wailing came up the pipes, as though a soul in torture below was trying to escape from the bowels of the earth.

The sound stopped. I went back to reading a book.

Then came a shout for help from my wife. I ran to her aid and found her in a horror-struck state, glaring at noisome evidence that the bowels of the earth were indeed in an uproar.

The sight of a septic tank backing up through toilets and tubs is unnerving. The primeval ooze just keeps slowly flooding up and over, oozing between cracks and over doorjambs, through ceilings, across rooms, down passages. The Good Earth seems to be wreaking revenge on the flush toilets, washing machines, showers, dishwashers and bathtubs.

It is a panic-making sight for a man with only his bare hands and an old-fashioned plunger with which to fight back the revenge of Mother Earth.

We summon help by phone. Steve Prentice, our favorite plumber and boating friend, arrives with a 50 foot snake.

"You need digging out, Bill," he says.

So we call another friend. Chester Rice, our selectman, arrives with a backhoe to dig up the lawn and uncover our septic tank. And right behind Chester's backhoe comes Louis French's septic tank truck and vacuum pump, with expert Keith Burns at the wheel.

They pump a fulsome 750 gallons of the "stuff" and haul it off.

Carrying that "stuff" off these days costs plenty. But when I complain to Louis French, he answers, "Now that the politicians are about through campaigning, it's hard to find use for the stuff."

State and federal bureaucrats are deep into the "stuff." They even have a language for it. They call it "septage."

The dictionaries don't have such a word. They call it "sewage." Louis French calls it "the honey pot." I call it "that stuff." But the bureaucrats call it "septage." And they are filling books with septage regulations.

Maine towns must provide septage disposal areas and state officials must license them. Officials say a good field will absorb 62,500 gallons of the potent stuff per acre per year. But the average Maine field licensed by DEP can take only half that amount — the waste of 180 families.

Twelve Maine towns are facing possible prosecution from the attorney general because they have not got septage dump fields licensed by the state.

To haul this stuff around by truck, you also must get a special state license, which costs you $50 and is colored yellow.

First laws about "the stuff" went on the books in 1926, the end result of the Herbert Hoover Commission on this baffling problem of what to do with that unmentionable stuff.

In 1975 Maine got a fine new set of laws, and regulations and bureaucrats. One result is that "the stuff" is highly concentrated in "septage." And that stuff is so potent, no one yet knows what to do with it after it is carried from a licensed septic tank to a licensed septage disposal field.

Federal grants are coming into Maine to see if it can be turned into cattle feed or field dressings or put on the back of federal postage stamps which will not stick.

"They ought to stockpile it for the next election," says the friend who carted off my septage.

Voting is More Fun if You're a Mainer

DAMARISCOTTA — In my town, it's easy to tell when they're politicking.

If the fire engines are parked outside on a weekday, you can be pretty sure they're voting inside.

We vote in the volunteer firehouse. On the spot where Engine Number 1 usually stands, Vera, Shirley, Polly, Harry, John and Erma will set up a card table. When we come to vote, most people take a minute to visit round the table. The officials-for-a-day are neighbors. They check off our names from the registration list. Mostly it's on a first name basis. "Barbara was in an hour ago. Said you'd be along. And Charlie is looking for you, about going hunting up north."

We take a paper ballot, go behind the red, white and blue curtain (where extra fire hose usually sits), and there we tell what we think as to who ought to be president of the United States, senator, congressman. Who ought to go to the state legislature or be our county sheriff. We lick our pencil again and mark what we feel about the bottle bill. And after solving world problems, we drop the paper into a slot that Anna opens up for us and then go looking for Charlie about that hunting trip up north.

Voting in Maine is fun. It is neighborly. It is seeing people, and swapping news, as well as being a citizen, choosing a president.

Maybe these are reasons why Maine is likely to vote more than most places.

Punching anonymous machines, identifying yourself to strangers and standing in line with people who don't talk to you, is no fun. So in big cities the vote is light.

Lorraine Fleury, one of the ablest, loveliest people in state government, has been running the election division for many years — no matter who is secretary of state. And Lorraine says that only 35 precincts in Maine have electronic voting devices or mechanical voting machines.

Maine voters mark paper ballots with pen or pencil in Maine's 611 other polling places — fire houses, school gyms, and so forth. You don't rig elections when all the neighbors are watching.

Maine had 628,440 registered voters when I talked to Lorraine. Of them 226,680 were Republicans, 224,753 were Democrats and 177,007 were Independents.

The blank ballots go to the towns mostly by mail, in packages of 75 ballots to a "batch." Precisely 633,697 paper ballots had been distributed by last Election day. To offset spoilage or last-minute registrations, 75 paper ballots are sent for every 50 registered voters.

On election night, the news media flash out election results. But none are official until Lorraine Fleury has tabulated and typed the figures, given them to the governor and council and they have certified them as true. That need not happen till Thanksgiving.

THAT NIGHT THE LIGHTS WENT OUT

DAMARISCOTTA — One night in winter the church spotlights failed. Darkness fell on the steeple of the Damariscotta Baptist Church.

Homecoming men sorely missed one of the loveliest sights of Maine — church steeples in their town pointing to the stars in heaven, gleaming white, illuminated in the early dark of winter nights. One such man wrote a sorrowful letter to his home town weekly, The Lincoln County News, suggesting that people from miles around who missed the lovely illuminated steeple would be eager to help turn on the lights again — if their help were merely asked.

The next issue of the paper carried a reply from the pastor of the Baptist church, John Holt. He told in such fine fashion the saga of how the lights went out on the Baptist church, that I'd like to share excerpts with you.

For now, thanks to the Rev. Holt, we see that even ordained ministers of the church working on the Lord's mansion, can be overcome and bedeviled by a light bulb. Even a Baptist preacher on top of a church roof admits he feels like taking a 50-pound hammer and smashing every light fixture in range.

Here are excerpts from Mr. Holt's letter.

"The saga of the Baptist church lights," wrote the Rev. Holt in the Lincoln County News, "is as human as the person who waits until the last day to get his car inspected and discovers only then that all the tires are bald, there are three holes in the muffler, there isn't enough gas in the tank to get to a garage, and it is Sunday, anyway, and closed . . .

"It was last Spring," wrote Pastor Holt, "when the first of the 500-watt roof lights illuminating the steeple expired. Its passing was duly reported to the church trustees at their next meeting. In April and May, the four porch lights, the spotlight on the dead elm, and another 500-watt spotlight on the roof died their programmed deaths. And these passings were duly noted at the June trustees meeting. And then came summer. You know summers. The lack of lights was not a pressing matter.

"Finally in the Fall, a deacon brought his 40-foot ladder and I climbed to the roof. The roof seems a lot closer to the ground when you are on the ground. With one hand clutching a rope which we had strung out from a peephole in the clock face (thereby stopping the town clock), I attempted with my free hand to remove the lamp. Without success. So the two of us climbed to the ridge of the roof and managed to rip the entire light assembly off the roof and smash the bulb in the process. At that moment I would have relished smashing every damn light with a 50-pound hammer.

"At the last trustees meeting, I reported all these events. We concluded a new, more easily serviced lighting system was called for. Naturally such systems must be ordered special. Naturally. That is where things stand now.

"Soliciting your prayers for the church lights, I am, Sincerely yours, JOHN HOLT, Pastor Damariscotta Baptist Church."

P.S. Guess what? The other night, half the weather vane blew off in one of those gale force winds. Got any suggestions?

As of May 20, 1977 the lights went on again.

How about some Haddock Pancakes?

NEWCASTLE — Fresh haddock can make a fine pancake.

I learned this at my church supper, on Shrove Tuesday.

Pancakes are the traditional dish for Shrove Tuesday. But at my church, we had fish chowder—some of the finest fish chowder ever made. "Wicked good" was the verdict of the minister and vestry.

After I had eaten two bowls so thick with fish that the chowder was solid I asked the fisherman who had prepared it for the recipe. Here is what he told me:

"Start by trying out five pounds of salt pork, nicely diced. You

gotta let that pork simmer slow. The fat will heat off, so after 30 minutes you'll have a fine batch of liquid. Take out the browned pork scraps and set 'em aside.

"Now, get the potatoes all cut to size you want. I use 50 pounds of potatoes. And I use 15 pounds of onions, cut up. And I put them in to simmer together in that pork fat.

"Now we come to the fish. You gotta start with good fish. I get 50 pounds of fresh haddock, right off the boat. Some like to cook the fish heads, tails and all. But for looks, I trim out the head and tail. Then be sly with the water. Don't drown those lovelies. Simmer till the skin peels off and then lift the flesh off the bones. Gently, gently. Don't let the flesh boil soft or it will break.

"Now your potatoes and onions are done. Add the stock, all the fat from the salt pork to the fish. Looks like butter, rises to the top, yellow globules. No need for butter when you use this pork fat. Then the fresh whole milk goes in, and a case of evaporated milk, to thicken it. Simmer slow, and watch close so it doesn't heat too hot and break up that fish too much.

"Then right at the last, when nobody is near, sneak in a splash of sherry . . . Make plenty. Eat on it a couple of days. By day three, it is at the peak . . But at a supper like this, there will be none left."

How About Some Haddock Pancakes? / 17

Well, that chowder, and the hot biscuits with it and then the three dozen assorted pies, was the best batch of Shrove Tuesday pancakes ever served.

Maybe fishermen and sailors need to bend a few religious traditions to suit the ways of the ocean.

I discovered the old seaman's version of the 23rd Psalm right after the church supper. It goes like this:

"The Lord is my Pilot; I shall not drift.

He lights me across the dark waters.

He steers me through the deep channels.

He keeps my log. He guides me by the Star of Holiness for His Name's sake.

As I sail through the storms and tempests of life, I will dread no danger; for You are near me; Your love and care shelter me.

You prepare a haven before me in the Homeland of Eternity; You quieten the waves with oil; my ship rides calmly.

Surely sunlight and starlight shall be with me wherever I sail, and at the end of my voyaging I shall rest in the port of my God."

This version of "The Lord is my Shepherd; I shall not want" was found written on a sheet of paper pinned to a prayer book. That prayer book was found when a great-aunt died a few years ago. She had close ties to seagoing men of long ago. Some say this version of the famous psalm was used quite a lot by 19th century seamen. Others think that great-aunt may have written it herself for the seagoing man she loved.

SOMETHING SPECIAL DIES WITH MABELLE

DAMARISCOTTA — Mabelle isn't selling the Sunday papers anymore. With Mabelle gone from the little store on the bridge over the Damariscotta River, somebody very special and somebody much loved is missing from Sundays in this part of Maine.

Mabelle Cotter Alexander Sherman died Jan. 6, 1977. She took away with her a precious chapter of Maine life and history. She would have been 90 in March, her son told me. That was hard to believe, for Mabelle, spry, blue-eyed, smiling, cheery and small, but staunchly independent to the last, was the very symbol of a lot of Maine to me.

She stood for reliability, permanence, continuity. I remember one early Sunday morning years ago, Mabelle told me, "My father, George Cotter, began handling Sunday papers on this spot in 1898 . . . As a young girl, I rode on father's horse and wagon to the depot in Newcastle to pick up the Sunday papers. They came on the 10:30 train. The Boston Post, the Boston Herald, the Boston Globe and the Boston American. Price was six cents, then."

Something Special Dies with Mabelle / 19

That's what I mean about Mabelle standing for permanence, continuity . . . . Those papers she fetched by horse and wagon 79 years ago carried the news that the battleship Maine was blown up in Havana Harbor, Feb. 15, 1898; that Admiral Dewey sank the Spanish fleet in Manila Bay, May 1, 1898; that Teddy Roosevelt led the Rough Riders charging up San Juan Hill on July 1 of the year Mabelle started selling papers. And when she sold her last Sunday paper, its news was about Carter's coming inauguration.

Mabelle was part of the lifeblood of Maine. More than 90 years ago, Mabelle's father, George L. Cotter, was running Cotter's Meat and Grocery store on the same spot where Mabelle was selling the Sunday Telegram.

But Mabelle's roots in Maine go back much farther. From a cove close to Mabelle's paper store, Mabelle's grandfather, Capt. Simon Cotter, launched his clipper ship Ocean Herald in 1853.

An oil painting of that 2,135 ton ship, hangs over the fireplace in the Damariscotta library today. Mabelle's grandmother was Sally Coffin Howe, and Sally's father, Col. Joel Howe, commanded a Massachusetts regiment in the War of 1812, then came to settle in Damariscotta before Maine became a state.

Early many a Sunday morning, Mabelle would talk to me about the early days, her eyes sparkling with fun and laughter as she remembered.

"My father taught me to be an expert butcher. Guess I was the first woman meat cutter anybody saw hereabouts. He'd put a side of beef on the block, and I would cut it into quarters. Best steak 40 cents; two pounds of hamburger 20 cents."

The year Lindbergh flew the Atlantic the Cotters took on selling the Sunday Telegram. "Father had a Model T Ford by then, and I'd ride with him delivering papers to South Bristol and Pemaquid." George Cotter died in 1929. Ever since, Mabelle has handled the Sunday papers.

When Mabelle was past 80, she'd be up soon after 4 a.m. every Sunday. By 5 a.m. she and her son Jimmy Alexander were down in the tiny store by the river, getting as many as 1,000 papers from Portland, Boston, New York ready for customers. From before daybreak till winter sunset, Mabelle had a smile with a twinkle and a bit of news to swap with every customer. Grief, sadness, sickness never took away that smile. Her lovely stubborn Maine independence would never let her quit.

Around Christmas Mabelle slipped, fell, broke a hip. Her son told me she wanted still to fend for herself, to run her own home and her own Sunday paper store. The day she was to go instead to a nursing home was the day Mabelle decided to die. With her she has taken a wonderful piece of Maine. She is mourned. She is missed. And Sunday without Mabelle lacks somebody wonderful.

DON'T PATRONIZE THE SMALL TOWNS

DAMARISCOTTA — I live in a small Maine town. And I am sick of being patronized. I wish to heaven Washington officials, Augusta planners, the New York Times, CBS, Harpers, Newsweek and all the rest would quit acting so doggone patronizing to Maine's small towns.

There is nothing 'quaint' about us. Small towns are the commonest kind of towns we've got in Maine. In the State of Maine there are 495 municipalities of one kind or another. And 454 of them are small towns, with populations of 5,000 and under. In fact, 412 out of the 498 towns in Maine have fewer than 2,500 people.

The smallest towns in Maine are the oldest. And the prettiest. And maybe the happiest. They have the longest lived people and the tightest knit families.

Maine is "small town," and thank God for that. Why? Because in this woebegone welfare world, there is still a human place in small town Maine where people need each other. A man needs a neighbor, a good neighbor. And so a man acts like a good neighbor, to get a good neighbor.

The man upstream from you doesn't foul your drinking water. The man on the mooring nearby watches out for your boat as well as his own. If a fellow's wife dies — or even if she only runs away — there are baked beans and a pie and a stew waiting on the back steps or kitchen table. If a house burns down, the neighbors pitch in to rebuild and the local church raises money. If a lobsterman's traps are wiped out in a storm or a draggerman's nets are ripped, his competition will lend him their gear.

That's a sense of values, a way of living. It cannot do everything that a government agency can do in the way of money. But it does wonders no agency can.

The real danger to Maine may be coming from well intentioned government agencies. They are breeding faster than starfish.

The fastest growing business in Maine for the past 10 years has been — government. More people are added to more state, municipal, local and federal payrolls than to any business in the state. Result? Soaring budgets and soaring taxes on income, property, cigarettes, liquor, gas and almost everything you buy.

For example, as I am writing, a State House official has brought me a seven page long list of Maine towns which will be hit with a 25 per cent increase in taxes this week to pay for increased education costs, as assessed on them by the State.

But the revolt in the small towns is not against increased taxes imposed from outside as much as it is against unwanted, uninformed, unproductive outside interference in their own self-government. The small towns are bitter at the way state and federal bureaucracies dictate to them how they should run their towns.

Look at the results of a survey of small town Maine opinion, polled along the coast of Maine. The Social Science Research Institute of the University of Maine made the survey. The results came as a shock to planners.

By a walloping margin of 79 percent to 13 percent, midcoast residents say they think that oil refineries and nuclear power plants will bring more needed jobs. They favor refineries and nuclear power plants along the coast, believing they can be made so they do not damage the environment.

These same midcoast residents say they are satisfied with the present day levels of vacation homes and tourism. While they support oil refineries and nuclear power developments, they do not want more growth in summer residents and vacationers.

Most Maine Coast residents think their local zoning codes and plumbing codes and building codes are adequate right now. And that the codes are fairly and well enforced by local town officials today. (Another blow for the planners who'd like to do that work.)

Worst blow to the state planners was this: Midcoast residents felt strongly that local government and not state or federal or regional government should be in charge of future planning.

More than 70 per cent want planning, especially close to the water. They want more public access to the coast. A large percentage favors a major new national park along the Maine coast, similar to Acadia. But the opinion loud and clear is "State planners stay away. We will do our own local planning!"

These coastal towns have been busy places for longer than there has been a United States of America, for far longer than there has been a State of Maine. They are among the oldest settlements in the nation. And they are still among the most beautiful.

Planners might ask why this is so. Has their beauty endured 200 and 300 years because these small towns knew how to preserve it? In a gruff, effective way, they revered their town, they loved their harbor; and they kept both beautiful for over 200 years. Now others want to tell them how to behave. How to "plan."

Planning is bred in the bones of most countrymen, most Maine coast fishermen. You can't farm and you can't fish and you can't raise a family or run a small town unless you plan pretty darn well. But it's never been done with bureaucrats and million dollar budgets. Opinion polls show an overwhelming majority of coastal residents want wise land use—planning as the survey calls it. But they want it done at the local level, by men and women they elect, whom they know, and who know the town and the people they are planning for. They want local knowledge, preferably a few generations of it.

Outside planners speak of the Damariscotta River, on which I live, as untouched, unspoiled, still the same river it was when Indians rode it in canoes. At a special meeting, these planners from a federal office made passionate speeches on that topic.

Some oldtimers near me smiled at that. They sent me copies of the old village Herald. I quote from Nov. 1877, an item in the paper which reads: "Within the last month, 16 vessels have cleared this port (of Damariscotta) for St. John, carrying 1,200,000 bricks valued at $6,000. This is largely due to the efforts of E. H. Glidden. Business at this port is on the increase."

May was the month of brick making along the Damariscotta. Clay was mixed with water in a hopper and loam was added in small amounts to prevent the bricks from cracking. The mixture was stirred by a horse harnessed to a large sweep arm arrangement. The men worked barefooted in the mud clay. The brick ovens or kilns were about 14 feet high. Large iron doors opened to the furnaces. Cord wood was fed night and day to keep the fires burning. Each kiln needed 150 to 200 cords. The average pay for working 14 to 16 hours a day, and including five meals daily at the cook house was $40.00 a month.

Then in May 1890, the village Herald carried this item: "An estimate of the brick making business on the Damariscotta River for the present season indicates that 1,100,000 bricks will be manufactured giving employment to 200 men and a market for 5,000 cords of wood and that 180 vessels will be required for their transportation."

Today, the planners would put a stop to any business like that before it started. "Ruin the river!" they'd say. Well, it didn't. The river is beautiful. And man is short-lived. And planners should read more history.

Here's to the Sale Ladies

NEWCASTLE — This is a column of praise for ladies who run rummage sales in Maine towns.

I never knew much about them until now. To tell the truth this man has been afraid to set foot inside a rummage sale, a fear many men in Maine share.

Rummage sales are scary to a man because they are clearly woman's special territory. In years past, I have hovered on the outskirts with other frightened men, waiting for wives to emerge from the fray.

But last week I got up courage and went into the basement of the Town hall, where ladies of the Miles Memorial Hospital League stage their yearly rummage sale.

I had a wonderful time. I laughed amid hundreds of ladies of all ages, sizes and shapes trying on coats, hats, etc. I learned to reach farther and faster than the competition at the racks and tables.

In the heat of the fray this man, who normally hates to shop, turned into the big spender. Proudly I hauled my loot home and spread it in the kitchen for my wife to admire — my proof that men make magnificent shoppers.

I splurged $11.25 cents and my trophies include a worn wooden garden chair, a long handled pitchfork, a 10 gallon gasoline drum (empty) and an iron wedge for splitting wood, all for outdoor work. For the indoor man, included in the $11.25 splurge, I got four gaudy sport shirts I would never dare to buy new but could not resist at 25 cents each; three pairs of Bermuda shorts, fine stuff with fancy labels, donated by summer folk; an 86 year old history of a Maine town I do not know; a huge but slightly cracked soup tureen and a chinese ginger jar.

But my prize piece of Maine rummage is a white velvet dinner jacket piped in gold and lined with silk, which I think a visiting Liberace left behind as revenge.

Mabel Gay, treasurer, says this rummage sale will earn more than $5,000. As it does every year, this money will help buy needed new equipment for Damariscotta's Miles Hospital. This year it will finance an $8,000 fetal monitor.

Dottie Billings, who recalls the first rummage sale raised just $500, says scores of thousands of dollars of vital medical improvements have been purchased with rummage money.

People in the region filled four barns with donations for the hospital rummage this year. Hilaire LeBon of Pemaquid Harbor says, "I guess we must have 10,000 pieces of clothing, from infants shirts to cocktail dresses, from ski boots to bikinis — plus beds, TV sets, costume jewelry. Name anything from attic to cellar and out to the woodshed, and we've got it somewhere."

Nancy Zahn, chairman, says the toughest work is sorting, sizing and folding clothes. "Perk Day went home to cook dinner so tired that she put her chicken in to heat and poured chocolate pudding over it, thinking it was gravy."

But the rummage sale does more good than raising money to benefit the Damariscotta hospital. Among the thousand or so women who come to buy, there are probably hundreds who count heavily on buying essentials here.

At the checkout, I saw young mothers who'd bought $100 worth of needed winter clothing for youngsters, and paid about $10. Some families depend on this sale to stock up on winter blankets, boots, coats, getting good quality and wide choice at very low prices — but not as charity or handouts from a welfare agency.

I'd like to get those high-domed economists and Washington experts out of their government bureaucracies and take them to see what happens at rummage sales in Maine basements.

The rummage ladies would show the bureaucrats how to beat inflation, with wool blankets and winter coats at one or two dollars; how to eliminate throw-away waste by recycling, how to help families to buy essentials well and cheaply; and how to help equip a hospital with an $8,000 fetal monitor. And above all, how Maine communities do all this without any federal grant, without putting people on a government payroll and without any new law on the books.

CURLING, THE BELFAST CRAZE

BELFAST — They are curling tonight in Belfast, Maine. In fact, they go curling in Belfast morning, noon, night and weekends, given the chance. This town of 6,000 souls can brag that about 200 of them are lost to curling.

"What is curling?" you may ask, for good reason.

Hardly anybody in their right mind in Maine has played the game. But in Belfast, they are crazy about curling. They have built the biggest and best curling club in Maine. (There is only one other, at Presque Isle, where they curl in a saner, more moderate way.)

We got exposed to Belfast curling all because of the southern charm of a persuasive, bearded surgeon-sailor in that town. He invited us (my wife Barbara was included in this bisexual sport) to Belfast Curling Club's "Ben Ames Williams Bonspiel."

Bonspiel is a code word for a curling party which lasts three days

and nights. For formality's sake it is called a curling competition. In February over 40 of the foremost curlers from Canada's Maritime Provinces drove down to hurl the stone and wield the broom and bend the elbow.

In Canada, curling is the top winter sport. More school kids curl than play basketball. Canadians start curling at eight years old and keep on curling till 88.

The Canadian men and women seemed, to this overseer, to outclass and outlast the Belfast crowd at all three pastimes, hurling, sweeping, bending.

Once the Belfast motel where the Canadian curlers stay — but only once — allowed other guests at the same time the Canadian curlers were there for the Ben Ames Williams Bonspiel. No longer.

Now during Belfast's Bonspiel, the motel turns away all other customers. Non-curlers simply cannot get into the spirit of the midnight to 5 a.m. sessions when the curlers like to throw their stones down the length of the corridor.

Curling was invented by the same people who brought you golf — the Scots. Legend has it that in mid-winter, dour and unhappy Scotsmen would go down to the frozen river; pour some of their native highland tonic down their gullets; then grab a big round rock and curl it down the ice covered river. Out of this, the Scots made a game and they call it curling.

When the summer came and ice melted, they substituted a smaller stone and moved onto the fields nearby the unfrozen river and got hold of a club and hit the little stone. Out of this, the Scots also made a game. And they called it golf.

How did the curling game get to Belfast, Maine? Well, about 170 years ago, Scottish regiments were shipped across the sea for duty in Quebec. When those Canadian winters came, the Scots wanted to curl. But they could not find the same fine, round, granite stones they used at home for curling.

So the inventive Scottish soldiery melted down their cannonballs. When tight fisted Scotch soldiers melt cannonballs to go curling, it is a sure sign that curling makes madmen out of sensible lads.

This same transformation happened to Belfast about 20 years ago, when Dr. Cobb came from Calais. The good doctor brought the infectious disease of curling in his blood. For the first few years, he'd load up cars with Belfasters on winter weekends and head for Canada and the curling rinks. It wasn't long before the Belfasters tired of all that driving to St. Stephens to play with Canadian rocks on Canadian ice.

So Belfast men and women built their own "Three-sheeter", or' three lanes of ice. Today it is a $100,000 clubhouse where they curl six nights and most days all winter long.

To get hooked on curling, you have to get out on the ice and try it for a week. Up until then, you may laugh. Laugh at the idea of skidding a 42 pound stone (they cost $150 a matched pair) to a target 138 feet away. Most of the time, players 'sweep'. They run ahead of the stone, frantically and furiously sweeping the clean ice with dirty brooms. They swear it changes the speed and direction of the stone. Well, they've gotta believe it.

Curling is like shuffleboard — but played on ice, with stones and with brooms. Above all with a vast amount of bonhomie and bonspiel and camaraderie. There are four players to a team; Skip, Mate, Second mate and Lead. A game lasts about 2½ hours. After 190 minutes on the ice, a nip of Scottish internal fortitude is needed by the players to keep the blood flowing warmly. That is the Bon-spiel part.

A final note of explanation; The Ben Ames Williams Bonspiel is the greatest of all Belfast Bonspiels; because that fine writer lived and wrote near Belfast, and he died on the ice, while curling. I wish he could see and take part in all the fun of the Bonspiel named in his honor and memory.

Making a Quilt to Raise a Steeple

BRISTOL — I wish you could have been there. It took you back 200 years.

Grannie Benner, 86, rocking slowly in her special chair, keeping a close and smiling eye on the Ladies Aid Society.

And the 11 ladies in period costume, seated and quilting around all four sides of the big old quilting frame.

The Ladies Aid Society of the First Congregational Church of Bristol often wear colonial costumes when they gather on Wednes-days and Fridays in the parish hall for a quilting bee.

Seeing their fingers perform intricate, lost skills, seeing their bon-neted heads bent over the frame, seeing their handembroidered, elaborate petticoats daringly hoisted two inches to reveal an ankle peeking out, hearing the gossip of the town, the scene could be 1776, instead of today.

The names around the quilting frame were names known along this coast 200 years ago:

Jennie Benner, Lillian Benner, Marian Burns, Dorothy Elling-wood, Mary Knapp, Adeline McLaughlin, Josephine Pendleton, Beatrice Sparrow, Josie Sproul, Mildred Weeks, Helen Woodward, Allison Allen.

They are making a Heritage quilt of Bristol. By the time this column runs, the 48-square-foot piece of work will be hanging in the First National Bank in Damariscotta, where more people can see it

and summer visitors can buy lots of dollar raffle tickets in the hope of winning this priceless covering.

The money earned by raffling the quilt will go toward repairing the steeple of the Bristol church and returning it to the top of the building.

"We are praying to raise better than $2,000" says Allison Allen, who has been directing the project.

The church steeple had become so weak with dry rot it recently had to be taken down for safety. Today it sits incongruously among the grass in a field near the church. Not often can you see a steeple sitting in a field. But if the Ladies Aid raises over $2,000 it will be repaired and set back atop the First Congregational Church, where it belongs.

That church is in the quilt along with 19 other Bristol landmarks which symbolize our American history in miniature.

At the top of the quilt the Indian chief Samoset is depicted handing over to John Brown an eight-mile tract of land now encompassing Bristol, Bremen, Damariscotta, Nobleboro and parts of Newcastle, Waldoboro and Jefferson. Brown got it all in 1625 for "fifty beaver skins."

This was the first land deed ever executed in New England. You can go to the court house in Wiscasset and look at an authenticated copy of the original deed.

In the upper left corner of the quilt is the Old Walpole Meeting House, built in 1772. Its paneled balcony has boards 30 inches wide. Negro servants sat there, while their masters sat in the enclosed pews below. This is the oldest church in Maine still being used in its original form.

Move among the ladies as they stitch and gossip and they will tell you what landmarks they are quilting, why and who lives there now.

Take the Curtis house, out on Pemaquid Point. It was built in 1830 by Robert Curtis, one of the first lighthouse keepers. His great granddaughter lives there now — Alice Potter, treasurer of the Town of Bristol.

Take the ship at the foot of the quilt. It shows the vessel "Angel Gabriel," which put into Pemaquid Harbor on Aug. 15, 1635, bringing passengers and supplies from England. Suddenly a hurricane struck, her anchors gave way and the vessel was dashed to pieces on the ledges.

All passengers except five were saved. Among the saved was the Blaisdell family. Now Mildred Weeks, a descendant of that family, quilts the Angel Gabriel which brought her ancestors here to Bristol 341 years ago.

These quilters are practical Bristol women. They decided to include the Ervine Tannery on their Heritage quilt. The tannery, begun in pre-Revolutionary days, was one of the earliest American industries. Records show the Town of Bristol was required to furnish 23 pairs of shoes for the Colonial Army, copper toes and all. The Ervine Tannery made them and shipped them by oxcart to Boston, our first export of shoes.

Fort William Henry, which commands Pemaquid, is on the quilt. A lot of blood was spilled around the site of this fort. The pirate Dixey Bull raided Shurte's Fort in 1630; it survived only to be destroyed by Indians in 1676, three hundred years before this writing. Fort Charles was built on the same site in 1677 and burned by Indians in 1689.

Then the Governor of Massachusetts ordered the strongest fort in all North America to be built in 1692 and named it Fort William Henry. Nevertheless the French and Indians captured it four years later, and destroyed it with the first bomb shells.

The King of England commissioned Col. David Dunbar to build Fort Frederick in 1729. It lasted 46 years, until the citizens of Bristol tore it down in 1775 to keep it out of British hands during the American Revolution. In 1908, the State of Maine built the present restoration of the old Fort William Henry.

Walk outside the quilting room and you face the original Liberty Pole on the Village Green, just nearby the Town House. Both are depicted in the quilt.

The fish atop the flagpole was designed by Shem Drowne, who designed the grasshopper weathervane atop Faneuil Hall in Boston. Drowne, listed in Encyclopedia Britannica as the first American sculptor, came to Bristol in 1736 and laid claims to the Pemaquid land patent. A few years ago, Drowne's original fish atop the Bristol Liberty Pole rusted out beyond repair and a new fish was copied exactly and forged by the local Westhaver Machine Shop.

The Town House depicted in the quilt was commissioned at town meeting on May 30, 1799, when the people of Bristol voted the sum of $295 for John Bogbee to construct it. The first meeting was held there on April Fool's Day, in the year 1800.

When it comes to quilts, I am a totally ignorant man. But this colorful, meaningful quilt is a joy to any eye.

Even more significant to me are the roots, the continuity and serenity embodied in the ladies who made this quilt.

They will, I am sure, get their steeple repaired and back onto their church.

My hope is simple as I watch these wonderful quilters in their becoming colonial bonnets and dresses. I hope that 100 and 200 years from now, their great-great-granddaughters will be in the Ladies Aid, quilting another Heritage quilt of the Bristol landmarks.

Dollar chances were sold on the finished quilt. The $2000 needed for the new steeple was raised. I went for the service of thanks.

Raising a new belfry

BRISTOL — I went to the dedication of a new belfry on the old Congregational church in Bristol Mills recently, and my eyes kept filling up with tears.

Not because of sadness, but because of goodness — the plain goodness of everyday people in small Maine towns.

It says something about life today that when you see ordinary, everyday goodness, it brings tears to your eyes.

A new belfry was going up. The old belfry, after more than a hundred years and a thousand sea storms and a hundred-thousand ringings of the big bell and the work of carpenter ants, had to go.

The Ladies Aid fashioned a beautiful bicentennial quilt and sold chances to raise the dollars needed to build this new belfry.

Everybody came for the dedication. The pews, filled to overflowing, creaked and groaned. The young Rev. William F. Dalke, with a southern drawl, a quick smile and a deep voice, heard the creaking in the timbers and said, "Never has so much weight from so many parishioners sat on those pews since the day they were dedicated, 137 years ago."

In that congregation were all the faces, men and women, old and young, that made New England, that sailed the Atlantic 378 years ago, that set the first anchor in Monhegan Island mud and hauled in the first cod and swapped first noises with the Indians.

The Ladies Aid came dressed in colonial costumes. In ruffled white hats, long print dresses and home-knit shawls, they looked lovely. The Bristol militia men came in brown knee breeches with long white stockings stretched over muscular calves. They wore blunt-toed black shoes with silver buckles and waistcoats of bottle green, decorated with big pearl buttons. They looked splendid. Seldom has my fisherman friend or the telephone repairman looked so well dressed and handsome.

As the people came in, the old bell in the new belfry rang out its ancient summons to hear the good news, the gospel. And soon, the plain lovely church was overflowing and the service began.

Paula Foster stood up front and sang "Bless This House". Little Sunday school kids came up front and sang "Gum-By-Ya," that ancient African song "Come back here, Lord".

Boy Scouts in uniform stood up and gave their Scout's oath. Then Harriet Redonnett at the organ struck up "Onward Christian Soldiers," and the whole congregation sang out loud and strong. Here everybody is the choir.

And when they sang the doxology, the name of the Lord was really praised. At the end, everybody turned to the American flag and sang out "The Star Spangled Banner" and felt right doing it.

Then the minister summoned Milton Russell to read from his history of the Bristol Congregational Church. In February 1839, 12

men joined to erect a suitable house for public worship of God, and they and their friends built it, 43 feet by 53 feet and 18 feet, six inches post in the clear.

A worn scrap of paper notes a plan to buy a 900-pound bell for $234. Another tells of wars. Another tells of smallpox. All tell of this church, center of this village for generations. Forefathers of those around me built this church and tended it, were baptized, married and buried here. Inside this church, the change from then to now is imperceptible.

Now in her colonial costume, Allison Allen, head of the Ladies Aid, stands up in church and presents a plaque of praise and gratitude to Milton Russell, turned 80.

Milton is bent, frail and white-haired now, a most-loved and kindly man. Allison Allen reads how Milton has been a servant of God and this church in every matter, large and small — janitor, organist, lay preacher, scoutmaster, trustee, deacon.

"Whatever needed doing, Milton did and did well," read Allison. "In any pinch, in any emergency, he always did whatever had to be done, quickly, quietly and to perfection. And Allison quoted those lines from Isaiah as she spoke about Milton . . . . "Here am I, Lord. Send me".

And all the congregation stood up inside the church. And they clapped and smiled with joy and applauded Milton Russell.

And the old bell in the new belfry rang with joy.

And tears welled up in my eyes at just seeing so much plain goodness in everyday people.

Milton Russell died a few months later. This church was filled again with his friends and the old bell in the new belfry tolled long for Milton.

A DAY IN DISTRICT COURT; LOCAL JUSTICE

WISCASSET — Davina Pearl, a distraught woman in blue jeans and sweat shirt, stumbled weeping and shaking into Lincoln County Courthouse, Wiscasset, before eight in the morning — before it was officially open for business. But that didn't matter. She teetered down the corridor, into the office of Barbara Cowan, clerk of the court, seeking help and justice.

She got both. With speed and with compassion. Which these days is a story worth a newspaper column.

Here's how it happened.

Davina Pearl — not her real name, incidentally — had been beaten by her husband and she wanted protection from him, she told Clerk Cowan.

Stripping off her sweat shirt, Davina showed welts caused by a beating from a belt. Bruises and blisters stood out fresh and savage.

Barbara Cowan is an experienced, composed and smartly groomed court official to whom wife beatings are nothing new. But she winced. Then she picked up the phone and spoke to Judge Paul MacDonald, the presiding judge, already in his office down the hall. She told him what Davina had said and how Davina's back looked.

I could hear MacDonald's answer snap out of the phone. "Call the local chief of police in his town, tell him to pick the husband up and get him in here fast. Issue an arrest warrant."

Davina Pearl, a big woman with cropped dark hair and huge, trusting brown eyes, was comforted and given a place to wait. "I'll stay with her," said a lady in a blue windbreaker.

Down the hall District Court was just beginning. The judge had opened proceedings on the dot of eight. His docket was full, 33 cases today — divorces, separations, driving under the influence, possession of deer out of season, criminal trespass, burglary, disorderly conduct, assault on an officer, operating after suspension, hunting in a game sanctuary, theft.

Daniel Webster fought for justice in this courthouse when we were a fledgling nation and Lincoln County stretched to Canada. That was 160 years ago. He'd like it here today, surprised as he'd be threading his way among the defendants in the corridor.

I guess 20 defendants are here early, each with an average of two supporters. I count 19 troopers, sheriffs and town police officers here to testify. And 17 lawyers are here too. Plus all the officers of the court. Justice is humming at a cost of a thousand dollars each hour.

At 10:15 a.m. the town police bring in Davina's husband from 15 miles away. Judge MacDonald, in black robe, white hair and horn rims, hears the case almost immediately.

Davina lumbers forward before the bench. In soft, short sentences she tells her side of the previous night's beating. "I don't care who sees it" she says and in front of the two dozen people sitting in the public benches of the court she strips off her shirt and displays her beaten back.

The judge invites the husband to tell his story. A big man in a red plaid shirt, baggy pants and workboots, he tells the judge he is a moral man. "I beat her because she needed it to teach her" is the gist of his testimony.

Some details from both sides indicate that in an eight year marriage this is the first bad beating, but not the first time the wife has run from home in fear. The defendant's story of why he was justified in beating his wife is cut short by the judge.

"We'll have nobody going around beating people like you admit to," says the judge. "I have a feeling you should go to jail, but the law today says you must have a lawyer to hold your hand on the way to the jailhouse . . . " The Judge turns to a court attendant and tells him to ask a local woman attorney to come in to court. "I think a lady lawyer ought to be good on a domestic problem such as this. She will be your court-appointed attorney, Mr. Pearl."

Suddenly a lady sitting in the courtroom gets to her feet and speaks out as a citizen. She tells the court that a small child is involved and that this ought to be considered.

Judge MacDonald recesses court and asks the lady to discuss the matter in his chambers.

It is now 11.20 a.m. and I am allowed into chambers to listen.

It is a sad story of unpleasant facts about life on the brink. The brink of everything from poverty to alcoholism to retardation to desperation. And central to it all — a four-year-old girl.

Judge MacDonald listens intently, then picks up his phone and asks for the Department of Human Services in Rockland. Quickly and quietly he recites the facts, the names and addresses. I hear him issue orders in a half whisper, "I want you to get down to this address as soon as you can. See the child. See the grandmother she is with. Size up the situation. Then come to court and tell me what you find and what you recommend."

It is now almost noon. The wheels of justice have been turning with compassion, fast but without fuss in this Maine people's court. The beaten wife is safe; the husband, under arrest now has a lawyer to defend him. She changes his plea from "Guilty" to "Not guilty." A social worker named Brian Gallagher is on his way to see about the young daughter.

The judge goes back to court to listen to other cases. His lunch hour has been short. A sandwich from a brown bag in his chambers. The cases roll on.

The courthouse corridor resembles a clubhouse. It is jammed with people with business before the District Court. The accused and their friends and supporters sit around and smoke, or stand and gossip. Mostly they are youngish, about 18 to 30.

Everybody seems friendly: police, attorneys, accused and hangers on. Nobody seems in awe of the court.

Once in a while court is recessed so the assistant district attorney can prepare his next case. For the 33 cases listed there are only two prosecutors. The defendants, however, are represented by 17 different attorneys.

The prosecutors meet with the arresting officer briefly before each case to hear the accusation and evidence. They lose often, perhaps because of lack of preparation: the men who represent the people of Maine must often do it on the fly.

Social worker Brian Gallagher gets in. He has seen the child. So Judge MacDonald again recesses court to hear his report.

The judge decides the child is safe for the moment with the paternal grandmother and calls in Davina Pearl. She is happy: she had been scared the state might take her child away from her. A place is arranged where the mother may stay safely.

Next the judge calls in the defendant and the lady lawyer. The husband is told he will be released on a $500 bond on his own recognizance but that he is forbidden from trying to see his wife until the case comes to court again in a week.

More arrangements are made for checkups on the daughter during the period the case has been continued.

The court officers go to prepare papers. The judge returns to the bench.

Soon after 5 p.m. the last case is over. Of the 33 cases scheduled, 23 have been acted upon and 10 continued or dismissed.

The judge drives off in a pickup truck with a load of firewood.

The lady lawyer drives off in a white jeep with a pulling winch in front.

The husband accused of beating his wife cadges a free ride home in a police cruiser.

The beaten wife leaves with a friend in an old blue Plymouth.

The court is quiet now. A lot has gone on here today. A lot more than most people realize. A lot of justice has been meted out, speedily and with compassion.

To a citizen who doesn't spend much time in these places, the day has been impressive. To the people who work here, it's just been another day of district court.

PEOPLE-TO-PEOPLE IN A SMALL TOWN

DAMARISCOTTA — Every Maine town should have one — a People-to-People Clothing Exchange like the one serving the people of Lincoln County out of the basement of the Baptist church in Damariscotta. This is a report on how it operates, warmly and efficiently, without one penny of state or federal funds.

Customers enter through a cellar door into a church basement that has been converted into a special kind of department store and nursery.

Around the main room are big, portable coat racks, hung with dresses, coats and jackets. Each rack is marked by sizes; for example, "Misses sizes 9-15", "Women, 10-18," "Men's suits and jackets," "Boy's clothes, 6-12." There are close to 200 garments on each rack, over 1200 in all.

In the center of the room are trestle tables, eight feet long. On each are eight baskets of clothes, again carefully sorted by type and size, all clearly marked. Then there are shelves of shoes and baskets of mittens and scarves. And a special section for infants clothing. Two volunteers staff "the floor."

At the back of the room is a nursery, complete with baby-sitters, cribs, playpens and all kinds of toys.

Partitioned from the "store" is the sorting room. Five volunteers work here several mornings a week, sorting the gifts of clothing and arranging them on the racks and tables.

They keep special stockpiles of blankets, sheets and mattresses for families who have been burned out. In one corner are layettes for girls expecting babies in a week or so but who have no clothes prepared for them.

A blonde girl of about 21, obviously pregnant, comes through the entrance door. Clinging to each hand is a small child.

It is her first visit. She gives her name and hometown to Dorothy Billings at the door. Dottie, who runs this People-to-People Exchange, writes the newcomer's name in pencil in a small school exercise book. "I like to call people by their names," she says. "Often customers call me on the phone about clothing their family and it helps to be able to put a face to the name, to see, in my mind, the mother and her kids . . . "

The pregnant mother of two asks about prices.

"No prices," says Mrs. Billings. "Everything comes in with love, and it goes out with love. Just take what you need, and while you're looking you can park the kids in the nursery at the back."

Girls from nearby Lincoln Academy do the babysitting. They worked it out with their principal, Arthur Dexter, so they get home ec. credit for it.

The nursery is a lively place: Fifteen kids were playing there when I visited last week. Between 8:30 and 11 a.m. a total of 65 people came to get clothing.

Some of the women coming for clothes also brought back clothes which their children had outgrown. These were set aside for sorting and cleaning if necessary before being put back into circulation. This emphasizes that what Lincoln County has is a clothing exchange, not a charity.

A dozen other people came with 20 boxes and bags of clothing to donate during the two hours I was there.

Nobody knows how many shoes, coats, clothes for babies, clothes for school kids and clothes for oldsters pass through this Baptist basement. But estimates are that it is around 15,000 to 20,000 articles in a year. Nobody knows the value, but clearly it is many tens of thousands of dollars.

And if a kid really has to have shoes or a winter coat and the right size is not available, the people who run the exchange buy them. Same for families who are burned out and have no bedding, says Dottie Billings. "Later we make phone calls and come up with the money to keep on. This kind of thing costs us $1200 a year."

People are cheery as they shop in this basement. There is no embarrassment, maybe because there is no atmosphere of Lady Bountiful or Sweet Charity here. There is no government social worker, no government form, no sense of patronage.

Mostly the shoppers are young mothers. But a few are grandmothers. About one in ten is a man — usually young, almost always a father but not always a husband.

A couple of girls tell Mrs. Billings that they expect their babies before Christmas, and they give her a short list of what they most need. Another mother says she has three kids sleeping on the floor and asks if there is a chance for a bed. Someone else wants a used pair of ski pants for an eight-year-old boy. Another says her place is so cold she needs four blankets for four kids. Another cannot find any shoes to fit her two-year-old.

All the requests are written into Dottie Billings' little exercise book. "I'll try. If I can get what you need, I'll put it aside for you for next week," she says. "If it's an emergency, call me the day after tomorrow, we may have it for you by then."

The People-to-People Exchange began five years ago in Betty Grindal's garage. Soon there was no room for her husband's truck. Now the exchange, which is open for business every Tuesday morning, keeps a dozen women occupied almost full time.

People come to the exchange from all over Lincoln County, every Tuesday from April till Christmas. Then by Dec. 20, the snow is apt to block the only entrance to the basement, and the plowing of the roads makes parking impossible. So the Exchange closes down till spring, although it continues to meet all emergency demands.

This coming Tuesday, there will be a windup Christmas party; toys and gifts for 400 children are being wrapped now.

Nobody here pretends this venture is, by itself, any big deal. But everyone putting in or taking out seems to appreciate it. Without any doubt it's a sensible, pleasant, decent and dignified way for one human being to work with another, without any government or social agency getting into the act.

Every town ought to have one, say the customers.

SAYING GOODBYE TO TWO GOOD MAINE MEN

DAMARISCOTTA — Spencer Gay had a voice as big as the Maine woods he loved and knew so well.

But his heart was bigger even than his voice. And, believe me, that means a big, big heart. Almost as many people had been helped by Spencer's big heart as had been scared by Spencer's big voice.

This week, Spencer Gay died in Damariscotta, where he had been born 78 years ago.

Damariscotta closed down in respect and in love for Spencer. From 10 a.m., Monday, until the funeral services were over, every store in Damariscotta was shut tight. And every seat in every pew in St. Andrews Church was filled. And friends stood packed six deep in the back.

Doris Marble, wife of Harry Marble, newscaster and Spencer's friend, is the organist at our church, and a fine musician she is. But this day at the end of service, Doris blasted out on the organ with Battle Hymn of the Republic. And our church was fluttering with white handkerchiefs before she played the last notes. For that music was Spencer Gay, all over.

Spencer spoke out loudly, proudly and often about his nation, and his state of Maine and his birthtown of Damariscotta. He loved 'em all. He served 'em all. And he'd not stand still and let anybody badmouth any one of 'em. That big voice would roar out. Then those blue eyes would smile.

Another nice thing about Spencer Gay was this. Few people said "Spencer" without saying "Mabel" in the same breath. Really, it was just about one name they shared: "Spencer-and-Mable-Gay". And that signifies.

Mabel ran that landmark — Gay's Groceries — for years. Her store was half-home to thousands. Spencer liked the woods and rivers more. His license plate was "Guide". And he'd done everything there is to do in Damariscotta, I guess. Including being state legislator and town harbormaster and two dozen other jobs as a citizen of Maine serving his town and state.

He was a good Maine man. For 78 years. Maine and Damariscotta are better for his coming. And poorer for his going.

Sad Monday, that was the way they called this Monday past in Damariscotta.

In the morning we said goodbye to Spencer.

Then in the afternoon we buried another hugely missed and wonderful man. Wilson Crook of Round Pond.

I was lucky enough to know Wilson from the first year I came to Maine. And saw him about every week at least since then. Maybe, in all 700 or 800 times, I saw Wilson's brown, bald head and his laughing eyes and his smiling face. Every one of those times, I felt better just from seeing that guy. There are few men like that, indeed. Wilson was one.

Wilson used to go lobstering in a black hulled boat. That black made it easy to spot Wilson hauling. When I was out on Muscongus Bay, I used to come alongside. And Wilson working in those yellow oilskins, somehow looked even cheerier than he did on land. But a trick heart forced him to quit lobstering these last few years. And there was a hole out on the bay without Wilson's black hull out on the water.

And now Wilson, 68, is not on shore either. And the hole he leaves there in so many lives will be felt sorely by many.

The funeral home in Damariscotta was clear out of chairs, so many came to say goodbye to Wilson. And the cemetery where he lies now down by the sea in Round Pond, where his boat had been moored, is a warm and friendly place to rest.

When men like Wilson and Spencer go, their friends galore come to services, and the towns where they lived just about close down. There is, I think, great goodness amidst all the sadness. And great naturalness.

Their lives, well lived, seem not to come to a sad sudden stop, but rather to be rounded out, finished, because they are complete.

Then in the small, old cemeteries where these good men go, they go not as strangers. They are among ancestors or friends and families who lived close by when they lived. Friends who fished and lobstered and hunted with them. Longtime friends who shared a school desk long ago in first grade and maybe got caught smoking behind the barn with them.

There is not the aloneness and bitterness to dying here, as in a city. There is something very good but very sad about the passing of a good man in a small Maine town. When this sad Monday was done, I sat on the back porch thinking about Wilson and Spencer.

And you know that mixture of sadness and gratefulness you feel at the end of a long, good, fine, worthwhile day, when you sit and watch the sun go down after it has shone long and well; and you are grateful for the sun and for being in its warmth. And yet you are sad it is setting. But you know that really it is not gone forever. Well, Spencer and Wilson went down over the horizon Monday. But in the Maine sky they shone long, and they shone well. And their good lives warmed and brightened the hearts of hundreds of people hereabouts, mine among them.

II /

The Boat, the Harbor, and the Fishermen

OUR BOAT has given us more fun and more trouble, more pleasure and more expense than anything we ever owned.

We began with a skiff, that first summer in Maine. We bought it second hand for $75 from Frank Farrin who runs a lobster pound at South Bristol. Using an outboard that came with our cottage, we chugged around John's Bay over to Pemaquid to Christmas Cove, once to Boothbay for Windjammer Day.

That trip was the mark of a senseless novice. Coming home, tide and wind had changed and the tiny skiff got caught in a chop at the mouth of the Damariscotta river, on an outgoing tide and an incoming wind. With my wife, my daughter, my dog and me in a 14 foot skiff, we had very little freeboard. With a small outboard, we had very little power. I get chills thinking now of how foolish we were then.

Our second year in Maine, we paid $1,000 for an old 28 foot lobster boat which Bill Carter used to fish out of Round Pond.

We loved that first boat with a special kind of love and pride. We called it Steer Clear. And here is how it got that name:

One afternoon in Round Pond, we had taken the boat off her mooring and brought her to the dock where we would get power to run a sander. We towed the boat in by rowing ahead in a *dinghy and holding a tow line. The boat had no power as we had the transmission out, repairing it.*

At sunset we headed back to the mooring, a mere 150 feet away with my son rowing the dinghy ahead and pulling us in the big boat. That is when the wind picked up and caught us broadside. Pulling hard as he could my son could not hold us against that wind. We began to blow across the harbor with no power to save us. Barbara yelled and blew hard on an ancient tin horn. "Steer Clear!" she cried to boats in our way.

Finally a friend, Charlie Bradley, came to rescue us in an outboard and towed us to our mooring.

We put in bunks and a cook stove on that old lobster boat. We went to night classes in seamanship and navigation, given at the local high school by Bill Danforth of the Wawenock Power Squadron. And in that lobster boat we learned to love and to cruise the Maine coast. On her we spent a 14 day-and-night vacation two years in succession. On her we visited islands every weekend. We had her for almost three years.

Then we sold her to buy Steer Clear II. This is the boat we have enjoyed for 10 years. She is 30 feet long, plus pulpit. She has such luxuries (for us) as a proper tiny galley, an electric head, twin screws and two Palmer engines and lots of room in a big main cabin. Each summer we seem to spend about 60 days and 40 nights aboard, taking all our holidays, our vacations and our weekends in Steer Clear II.

Her home port is New Harbor, which means that New Harbor is our second home. And the fishermen there are among our best and closest friends.

LOBSTERING: A PRIMER FOR EATERS AND WATCHERS

NEW HARBOR — I keep my boat down at New Harbor, which is about the prettiest, most photographed and most painted working harbor in Maine.

We get lots of visitors. Partly because the harbor is so pretty and partly because you can eat fresh-caught lobsters and clams right over the water and watch the fishing boats unload while you eat.

Rightly, people are curious about the world of lobstering, seining and clamming. They want to know about the bright colored lobster marker buoys and the shape of the traps with the heads knitted into them. They want to know why the bow of a lobster boat is so high, why the bait smells so strong and even what kind of living a lobsterman makes.

And, they want to know about the birds swarming around the boats unloading fish, the enormous nets hung high from the draggers, the 200 mile limit and the Russians.

The shags stop visitors cold. A shag sitting on a ledge, wings outspread to dry, is a pretty strange sight. But a shag, neck outstretched so far that it looks a yard long, flying just 12 inches over the sea is a strange sight, too. Shag is the Maine name for cormorants. They are fine fishermen, as are the herring and laughing gulls.

At New Harbor, a shag often sits atop the big red buoy close to the harbor entrance, which relates to other visitor questions. Why are some buoys black and others red? Why are some square and some pointed? What does the long pole with the square box on top mean? (It is a radar reflector, and it marks a ledge too)

If there is a fisherman on the wharf, he'll usually answer all questions — if he is not loading bait, selling fish, icing up, getting gas or water, getting ready to go out or go onto his mooring.

Knowing a bit about what you see along the wharves and harbors and fishing villages of Maine makes it more enjoyable.

That is what these reports are about: Making Maine more enjoyable by explaining briefly and simply, some of the sights.

First, about those brightly painted buoys. Every lobsterman has his own colors. The buoys mark his traps, so he knows which to haul by their colors.

And a recent Maine law requires that these same colors be shown on his lobster boat. Sometimes you'll see a marker buoy nailed on the bow or the house of the boat. Sometimes the colors are just painted on. This way, a warden or another lobsterman can match up boat and traps, and be sure that a boat with a red and green identification on it is not pulling traps that are orange and yellow.

Lobsters are close in to shore in the first months of summer. They come where the water is warmish. In winter, when the water is icy, lobsters burrow into the mud. Then in spring and early summer, when the temperature warms up, the lobsters crawl out of the mud and migrate to the hard bottom and crawl among holes in the rocks.

In July Maine lobsters start shedding. As a lobster grows, it gets too big for its present shell. So it sheds that shell, and grows a new and bigger one which will last till it needs the next size up.

When shedding, lobsters are vulnerable and helpless without any protection until the new shell begins to harden. When it is brand new, the shell is no harder or thicker than tissue paper. So the lobsters stay hidden during this danger period.

When the shell hardens and it is safe to come out, they are hungry. So they trap easily. And the lobster market about this time of year gets flooded with 'shedders' or 'soft shells'. They are usually priced a bit lower than hard shells. The meat is softer and sweet.

This is one reason thousands of traps are so close in to shore in summer. Another reason is that young lobstermen, 10 or 12 years old, are making some money with only a little boat and outboard and 20 or 30 traps. They set their traps close in.

There are almost two million traps out this summer along the coast of Maine. Too many, say the experts. All you need to go lobstering is a $20 license, some traps and a boat to fish from. Maine lobsters are seriously overfished today, and each year there are proposals in the legislature to limit the number of licenses and limit the

number of traps per boat. Some big boats, with two men aboard, may fish as many as 500 traps. Most fish 200 or 300 traps.

Those bright painted markers, as crowded as daisies in a field, all indicate traps below. At this time of year they are so close together they often tangle with each other as the wind blows or the tide shifts. Their lines wrap around the propellers of boats, and can easily put a boat out of action.

Most lobster boats have cages around their propellors to prevent this. The cage cuts down speed and efficiency, but it saves having to dive overboard and swim under the boat to cut off the pot warp wrapped around the propeller or rudder — a cold business.

A man's lobster buoys used to be made of cedar, shaped by him, painted by him. But today they are mostly styrofoam, which is lighter to handle and lasts longer. The shape varies according to preference. But a blunt buoy catches seaweed, and so gets heavy. In a storm, the trap might be lugged off by the added weight.

This is why most markers are pointed, so that seaweed and debris will not get hung up and create too much drag.

The trap, marker buoy and the pot warp (or rope) add up to an investment worth about $15 these days. A man with 500 traps out has $7500 tied up in traps alone, and maybe another $30,000 more in his boat and electronics. Which is one reason lobster dinners cost a pretty penny these days.

FISHERMEN WATCH OUT FOR EACH OTHER

NEW HARBOR — Among fishermen out of the same harbor, there is usually a close camaraderie unknown to men who work on shore.

One lobsterman and his boat depend on the others sometimes for his very life and for the life of his boat.

So fishermen look after one another.

They never say much about it. They don't need to. Their actions speak volumes.

Take the way it works down in New Harbor, where I keep my boat, "Steer Clear."

Once in a while we get word that so-and-so has not come back in when expected.

The word gets around fast on some inexplicable grapevine made up of wharf talk, CB radio, and maybe a rap at the door.

"Charlie's not back. I'm going. You want to?"

That's about all that is said.

And then at dark of night, you hear the oarlocks creaking as punts make out to the moorings.

Then you hear engines break to life, and boats begin moving out as if it were dawn instead of night.

The the CB radios get busy. And everyone is listening if they are not talking, arranging who will search where.

Soon the bigger draggers are joining in. It doesn't matter a tinker's damn if they just got home. Out they go. Everybody out to look.

And I guess the guy who is lost, who hasn't made it back to harbor, knows all this will happen.

He knows it doesn't matter now that he was feuding with this fellow, or owed that one money, or had a fight last week with another. They'll all be out looking just as he'd be out looking for any of them.

Or take a different condition.

It is summer weather and the lobsters are crawling in close to the rocks. So your traps are close in. And one day you are close in and your engine quits, and it's a lee shore and the sea is running. You are in a mess. Likely to lose your boat, if not yourself. So you heave an anchor and get on the radio and call other boats from your harbor.

They'll come, whatever the weather, whatever the sea. They'll come in close enough to somehow get a line on you. And then they'll haul you off, out of the danger, and tow you back in.

Of course no money passes. In fact not even a lot of words are exchanged.

Fishermen Watch Out For Each Other / 57

Most times, the man or his boat or both are rescued. Once in a while both are lost.

When that happens down here at New Harbor, there is a service in the church. And the church is packed solid. It's hard to recognize all those faces popping up from jackets and ties and shirts.

And the minister reads the old prayers of the sea, prayers read in seaports for missing men as long as Bibles have been in print. Then the organist plays those hymns of the sea. And you see Adam's apples bobbing, and eyes filling up and throats doing a lot of swallowing, and thick, strong, calloused hands rub overflowing eyes.

And the men who fished with the lost fisherman go and talk a few words to the widow and her youngsters.

And this Maine fishing village comes together, strong, helping, supportive to their own in need.

The sadness is terrible. But the good that comes out of it is enormous.

The suits and ties are shed. The work clothes are put back on. And before long you hear the engines, and the boats are going out again. Minus one.

Copper bottomed love

RIVERSIDE BOATYARD, Newcastle — This boat was 30 feet long and 10 feet wide when I bought her. Today I finished painting and coppering.

Now I swear she is 328 feet long, four stories high, and broad in the beam as the wide Missouri.

If the Coast Guard keeps on calling her a "small craft", then I say "Nuts to the Coast Guard!" Let them caulk her seams, which today seem long enough to stretch end-to-end across Lincoln and Knox counties; let the Coast Guard sand down her decks to bare wood (they'd rather scrub the Portland Light with a toothbrush).

With the red paint I stroked on her everlasting bottom, a bawdy sailor could paint every port east of Suez crimson.

"It's the work that makes you love her," smirks the fellow who owns the boat in the next cradle. "The more work she costs you, the more you love her. Like marriage."

He climbs aboard. And helps himself to an inspection tour. Checks the pulpit, flying off the bow. Manhandles Danforth anchor and fathoms of chain. Stretches out on the foam rubber bunks. Tickles the electric button (very fancy) which makes the 'head' perform. Toys with a Transcentury depthfinder. Primes the Perko stove in the galley. Lifts the hatches and peers professionally at the private parts of the twin Palmer engines. He blows a blast on the horn to check its voice. He opens the fish well and gloats over an imaginary catch. He prods the light metal of the 100 gallon gas tanks and runs his critical eye over their shining contours.

I wince at the faults he may be finding. He looks too closely, too professionally, too critically at a boat I love.

"You say it's work that makes you love a boat" I snarl. "So why don't you go love your own?"

"No harm meant" he answers, climbing off. "A boat is like marriage, you love your own. But it's still fun to look at someone else's!"

A boat up in her cradle in the boatyard is exposed like a woman on her stool in front of a dressing table.

The boat owner peers at his boat critically, searching her beauty for faults to remedy. Near him are arrays of pots and jars, filled paints and cure-alls. Just as the girl at the mirror peers with disapproval at her lovely face, the boat owner can't resist dabbing and dabbing at faults only his eye sees.

Finally the moment comes for launching the boat, as it comes for launching the girl. The boat goes careening down the ways to join the others in the harbor. The girl goes floating down the stairs to join the others at the party.

Suddenly all the faults vanish. The girl, bobbing amongst her friends, looks lovely.

The boat, bobbing at her mooring, looks pretty as a picture. And joy bursts out. Forgotten by the girl are those horrid hours under the dryer, that horrid wrinkle near her left eye. Forgotten by the boat owner are the tortures of the sander which bites, the paint which clogs, the caulking compound that glubs up.

Gone is all the ache of preparatory drudgery. The glowing girl perhaps may thrill at the touch of arms which come to encircle her for a dance or a greeting. But a man whose boat is going 'overboard' has a thrill no mere woman ever knew. Oh! the beauty of the first wind filling the first unfurled sails. Oh! the music of the first water rushing by the spray rail! Even to a lowly power-man, no cello notes from Pablo Casals throb more movingly than the first resonance of his engines, the first whirl of his drive shafts, the first churn of his propeller blades biting again into salt blue water.

There is a magic metamorphosis for a man in those first moments when he and his boat regain freedom from the land.

The lobster sheds its shell, the snake sloughs its skin, flowers burst from bud to blossom and bees get their first glorious taste of nectar, even drab chrysalids are born again into beautiful butterflies.

Bully for them all!

Girls tingle as they walk down the church aisle to marriage; women come to fulfillment with newborn babies in their arms; candidates wake up elated when elected to office; even eggshells get ecstatic as they feel a rapping and out pop birds; horses you back sometimes win, stocks you buy sometimes climb, even peach pips you toss off the porch may turn into peach trees.

Bully for all of them too!

But no magic matches that idiotic but wise, silent but raucous, physical but spiritual, childish but ancient magic a man feels getting back home aboard his boat after a long winter in an alien land ashore.

This is the way it is. And this is the way it must always be. Without this hypnotic love-affair, why would any sane man keep on running up those outrageous boatyard bills? Why on wet stormy days ashore will he seek his refuge in marine hardware stores? Why even in cold winter nights will he warm himself by the glow of an ocean chart, foolishly plotting courses he may never sail?

Boat-owning is a disease, almost incurable. No doctor can operate to cut the infection out. The virus lives in the heart. It flourishes undetectable, but virulent, among the corpuscles. Even a psychiatrist cannot close in on the aberration. For boat-owning is not a mundane state-of-mind.

Boat-owning is a paradise and purgatory of hope; of hopes that can never be fulfilled and never be put out. One perennial hope is that you will be 'overboard' earlier; another that fog won't lock you in harbor; that the anchor won't drag, sail won't split, engine won't fail, leaks won't spring.

When the hopes turn sour, does a boat owner quit in disgust? No. Either he just sits on his deck and loves being there or begs off sick from his business and spends the day with his head in the bilge, working like a slave.

"It's like marriage" says the man from the boat cradle next door. But it is worse. Being married to a boat is like being hooked on the dumbest broad in the world. A boat keeps your bank book flat, your back aching, your fingers sore. A boat steals you away from your home and family. And the damn floating wench can't even cook!

Six Dozen Mussels Please

BUTTER ISLAND — We ate mussels aboard our boat last night and enjoyed one of the finest meals you can gather along the Maine coast absolutely free.

On the low tide at morning, I picked six dozen select blue mussels from a mussel bed far from any pollution, below the low tide mark, and well washed by cold ocean tides.

The mussels were big and they were dense. Inside 20 minutes I had picked enough big mussels to give us three dozen each.

A flourishing mussel bed represents one of the densest, richest food sources in the world. One acre of good mussel bed can produce 40,000 pounds of mussels.

We let our mussels sit in cold sea water, cleaning themselves for hours. Then at dinner time Barbara makes a broth, consisting of one cup of white wine, chopped onion, some garlic, oregano, thyme, pepper and bay leaves which we pick from island bushes. She brings this mixture slowly to a boil. While she is doing that, my job is to trim the beards off the mussels, scrub them thoroughly and get them wholly clean.

Then in the pot they go, all six dozen tumbled into the white wine mixture. Slap on a lid, and let them boil and steam for six minutes. Use a big spoon to stir up the mussels, so they all get a chance to get the hottest steam and the finest sauce. Every mussel opens up and the juices of the mussel itself add immeasurably to the broth.

Now sit in the stern cockpit of the boat and enjoy the feast.

Barbara brings a long loaf of crusty French bread out of the ship's oven. We dip this into the sauce, as we eat three dozen mussels each happily tossing the shells overboard into the ocean, whence they came.

There are two drawbacks to mussels.

One is you get tired of them. About once a week is enough. Second is they are occasionally victims of the red tide. Check with local fishermen before you gather.

This column is being written during our yearly vacation cruise among Maine islands. And while we stock our icebox well before leaving shore and replenish it often, it is fun to enjoy some of the free, wild produce and shellfish and fish that abound.

Right now, the islands are ablaze with wild rose hips. The wild roses on these thorny bushes are well past their peak, and the bees no longer offer tough competition. So now is the time to gather the red and orange fruit, which look like tiny tomatoes. On shore, they can be made into jams. But on the islands, they are a good addition to a wild salad, and filled with vitamin C.

Hot wild mustard is in bloom now, growing among the jetsam at high tide mark. The leaves are a pungent addition to a fine salad. But the mustard greens are best in the springtime, and are very good cooked. The best of island foods are the berries: wild raspberries, blueberries, blackberries, even wild gooseberries and strawberries.

How to Know a Rock 10 Million Years Old

KENNEBUNKPORT — It is heady stuff to find out that the rock you picked up on the beach yesterday may be 10 million years old.

My wife Barbara is a beachcomber, hooked beyond hope on picking up odd shaped, lovely colored stones. So we have been learning a bit about rocks along Maine's coast. And it is mind boggling.

First, this lovely coast of Maine was 400 million years in the making.

And written in the rocks you pick up or the ledges of granite you laze on in the sun is the savage story of the how and the when and the why of Maine's rugged coast.

These rocks were torn from the throats of volcanoes. Millions of years ago fiery explosions of atomic force hurled the boiling innards of the earth skyward, and they fell sizzling into the sea and sank. That molten granite, so hot it ran as a fiery liquid, chilled and solidified and became, finally the ledges along the beach on which you may have climbed and sunned.

Maine rocks change as you go along the coast. Far downeast by Quoddy Head the rocks are dark green, dark gray or black, massive and unfractured, quite different from the layered rocks in Casco and Penobscot Bays. The massive black rocks are called "gabbro."

But look at "gabbro" through a magnifying glass and the seemingly solid rock isn't solid at all. It is revealed as a mass of interlocking crystals of different colors—white, green, black and gray.

I've learned these "gabbro" rocks are "igneous rock." This means rocks created by fire (as in the word "ignition"). That fire was the center of the earth erupting millions of years ago.

In Casco and Penobscot and Muscongus Bays the rock instead of looking solid looks like it is made up in layers.

And it is. These rocks have been built up over millions of years, a layer at a time. A layer of mud joined to a layer of sand joined to a layer of volcanic ash. These layers were once separate sediments on the ocean floor. As millions of years passed, they fused together. The result is called "sedimentary rock." You can often break the layers apart, even now.

But the king of all Maine rock is granite, especially Maine's pink granite. Put a magnifying glass to this, and you find very pink feldspar, pink because it is loaded with potassium. You also find flakes of quartz which shine like glass and specks of mica and white calcic.

This Maine granite built thousands of American monuments, cathedrals and great office buildings.

Go ashore on dozens of Maine islands and you'll see great quarries where hundreds of thousands of tons were taken out to build cathedrals such as St. John's in New York, and railroad stations such as Grand Central.

The Maine coast was a chain of mountains 200 million years ago, say geologists. Erosion cut down those high mountains to rolling uplands inshore. What were once the valleys of those ancient mountains are now filled by the sea. And we know them as the great bays of Maine — Casco, Muscongus, Penobscot, Blue Hill, Frenchman, Machias.

Look up from a small boat at the granite atop Mt. Desert and be amazed by the fact that the granite on top was once sediment lying on the ocean floor. Over millions of years it worked its way up to become the top of Mt. Desert.

Now history is coming full cycle. Streams on Mt. Desert are slowly eroding that same granite and returning it to the ocean as sand and clay. Millions of years from now it may end almost back where it began.

SAVORING THE SHEDDER

MT. DESERT — Now that 'shedders' are in strong in August, the price of lobsters is dropping. Even Maine people can afford a few.

The other night I served a batch of shedders to Maine friends from inland. And they did not know how shedders get that way, or even what they are and why they cost about 20 per cent less than hard shell lobsters.

In fact my friends didn't know much about lobsters, except that they like 'em. In case you are in the same fix, this is a short primer on lobsters.

By the time a little one-pound lobster lands on your plate, it is probably six or seven years old. And the shell you tear off may be the seventh or eighth shell that lobster has lived in as an 'adult'.

Shells do not grow like a skin does. So each time a growing lobster puts on a bit of weight or size, it has to shed its too-tight shell; and then grow a new, bigger one with room to grow inside it. This is shedding. Lobsters shed about once a year, more often when tiny. And the shedding usually takes place in August and September.

Climbing out of that old carapace or shell, and leaving the whole shell empty and intact behind him, is an incredibly exhausting job. It takes about 20 minutes. The moment it is done, the lobster is naked, unprotected and easy prey to fish or other cannibal lobsters. Sometimes down at the wharf, you may see a fresh caught lobster right in the midst of climbing out of his skin.

They grow a new shell quickly. But it takes weeks to harden into strong protective armor. Lobsters eat clam shells and mussel shells to get the calcium needed to make their own shells hard. But while the shell is soft, they are called 'shedders' or soft shells. And because they cannot travel well out of state, shedders are cheaper to buy than hardshells. I like them even better. They are easy to open. The meat is sweet. The meat is tender. The lobster juice is plenteous.

About 60 per cent of the entire Maine lobster catch are shedders, or soft-shell lobsters. But off Monhegan Island and in Canadian waters, there is a closed season in the months lobsters shed. But in Maine, shedders or soft shells may account for 10 million pounds out of an 18-million-pound catch.

While less than 20 million pounds of lobster are caught here in a year, experts say that at least 25 billion — repeat billion baby lobsters are born in Maine waters each year. Most are eaten by other fish in infancy.

Female lobsters carry up to 40,000 eggs in a sticky mass outside the shell, attached to furry swimmerets or claws. Lobsters mate only in the brief moments after an egg-bearing female sheds.

Just prior to mating, lobsters whip each other with their antennae. That whipping is a ritual of courtship.

Lobsters spend their life in the ocean, but they are badly designed for swimming. By using eight crawling legs, they walk slowly over the ocean floor, eating plants, trash, clams and sometimes crawling into lobster traps to eat the bait. They have strong concave teeth and digestive tracts rugged enough to handle stone. Their biting claw is so strong that the first thing a lobsterman does is to 'plug' the biting claw with a wooden peg or bind it shut with a strong rubber band.

Laws regulate the minimum and maximum size of lobsters that

can be sold in Maine. The minimum is 3 3/16 inches and the maximum is five inches, measured from eye socket to end of body shell. All lobstermen carry special gauges for measuring 'keepers.' Too often you throw three or four lobsters away before getting a keeper. But in Massachusetts they keep lobsters weighing 35 pounds, caught far to sea in draggers' nets. Such a giant may be 50 years old. Men who have eaten them say the meat is tender and delicious.

Hang around lobster wharfs long enough and you will see some of the oddities. For instance, while lobsters on your dinner plate are cardinal red, and lobsters in the sea are normally bluish green with some brown and black, freak lobsters come in all colors. Sometimes you get a sky-blue lobster, or an albino, or a calico, and very rarely a lobster that is bright red before it is cooked.

But any shape, size or sex, Maine lobsters are a Lucullan feast. I'd like four, right now.

Harbor seals have the friendliest faces

ROCKPORT — My heart jumps every time I see a seal's funny face pop out of the sea and look quizzically at me and my boat.

There is something about those long droopy whiskers and those liquid bulbous eyes and the tilt of that sleek shining head that fills me with affection and laughter every time I see a seal.

And you see seals almost every day you are out on Maine salt waters. Lew Dietz and Harry Goodridge, guardians of Andre the Rockport seal, say there are between 7,000 and 9,000 seals in Maine — all of them harbor seals.

The Maine harbor seal is a fish-eating mammal of the group called 'pinnipedia', which is Latin for "fin-footed."

There are 15,000 species of mammals, including man. Mammals

are distinct from all other animals because they have vertebrae, hair, and self-regulating body temperatures. The females have milk producing mammae.

Maine is the breeding ground for the harbor seals of the entire eastern United States.

The females come up the rivers to give birth. From my house, I look onto ledges in the Damariscotta River where mothers and their new born pups sun and frolic in springtime.

The fathers are not around. They stay at sea, lolling on offshore rocks and ledges, fishing.

Seal pups can't swim when they are born. The mothers nudge them into the water and teach them how. When they are tired, the pups climb on their mothers' backs and hitch a ride home.

When born, the pups are a light grey, almost white. For the first four to six weeks, they nurse rather like a newborn puppy nurses. The milk of a seal mother is ten times as rich as cow's milk.

Seals are so widespread in Maine that more than 40 harbors, islands and coves are named "Seal." Indians used seal oil as a skin beauty treatment, as medicine to heal burns and also to bring people out of fits. Seal steaks were served at weddings. And, of course, seal skins have always made fine coats.

But seals eat tremendous quantities of fish, and they can ruin fish nets. So Maine passed a law in 1900 placing a bounty on harbor seals. Town clerks paid a dollar for each seal nose brought in as evidence of destruction. But smart Indians killed one seal and made a dozen 'noses' out of a single skin and collected $12. After five years and $25,000, the state rescinded the bounty.

Because of the damage to their nets, fishermen often shoot seals. In 1972 a federal law was passed to protect seals and other marine mammals. Now anyone touching, let alone shooting, a seal is liable to a $10,000 fine.

The Navy and other government agencies train seals to locate distant divers and to carry tools back and forth on command. Trained seals could save lives and become man's underwater helpers. But they also might be trained as a deadly and unsuspected torpedo.

Till then the friendliest face in the sea is the seal's.

How salty is Maine's ocean?

ISLE AU HAUT — There is exhilaration in feeling salt spray blow across your face. The briny taste and the tangy smell of the sea are tonics for body and soul. And I wonder if this is instinct, since our ancestors and indeed all life, came from the salt sea.

Yet if mankind originated in the sea, why is it that we cannot tolerate drinking sea water now?

One answer is that the sea has become saltier and saltier.

The ocean off Maine contains three times as much salt as our blood. This is why we cannot quench our thirst by drinking sea water. In fact, drinking sea water makes a man thirstier. Sea water is now so much saltier than our blood that it takes up more water from our system than it gives.

Yet it is tremendously refreshing to rinse your mouth with cold sea water from the Maine ocean. It is a far better taste than you get from putting salt in drinking water.

The reason is that sea water contains several different kinds of salts. Sure, it contains plenty of common table salt, sodium chloride. But it also contains magnesium sulphate, the same as the Epsom salts, which some people take as medicine.

The salts in the sea come from the land. The salt in the crust of the earth is dissolved by rains and streams and rivers and these salts finally run down into the sea. Other salts come from the giant volcanoes which erupt unseen far down on the sea floor, thousands of feet below the surface. These two actions continuing over millions of years have made the sea saltier and saltier. Now this salt content is high enough to kill much of the land life which sprang from the sea when it was less salty.

Comb any Maine beach and you see scores of empty black cases, like coin purses with a sharp prong at each corner. But you never see anything like them alive in the ocean. What are they?

They are the egg shells of skates, that big flat fish with a long tail. Skates lay two eggs, each about the size of a pigeon's egg, and the eggs are protected inside the black purses. When the eggs hatch, the empty purses drift loose from the sea floor and end up on the beaches.

Another weird shell washed up on our beaches is that of the horseshoe crab. They are not skeletons of dead horseshoe crabs. Rather they are cast-off shells which horseshoe crabs outgrew and shed. These creatures haven't changed in 200 million years. They are living fossils of prehistoric times. No other animal has endured unchanged like this ugly creature. They are not really crabs. Their closest relatives are land-based scorpions and spiders.

Lobsters and crabs pull out of their cast-off shells by moving backward. But not this 200 million year old horseshoe crab. He slides out by going forward.

The big tides make Maine shores a happy hunting ground for flotsam and jetsam. What's the difference between 'em? Flotsam is the floating wreckage of ships and boats. Jetsam, some purists say, is the stuff jettisoned, thrown overboard, by an endangered ship. But some experts on life along the shore use "jetsam" to describe those lines of dried seaweed and shells left behind by the tides.

How Salty Is Maine's Ocean? / 71

Boat houses: cheap, warm and happy

EAST BOOTHBAY — Tom O'Neil, 28, and Karen Varney, 24, are beating the high cost of living on shore. Instead they are living happily and economically aboard a 31-foot sailboat, and doing it in comfort through Maine's coldest winter.

Tom is a mechanical engineer, a graduate of Wisconsin, who works as a draftsman at the Bath Iron Works. Karen is from Brewer, Maine, and she works in Bath too, with a state agency providing help to the families of retarded or handicapped children. Their sailboat-home is tied up to a sheltered dock in East Boothbay.

"I paid $5,000 for "Boldwater" six years ago," says Tom. "She is a Casey cutter, built of wood in 1942. That makes her seven years older than me. This is my third winter living on her in Maine. That first winter we sailed south to the Bahamas, stopped on the way to earn money and then for a year we worked in the islands. We came slowly home, stopping again to earn as we sailed. We got back to Maine in November 1974. We far prefer living on a boat," says Tom, a lithe, bearded, able and agreeable host.

Living aboard "Boldwater," Tom and Karen have the finest of ocean views, but do not pay much in property taxes. "Ocean front homes start at about $50,000 hereabouts, and taxes run around $1,-200 a year," Tom says. "Plus the oil to heat 'em in winter and the ploughing of drives; and then the mowing of lawns in summer; and the paying of mortgages, all year every year. We got our home for $5,000. Low taxes, no oil burner, no lawns."

Tom O'Neil shows me around his home on the water. "I encase the whole boat above the deck in heavy plastic, from November to May so we are warm and don't heat the outdoors. I have my workshop here on deck in winter, plus all tools and maintenance gear. That gives us more room below. On bright sunny days in winter, it is hot on deck under the plastic." We go below, where there is a comfortable sleeping cabin in the bow; then a main salon or sitting room, complete with a Shipmate coal stove for extra warmth; then there is a galley or little kitchen; then a head or small toilet.

"We have electric power and fresh water piped on board from dockside," says Tom. "Here is our TV and our stereo, and we have electric lights for reading and an electric heater for fast heat. When we need a shower in winter, we go to the Y. In summer, we dive off the deck."

Life aboard is simple, but comfortable. There is no space for unnecessary frills. "We read, watch TV, listen to music, and do repairs. We go to bed about 9:30 p.m. and get up at 5:30 a.m. for work. We see sunsets and sunrises here most of the year. And only a hard blow right out of the east tosses us around. Otherwise we are well sheltered here and there is no ice. We pay about $30 a month rent to tie up and get the utilities. In summer, we cruise the coast on weekends in our home. Some winter we may sail off again to the warm Bahamas. . .shipboard life is the best for us."

Another family living aboard ship through this winter is the Frank Gibbs, down in the region of Harpswell. Up to five kids live aboard this 40-foot trawler converted for family living. Gibbs is a well known radio personality in Maine.

Probably dozens of families are living year 'round on boats in Maine and loving it.

Soon my daughter and her husband will give it a try. Bill and Susan Fagan are buying a classic 38-foot cabin cruiser — a Whitney built in 1931, and kept in mint condition by one family for over 40 years. She cruised Maine waters last summer, but is now at Mystic. She has two sleeping cabins, a salon, two 'heads', a fine galley. Above all she has the elegance in woods, brass, and bronze that were built into boats 40 to 50 years ago, but are scarce today.

I am full of envy. I love the idea of living year 'round on a well made, well kept, classic boat. It may be the best way to combine romance, adventure, gorgeous views, a good life-style with rock bottom costs.

Sea urchins, starfish and sand dollars

NORTH HAVEN — When I leaned down over the wharf to help Piper, my Dalmatian, jump up from the float below, my last pair of eyeglasses slipped off the string and fell out of my shirt pocket. Helpless and cursing, I watched them sink and spin slowly down through the sea to the bottom.

Since I had another week of cruising on my vacation, I needed glasses badly enough to go diving to retrieve the sunken pair. The water was only 12 feet deep, but it was cold and dark down there on the bottom where starfish and sea urchins and sand dollars thrive. By feel more than by sight, my fingers finally located my glasses, which I am using now as I write this column, anchored off an island beach in Penobscot Bay.

Some sharp spines of the sea urchins broke off and stuck in the tips of my searching fingers. But these Maine urchins are not poisonous, like the black spined urchins in Florida and the West Indies which sting as viciously as a hornet.

I brought a couple of urchins and sand dollars and starfish up to examine on the deck of my boat "Steer Clear." They are all kissing cousins, members of the same family, despite totally different outward looks.

Take the needles or spine off a sea urchin and you find the five-rayed design and the holes through which five tube feet protrude — miniatures of the five longer feet of starfish. Now open up the green shell, and you come to the roe. We don't eat the roe of sea urchins in Maine, but they are a prize delicacy on the shores of the Mediterranean, and among Italian and French colonies in Boston and New York. Eaten raw, with hot, fresh, crusty French bread, they are extremely rich and some gourmets say they have a flavor more subtle than caviar.

I tried a few, after reading Euell Gibbons, who wrote about them in "Stalking the Blue Eyed Scallop" and in his pamphlet "A Wild Way to Eat," written for Maine's Hurricane Island School. The orange-yellow roes taste of seafood, slightly sweet, with a hint of cantaloupe.

Starfish are hated by most fishermen. They can eat and destroy a huge oyster or mussel or clam bed overnight. The starfish just climbs on top of a bivalve, spreads its five tentacle feet so they cover each side of the oyster, mussel or clam shell, and then pulls in opposite directions. Sooner or later the single muscle by which clams, oysters and mussels keep their shells closed, gives way. And the starfish devours its prey.

Fishermen used to cut starfish to pieces when they hauled them in their nets, and then threw them back into the ocean.

But no more. Now everyone knows that starfish grow new rays or tentacles. Sometimes when one starfish is cut or torn into five separate rays, each ray can grow into a new starfish, provided it had a piece of the central body. This is one reason there are so many millions of starfish in the ocean. Another reason is that they have no enemies, outside of gulls. And they are of no commercial value.

Sand dollars are a beautiful treasure of the sea, often made into decorations. Examine them closely and you see they are a cousin to sea urchins. The sea urchin spines are just a small soft coating on a sand dollar. You also see the same five grooves for five feet as in the starfish and sea urchins. And they reproduce in the same way as sea urchins, by shedding eggs or sperm into the water from these five gonads. Although they both are part of the same family, these voracious starfish eat sand dollars.

Shake the shell of a dead sand dollar, and you hear a rattle. The rattle is the noise of five teeth with which the sand dollars eats. This chewing apparatus has a lovely name: Aristotle's Lantern.

But diving for glasses is a hard way to find out these things.

Dragging with Charlie

ABOARD LOUISE G. — My alarm shrills at 2:15 a.m. I dress, get together my gear and drive an hour to the fish wharf at Cundy's Harbor.

There at 3:30 a.m., behind the big white house and in front of Holbrook's store, another car pulls up, douses its headlights. In the dark a voice calls out — "If you're coming dragging with Charlie Saunders, I'm here! Grab your gear and follow me!"

In the darkness, we follow Charlie, slithering down the ledge, over unknown rocks and mud to the shoreline. We move along. A flashlight shines on the water's edge and the last rock for a jump into the skiff. Thence out to the dragger Louise G., a black bulk outlined against the night sky, hanging on her mooring.

Charlie jumps aboard, pulls the switch to turn on the ship's lights. For the first time we see each other. I see Charlie Saunders, black haired, 35. Until he took to fishing full time, Charlie Saunders taught school—math and biology at Freeport and Bath. I see his helper Lendell Alexander, 16, big in high rubber boots, oilskin pants, long blond hair. We shake and say hello fast and Charlie goes into his pilot house and Lendell goes forward to the bow. Soon Charlie has the diesel coming noisily to life. Lendell ties in the skiff to the mooring line. Charlie yells and Lenny casts off and the Louise

G. is underway, gliding through the black night, headed to sea and the fish, whiting today.

Stars shine down brightly as we glide south past Bear and Harbor and Burnt Coat islands, past Carrying Place Head. It is turning 4 a.m. as we pass the bombing range marker on Cape Small.

The light atop Seguin island beams brightly across the dark sea. Its 100,000 candlepower beam shines from 180 feet above the sea, visible from 25 miles. George Washington commissioned Seguin Light.

Off Seguin dawn breaks. It reveals eight other Maine draggers already at work. This stretch of water is transformed from lead grey to burnished bronze as the first rays of the sun strike us. We set out the nets for our first trawl.

In the fishing business, you start work early. And keep working 'til late. When banks and offices open at 9 a.m., Maine draggermen have already done five or six hours work. When banks and office workers head home at 5 p.m., the men on the draggers have three hours more work to do. This day on the Louise G, began at 3:30 a.m.; and we will finish just before 8 p.m. A Maine draggerman puts in a work day 16 hours long.

This is a report on one such day in August on a dragger. In February, it's about the same 16 hour day, with these changes. Deduct 70 degrees from the air temperature; add a knifing wind, a running sea and white vapor, more blinding than any fog; a wicked salt spray that stings like grains of ice as it whips against your face and runs down your neck, along your spine under your oilskins. In February, dark comes four hours sooner, so you may make your last haul-back and pick over the last trawl of fish in the dark, under deck lights, in the freezing blackness. The money is better in February than in August, if you can stand the work. This winter the helper on this dragger took home about $6000 in six months cold hard wet work. But the number of draggers keeps going down because prices keep going lower and fish get scarcer and smaller.

"In Rockland, half the big fishing fleet—150 footers—are idle. Tied up," says Charlie Saunders. "Our 50 foot draggers get fewer. Down from around 75 two years back to 45 today. And some of those are up for sale." Charlie Saunders is secretary of the Maine Draggermens Association. He is also an active leader in the new fishermen's co-op at Cundys Harbor.

Our first trawl, set out at 5:30 a.m. is hauled back at 8 a.m. The nets come alongside. There is no smile on Charlie's face. It is too easy a hoist to swing half-filled nets onto the deck, jerk the lines open and spill out the fish. The pile is not big. Maybe 400 pounds. Inside 20 minutes, Charlie and Lendell are setting out again.

Nets for whiting are paid out from the side of his vessel. They are weighted down to the bottom by the two big wood and steel doors, that hold down each side of the mouth of the net. These doors each weigh over 750 pounds. Handle them wrong as they come slamming up out of the sea and you'll smash a hand.

Our net, like a huge stocking cap, streams out astern, dragging along the ocean bottom, hundreds of feet below. Our speed is down to 2½ miles an hour. In the pilot house, Charlie Saunders watches and listens to $16,000 worth of electronics. "One day" he says "I counted all the dials and knobs inside this pressure cooker where I work. Came to more than 100."

Today the $6000 scanner—an underwater radar that shows the rockpiles ahead and to the sides—is out of order. Charlie is working from another instrument that shows in smudgy grey marks on a moving sheet of paper, the formations of rocks and fish along the bottom, down where his net is dragging.

That net is worth at least $6000. If Charlie lets it get hung up on a rockpile, it can be ripped to pieces. He will lose the fish. And lose the rest of this fishing day and maybe others while he repairs it.

So he watches the instruments closely. The line depicting the bottom slopes up; and then down; then runs flat. Suddenly a line shoots steeply up, like the peak fever on a temperature chart. On this chart, that peak spells "rockpile below." Charlie must turn his boat; his net behind avoids the danger in time. If the $6000 scanner was operating, Charlie would know much more about the fish and the terrain down there. It is rough, mountainous, pocked with steep hills, high ledges and rockpiles, and valleys where fish hide.

"Call it a game of cowboys and Indians. In chasing the fish between the rockpiles. Daring how close I can come to the rockpiles to get those fish without the scanner, I will play it safe today." Flat calm, hot, we drag for 2½ hours.

Second haul-back is ordered by Charlie at 11 a.m. With a side trawler like this 35 year old Louise G, hauling back can be a time when you lose fish out of the nets. The boat lies almost dead in the water, out of gear, while Lendell works the winches, hauling in the 700 to 900 feet of expensive wire hawser out on each side of the net. "If we had a stern-trawler, we'd have power enough to haul-back and keep forward speed too. That way there is no risk of fish escaping . . . " says Charlie.

Lendell, the helper, moves to the midship rails to handle those huge 750 pound doors as they slam up out of the sea. He grabs, twists, unhooks the net, then hooks the door back into a steel rack. Repeats with the next door, just moments behind. Charlie is working the winches now, bringing up the laden nets. Finally—fish. One huge bulging bag, filled to bursting with silver fish. On deck, they explode it open by pulling loose the tie knots and a torrent of fish pours out. Then another bulging bag. Charlie is smiling at his third bulging bag. He whoops with glee. This haulback brings up 6000 pounds. The decks are awash with fish, knee deep in whiting.

Nets carefully emptied, carefully folded, Charlie and Lenny work together, setting out the third trawl of the day. Again our dragger steams slowly, turning, twisting to avoid rockpiles, playing cowboy and Indian, hunter and hunted with the schools of fish far below. Smudges on the instrument paper in the pilot house show what the electronic beams are picking up underneath us. In the pilot-house Charlie moves his boat in careful pursuit. For lunch, he eats a can of pears.

Lendell Alexander spends the next five hours "picking." By hand he sorts the fish, throwing the good sized whiting into the fish hold below; piling the edible, marketable ground fish separately; then kicking overboard the unwanted, unmarketable fish. Nearby five thousand gulls wait. When Lenny kicks the unmarketable fish overboard, our boat is the eye of a snowstorm of white gulls, screaming and diving. They scavenge everything.

But the waste is terrible. Charlie Saunders, like most Maine fishermen is bitter about the waste. "It is criminal" he says "to throw back thousands of pounds of fish protein from just one small boat on one day . . Multiply it out by all other boats doing the same . . . The world needs the food. But if we take it ashore, no one will buy it in the U.S."

Earlier this summer I had flown out with the Coast Guard to see Russian fleets fishing on Georges Banks. Hundreds of vessels, 300 feet long, compared to the 52 feet of Louise G, fishing day and night, month after month — and wasting nothing. The foreign fishing fleets process it all. We waste, throw back, almost half. And all those fish are dead, useless. The Russians use every fish, big, small, of whatever species.

Third haul back brings in another bonanza. "More fish than we've had in a year!" shouts a happy Charlie Saunders, as another 5,000 pounds or so are dropped on deck.

Picking them over, throwing overboard the unwanted thousands of fish is too much work for an exhausted Lenny to do alone. Charlie turns the wheel over to me, to bring the boat home to Cundy's Harbor, while he picks with Lenny.

Finally at dockside, the dirtiest work of all . . the 'lumper' goes down into the hold and, waist deep in fish, loads them into baskets.

Price to the fishermen is 5 cents a pound today. This has been a good day. Roughly $250 for the boat, half the earnings. (To replace the Louise G new and all her gear would take $150,000). Then take out for the food and fuel used today. Then split the remaining $200 or so between Charlie and his helper. It's been a good day. Say $100 each for 16 hours, tough work. That comes to $6 an hour. Sometimes it works out to only a dollar.

At 8 p.m., back to the mooring, we finish hosing down, cleaning up, leaving stuff ship shape to leave at 3:30 a.m. tomorrow. That is only 7½ hours away; and a man must see his family, clean up, have his dinner, sleep and get up to go again, for 16 more hours tomorrow. Maybe the price will be a nickel a pound, maybe. Maybe the catch will be good, maybe. Maybe it will be zero. Maybe the net will get ripped to shreds. That is fishing.

III /

North Country

Aroostook

J AKE DAY GOT US to the North Country during our second winter in Maine. And we were hooked.

Jake—who has turned 80 now—last climbed Mt. Katahdin, the highest mountain in Maine, when he was 75. Went up with Governor Ken Curtis who was heading up to 40. Jake is a Damariscotta boy, just like his grandfather; but went west to Hollywood and helped Walt Disney make "Bambi", that classic movie about the white-tailed deer. But Jake's first love and real fame is rooted in Maine and his paintings of the country and the animals at all seasons.

Well, Jake loved the north country so much that he founded Jake's Rangers, a group of Damariscotta men who went fishing and hunting together in Jake's north woods. Justice William O. Douglas was proud to be the only outsider ever to become a "Jake's Ranger".

Jake got us to Mattagamon Lake, beyond Patten, and we stayed with Chub and Fran Foster, who ran a hunting camp there. Chub is one of the finest guides and Fran is one of the finest cooks in Maine. So Jake started us off right.

That trip was an eye-opener for newcomers. First, just getting from Damariscotta to Mattagamon Lake in February is neither quick nor easy. The snow was piled 12 feet high along the roadsides *in the north country. Cars flew red flags from the tip of their radio antennas, so you could see the flag coming over the snowbank.*

Fran and Chub met us with snowmobiles, and we left our car on the "civilized" side of the lake, and piled our gear and ourselves on those snowmobiles and headed across the big, frozen lake into the teeth of a bitter north wind.

That was before we learned about the right way to dress to keep warm. We had on layers of the wrong stuff. Each of us had a gap somewhere. And that subzero air, plus the north wind, got in. Now, years later, I still ache at the remembrance of that cold, cold ride.

Since then, the North Country has been a magnet. It is a world wholly different from the rest of Maine.

SLED DOG

GREENVILLE — For the third time in one morning "Red Sam", a well trained dog in McIver's famous "red" sled-dog team, disobeyed a command from McIver.

McIver halted his 12 dog freighter team, which hauled supplies out of Churchill over 50 miles of snow-packed wasteland to men on remote weather stations. And he walked down the sled line to "Red Sam". And he cut the dog out of his pulling harness. Then he hefted the 68 pound animal high into the air; and smashed "Red Sam" down across his knee, breaking his back and killing the dog instantly.

State-side G.I.'s winced like women at the sight. Big men in parkas, they moved in a circle, moaning around the cracked body of the husky in the snow. And glowered at Angus McIver, the dog-driver.

But the other sled-dog drivers stood silent. They understood. They knew no man loved his teams more than McIver. They knew about the bag of doughnuts which Angus McIver, a raw boned Scot, carried on his sled — where every ounce of weight meant gold, and how as a special sundown treat McIver fed doughnuts to his strong reddish dogs who had pulled their hearts out for him all the long day.

"Angus did what he had to do," explained an old dog driver. "Out in the Arctic snow men's lives depend on a sled dog. And that grown, trained dog disobeyed orders three times."

Ron Riley, a sled dog driver from Sidney, Maine, leans to fondle his lead dog, readying for the start of a gruelling marathon sled dog race in Greenville's winter carnival.

"A thousand dollars couldn't part me from this dog," says the gruff and weather-lined Riley as he digs fingers into the dog's guard hair, through the layers of wool and feels for tell-tale fat on muscled ribs. "Most lead dogs know commands. This dog obeys them. Always!"

Riley loosens the collar, rubs the dog's big chest. "She's turned seven years old now. And the speed is going out of her. I'm afraid the younger dogs will over-run her any day. And a sad day that will be!"

That day came at Greenville. The young dogs overran their leader. And when the long race was done, there was no joy in it for Riley. No matter how many teams he had beaten, his loved lead dog had lost. And he would have to pick a younger, stronger dog with bigger wind to move up the sled line to become the new lead dog. "And will the new lead dog obey — always? And how will the old dog feel left home in the kennel?" These questions throb like an ache in Riley's mind, spoiling the day.

"We keep 30 sled dogs in our family. Been at it for years and years. I had 'best of breed' in other breeds many times in Maine before I came to sled dogs, though."

The Maine Sled Dog Club, organized in 1959, is spreading enthusiasm for this great sport across the state. But it takes plenty of work and plenty of cash. Untrained Siberians (blue eyes 35-60 lbs.), white Samoyeds (38-68 lbs), silver-grey Alaskan Malamutes (50-85 lbs.), Eskimo dogs (up to 135 lbs, but usually closer to 80 lbs) all cost well over $100 each as furry, butter fat pups. A trained lead dog, even the mongrel Indian dogs, can cost up to $1000 each. Teams must run a 15 or 20 mile course five days a week to be in winning shape (tough pads, no fat, plenty of wind and endurance.) They must be fed well and groomed carefully and weighed constantly and vetted year-round; and housed at home; and transported by special truck to race sites. Care and exercise take upwards of two hours a day; food and vet bills for 30 dogs may run close to $2000 a year. So when you see a well trained 12 dog team flash by, complete with a sled worth $150, you are looking at a total investment of $20,000 or more.

But a dog is only as good as his feet. Racing over wet snow can soften pads; ragged ice can cut them; or toenails, used for gripping, can be torn back. The result is infection. Hence special boots are sometimes used over the thick pads. A sled dog's pads have tufts of hair between the toes, which serve as snow-shoes.

All huskies can pull loads twice their weight. The record was set by a 93-pound Malamute which moved an incredible load of 2,103 pounds. One team, using a wheeled sled, travelled from Fairbanks, Alaska, to Lewiston, Maine, a distance of 6,000 miles. Speed depending on load, is up to 12 miles an hour.

Admiral Peary would never have reached the North Pole without his sled dogs. "Day after day" he wrote "they struggled across that awful frozen desert, fighting for their lives and ours; day after day they worked till the last ounce of work was gone from them, and they fell dead in their tracks without a sound . . ."

Training for a sled dog starts when the dog is about 8 months old. The pup is harnessed amid experienced dogs and learns from them. Biggest dogs are used in the "wheel positions", directly ahead of the sled, and do the heaviest pulling. Lightest dogs may be trained as lead dogs or work in the pivot position, just stern of the leader.

Commands are few. "Gee!" (meaning "Right!") "Haw!" (Left) and "Whoa!" (Stop). There is no command for "Go!" — Sled dogs must be staked down to keep them from running. "Mush!" is just for movies. Each driver develops his own special, undecipherable language for his own teams. But dogs must learn to pull with each other. When they fight, the wolf way back in their blood stream comes out. They fight to kill.

Nature's protection against death in the jugular vein as well as cold in the Arctic are the 4 to 7 inches of "guard hair". Underneath this outer-layer is a double-layer of soft, tight wool, insulated with oil. In a sleeping bag like this, huskies can sleep outdoors at 50° below zero, snuggled into a snow bank for extra warmth.

Snow-blindness is a tragic threat to these magnificent working dogs. The strains which develop blue eyes seem to be immune from this sad malady.

In Maine, sled dog owners guard as a trade secret the precise diet they feed their teams, though the basis is usually a first class commercial dog food. In the Arctic however dogs are fed caribou, seal meat, whale meal, Arctic char and other high-energy, high-protein food. Instead of drinking water, they eat snow. (Water freezes). Weight-watching is an almost daily chore for team owners, who fear fat on their dogs, yet need them strong and filled with fuel-food.

Bright eyed girls with turned-up noses and copper colored pigtails and only 10 or 12 winters behind them gave the lie at Greenville to the idea that sled dog racing is only for a tough breed of men. The girls' soprano screeches drive their three dog teams with a frenzy, to galloping speeds covering a 3 mile course in close to 15 minutes.

There is a mystical, primeval splendor in seeing man and his sled dogs work. And, thanks to the Down East Sled Dog Club, you have the chance most weekends in winter.

LUMBERJACKS—THE REAL PIONEERS

ALLAGASH—Sitting by a warm fire these winter nights, I think of Maine's north woods, where dead of winter was the busiest time for lumberjacks.

What a breed they were! The Maine lumberjack was tougher, rougher, more daring, and endured more hardship and tamed more wild land than any cowboy of the West.

How did the cowboy get to be the symbol of the hard, sentimental, freewheeling American male who tamed the great spaces?

The Maine lumberjacks, the river drive bosses, the loggers, the timber cruisers, the cant-dog men, the choppers, the sawyers, the filers, the teamsters, the brawling lumber kings — these are the very stuff of the American spirit and the Yankee pioneer.

But cowboys got to be the legend. Good sun and flat land made life easy for the moviemakers. So the movies glorified the cowboy, and the Maine lumberjacks lost out to glory because their land was too rugged and their weather too cold for Hollywood.

Now I like the cowboys. I like their cowponies even more. But the dismal end is the nasal, tinny, whining music that cowboys sing around the old corral. Coyotes wailing are sweeter to the ear.

The ballads of Maine lumberjacks are music and poetry from heaven, by comparison with those western wails.

Hey-day of the great lumber camps was in the 1920's and 1930's. Before radio came to those rough and ready camps, hundreds of lumberjacks would sing around the stoves at night. Some wailed. Some roared. And some sang with simple beauty. And the songs they sang were about the last truths — Rum, Love, Death on the logging drives, Home and Mother, and the Gorgeous Girls of Bangor.

Thank heaven some of their verses are preserved forever. Mrs. Fannie Eckstrom's books — especially "Minstrelsy of Maine" — give us the words and the sad tales behind the long lumberjack poems . . . "The Jam on Gerry's Rock," "Canaday-I-Oh," and especially that tragic ballad "The Hoboes of Maine."

Our wilderness camps produced their poets. Larry Gorman was perhaps the best known of Maine's lumberjack poets. He died in 1923, but is kept alive forever in a book about him by Prof. Edward S. Ives. And there is Joe Scott, dead in 1916, who wrote songs on demand for a couple of dollars each — love songs, drinking songs, raucous songs and bawdy songs. Among his best is "The Whore's Lament."

One logger's favorite song is about Dan Day who lived on Perry Stream, who fathered 18 kids and then sired triplets named Peen, Lay and Lum. Loggers commemorated the birth of the Day triplets with this classic: "The Day Settlement on Perry Stream is the only place in the world where they ever made three Days in one night."

The lumberjack songs would fill several big books. Prof. Robert Pike, who has written so well about the North woods says his favorite is "When the Drive Comes to Town." The first verse of it goes this way:

"Come all ye gallant shanty boys and listen while I sing,

We've worked six months in cruel frosts but soon we'll take our fling.

The ice is black and rotten and the rollways are piled high;

So boost upon your peavey sticks while I do tell you why:

For it's break the rollways out, my boys, and let the big sticks slide!

And file your calks and grease your boots and start upon the drive.

A hundred miles of water is the nearest way to town;

So tie into the tail of her and keep her hustling down!"

The axes that built Maine

PATTEN — George Parsons sharpens axes. Go into his wooden work shed. It is an eye-opener into the world of axes.

These tools are not just things with sharp edges you keep in the garage for chopping firewood. They are gems; they are surgeon's scalpels; and they built Maine.

About as good a woods museum as you can find anywhere is the Lumberman's Museum in Patten. Spend a few fascinating hours there, and you'll get an insider's look at life in the old lumbering camps, in those never-to-be-forgotten days when axe was king of the Maine woods.

Men used three kinds of axes in those days — the single-bitted, or pole-axe, the double-bitted axe and the broad axe.

The first two weighed about four pounds. The double-edged axe had the great advantage of two bits, or cutting edges. One could be ground fine for cutting, the other left bevelled for splitting.

The biggest advantage of the single-edged axe may be safety;

carrying it on your back through the brush, you were not so likely to get gashed in the neck.

The broad axe is too much for me. It weighs 12 pounds or more. Its blade is very wide, and its handle is curved and short.

In the early days of Maine lumbering, a cutting crew in the woods consisted of three men — a liner, a scorer and a hewer. The liner cut off the bark. Next, the scorer stood on the log, cut very close to what would be the finished face of the log, scoring it for the next man. Then came the artist with the broad axe, who "hewed the line" made by the scorer.

Harry Foster from Nova Scotia was a famous broad-axe artist. He could hew a board 12 feet long by one inch by eight inches with his broad axe. Men say he could hew a line so straight that on a 20-foot log, he could hew the chalk line and never be one eighth of an inch off the mark.

Axemen, the year round professionals in the trade, cherished their axes the way a marksman cherishes his rifle. They shaved down their axe handles till they sprang like whalebone. They carried their own oilstones to keep a keen edge on their weapon. They made and hung their own handles to fit their own axes, tailored to suit their swing.

Their skill was a matter of pride and joy. They did far more than cut down trees with their axes. They made small, decorative furniture. When they went into the Maine woods, their axes built camps for the lumberjacks and hovels for the horses and wooden sinks for the cook shack and chairs to sit on, tables to eat off and bunks to sleep upon.

These men kept their axes so sharp that they could shave a match stick into a dozen slim slivers. Or taking the axe head between two hands, they'd use it as a smoothing plane or as a knife to carve delicate patterns into wood.

Trees and timber cut by such magnificent axemen became masts in great schooners and planking for ships that circled the globe, and houses for colonial Americans. The axe more than the rifle won the North American continent.

But a couple of fellows got rich from trees in more frivolous ways.

Harry Davis, of Monson, who lived to be well over 90, was the Spruce-Gum King. The clear tit gum came from the spruce tree ready for chewing and sold in penny sticks from Maine to Texas. Harry also sold the balsam pitch for $55 a gallon to the Defense Department. In World War II they used it for fusing together the glass in gun sights and microscopes, as it was the most transparent "glue" known in those days.

And then there is the toothpick, probably the greatest social innovation of the 19th century next to the spittoon.

The toothpick was the "invention" of a Yankee trader from Strong, Maine, named Forster. Forster found natives in South America, where he was travelling, picking their teeth with wooden toothpicks instead of knives or goose quills.

He sent a box to his wife back home. A hotel man got them by mistake and ordered more. Forster came home, made toothpicks from Maine white birch and sold 250,000 the first year. By the 1860's he had factories making the things by the millions.

Now toothpicks are shipped out of Maine in carload lots almost every day of the year.

Ed Lacroix's Allagash Locomotive

ST. FRANCIS — On the stormiest, snowiest day of winter, somebody ought to take the Corps of Army Engineers into the Allagash wilderness and show them King Ed Lacroix's engineering miracle.

Ed Lacroix, a lumber king from the St. John River region, built a railroad 13 miles long, there in the wilderness. That was 50 years ago.

Now, all to hell and gone in the wilderness, you can still see the 90-ton steam locomotive which Ed Lacroix brought in. When he had finished hauling a million cords of wood with that monster, King

Ed Lacroix moved on to cut timber elsewhere — and didn't bother taking that 90-ton steam locomotive with him.

So there she stands, bang in the middle of the Allagash wilderness. Piled with snow in winter, she must look weird even to the few wild animals stirring. In the summer canoeists look up from the Allagash waterway and gawk and gasp when they see a huge locomotive in the forest, miles from nowhere.

Fifty years ago — in the winter of 1926 — King Ed Lacroix brought all his workers, all his supplies, all his equipment through 50 miles of forest to begin building a 13-mile railroad from Eagle Lake to Umbazooksus (roll that wondrous word around your tongue three times fast!)

Lacroix moved them in across tote roads bedded in ice and over lakes frozen yards deep.

He needed 60 flatcars, each 32 feet long, to carry his lumber along the railroad, once it was built. So he built huge sleds and hauled the flatcars in on them. And his crews and his sleds brought that monstrous 90-ton steam locomotive from Lac Frontiere on the Quebec border across those 50 winter miles of forest wilderness, tote road and frozen lakes.

Ed Lacroix's Allagash Locomotive / 95

Building the 13-mile railroad through that rough country took guts, daring, muscle and backwoods knowhow. Today you can see the remnants of the giant trestles Lacroix built. He built one 600 feet long out into the waters of Umbazooksus, and he built another giant trestle 1,500 feet long, spanning the Allagash stream. And to get his logs up out of Eagle Lake onto his flatcars which were 25 feet higher, up on the rail bed, Lacroix built three huge conveyors, each 225 feet long. These conveyors, powered by diesels, delivered a cord of wood every 90 seconds into the waiting flatcars. It took Lacroix just 18 minutes to load each 32-foot-long car with 12½ cords of wood. As soon as he had a 12-car train loaded with 130 cords, the 90-ton locomotive would take off. It was a dangerous 13-mile ride, and the engineer took it mighty carefully. He took three hours to travel the 13 miles to Umbazooksus. Once there, Lacroix speeded up the work. He'd unload the entire train in 60 minutes, dumping the wood into the stream, sending it on its way to Great Northern mills. Lacroix scheduled three trips of 12 cars every day.

In six years, 1927 to 1933, King Ed Lacroix moved out a million cords of pulpwood. He cut the area clean. Then he moved on.

But his 90-ton steam locomotive still stands there in the Allagash wilderness where he left her. Too big big to move, she is an amazing monument to the men who did the impossible in Maine's north woods half a century ago.

BEARS: 9,000 IN THE DEEP WOODS

GREENVILLE — The very words "black bear" conjure up the deep woods. Maine, I am happy to report, has more black bears than any state east of the Mississippi, between 7,000 and 9,000 of them.

But we really don't know much about our bears. To find out more, Roy Hugie, 30, a big game research leader in the Department of Inland Fish and Wildlife, is running a 'bear management' program in Baxter Park.

In June and July, more than 32 bears have been trapped and tagged and another 30 will be caught and tagged before they den-up for winter in November.

In addition, eight bears are radio-equipped. From planes, Roy and others will track them, find where they travel and what they eat most and other details of their lifestyle.

Bear hunting in Maine is big business. About a thousand bears are killed by hunters, more than half of them by out-of-staters, some 33,300 of whom are paying $60 for a license to hunt bear this year. (In the state of Washington, they kill 14,000 bears during a hunting season)

To make up for this loss, about 1,500 bear cubs are born in Maine each January. And a baby bear is an amazing creature.

First, it is tiny. A mother bear weighing 250 pounds may produce a baby weighing only eight ounces, blind and hairless.

Last year a 300-pound female produced a 12 ounce cub. That is the equivalent of a 110 pound human mother giving birth to a baby weighing only about four ounces.

Born tiny in January, denned up with momma, the two or three cubs in a litter each weigh about six pounds by April or May when they begin to move out and feed on something other than mother's milk. They spend the whole first year with their mother, and den up with her again in the next winter.

Bears make good mothers. Infant mortality is low. And mother bears will fight to the death to protect the cubs from old male bears who would eat them, even their own.

Bears mate, but they don't really marry. In fact, bears are basically loners. The only social occasion in a bear's life may be that brief mating in June.

An odd thing about bears is that after mating, nothing much happens to the fertilized egg between June and November. It just stays there, waiting till November, when the female dens up. Then it begins to develop.

Bears do not really hibernate, despite all the tales about hibernating bears. Rather when a bear 'dens-up' for winter, he or she goes into a moderate, long sleep. For example a bear's body temperature stays about 102 degrees, whereas a hibernating woodchuck drops its temperature to 60 degrees.

A woodchuck breathes about once a minute when hibernating. But a merely dormant bear breathes 10 or even 20 times as often. In fact, you can sometimes spot a dormant bear in winter by seeing steam coming up through the snow where a bear is denned up.

They survive winter by living off the enormous amount of vegetation and insects and trash they have eaten in early November. Going in at 250 pounds, a big bear may emerge at 175 pounds.

Most Maine bears weigh about 140 pounds and stand about six feet high on their hind legs. The biggest Maine bear found recently was 410 pounds, though old time monsters weighed in at 500 pounds.

Normally, Maine bears live to about 12 years, but a few have lived to be 25.

No more bears will feed at Baxter Park dumps. The dumps are gone. And the problem bears who bothered campers for food have been taken 100 miles away to learn how to fend for themselves.

No one should mess around with a bear. But happily Maine bears have never mauled human beings, as western bears do. They are gentler here in Maine, partly because no grizzlies are here to attack them and make them ferocious. Some guides say that in Maine, only an old male bear or a man will kill another bear.

GHOSTS OWN THE ALLAGASH

ALLAGASH WILDERNESS WATERWAY — If rocks could rub their bruises, every rock in the Allagash would smell of Ben Gay ointment. This was the "summer of hard knocks" for Allagash rocks. Every one is bruised black, white, green and red, the paint scars of a thousand canoes show where they hit and hit and hit.

"We put 18 canoes in at Churchill Dam to run the Chase Rapids; and pulled 16 out of the river" says the Texas wife of ranger Steve Cram.

Novices with more courage than sense try going down the rapids without knowing how to handle a canoe. "They don't know how to back paddle; how to keep a canoe pointed; how to watch ahead and pick a course; how to stop dead; how to go real, real slow" says my guide Bert O'Leary. Bert was born a river man, in St. Francis.

Bert, like all good rivermen, uses a pole, a light ash pole 10 or 12 feet long with a strong metal tip. He scorns a paddle in fast shallow water. With that pole, he keeps us pointed where the rocks aren't; he stops us short and looks ahead.

Speed is not for the riverman; he takes it slow, slow, his canoe under total control all the way.

Rivermen like Ben O'Leary and Ed Pelletier, who together have spent over 80 years around the Allagash, use canoes 20 feet long or more—Old Town, canvas canoes.

But most of the 8000 who canoe the Allagash in summer, use metal canoes, 16 feet long, which rent for $7 a day or so. And they are hard to handle in the rapids. The metal sticks to the rocks. The metal is hard on the buttocks. The metal gets punched out of shape. And 16 foot is an awkward length. So when amateurs in metal canoes get in the rapids—there has to be a way to rescue them and their boat.

There is. They just turn the water off.

The word gets passed back to Ranger Cram at Churchill "Turn off the water. Canoes are stuck." He closes the dam. In a minute or two, the fast flowing Allagash rapids are bone dry. The stranded canoeists pick their canoe off the rocks where water pressure had jammed it, and carry it across a now dry river bed to the bank. "OK now. Turn the water on again!" Ranger Cram lifts the dam— and back to life come Chase Rapids.

The Allagash is more than a beautiful river in the wilderness. There is a mood, a spirit, a meaning to the Allagash no other river has—not the Snake in Colorado nor the Nile of Egypt nor the great Mississippi. What makes the Allagash different are the Allagash ghosts.

Standing off from the flame of the campfire one night, Bert and Len and Ben and I saw the ghosts which make the Allagash special.

We stood silent on a high rock, looking out over the black river water burnished bright silver by moonglow. And we saw the ghosts of the Allagash. First came the ghosts of the Indians, whose river this will always be. Allagash in Abenaki means "place of the hunting camp" or "bark-cabin lake." (And that weird word for a lake in the Allagash—Umsaskis—means linked like a sausage.) Listen, and between cries of the loon you can hear the swish of Indian paddles, gliding a birch bark canoe through the moonlight.

The next ghosts come . . , ghost of the incredible Joseph Chadwick, who mapped this country 210 years ago. He made survey maps two inches to the mile. He came here; but on the Allagash the Indians would not let him make a map. This was their holy hunting ground . . . Now, the ghost of Moses Greenleaf, the visionary who hoped to lead settlers into this wilderness, but died of typhoid. But what Moses Greenleaf reported in 1815 of these natural riches led in part to Maine gaining statehood in 1820.

But the ghosts that Leonard and Bert see best are the newer ghosts of big fisted, strong legged river men who ran the log drives and the horseboats, who worked and fought and hunted and died along the Allagash.

They are not quiet ghosts. They come with a roar and deafen you with noise. See the man steering Mary Ann, the first Lombard tractor, brainchild of the Waterville blacksmith. This forerunner of the first military tank and the first caterpillar farm tractor was born in the Allagash . . . One logger wrote: "To meet a Lombard locomotive on a still, bitter night deep in the woods, the headlight cutting through the darkness, chugging and rocking as it towed a train 500 feet long—blowing steam and smoke and fire to the treetops, was something indeed to remember."

The Lombards weighed 30 tons, did the work of 60 horses. But when those 30 tons, skis in front, tractors behind, hit an icy downgrade, prayers went up to heaven like rockets. The first Lombard worked the wilderness woods in 1907, the last in 1929. And the great iron bones, the skeletons, rest even now in the woods where they worked.

Noisy, banging ghosts of the tramway and the wilderness railway; feats of engineering and invention that no college man could dare. Inventions which had to be patched and made to run in the wilderness using only the wire which baled the hay for the horses . . . Here was born the American word 'haywire' . . .

Ghosts of the harshest of drivers, Will Cunliffe; and the best of lumbermen, and King Ed Lacroix, who paid better, fed better, and hauled more wood than any man. On the last long log drive on the Allagash, King Lacroix drove out 30 million feet of long log spruce.

These ghosts are here on the Allagash forever. The river is theirs, if it is ever anybody's but the Indians' river, and the river of the moose and the deer and the trout and the foxes and the loons. Yet the kids who bang up canoes rented for $7 a day and lose their dunnage and get tipped and soaked and keep on going and keep on sleeping on the rocky spots each night—these kids fit the Allagash too, in a different way. So do the "sports" who pay $1000 for the trip, fly in with guides and motors and fancy tents and charcoal steaks for dinner. There is room on the Allagash for everyone who loves it.

My friend turns, all muscle and tough river man, and smiling says: "Now that's a damfool thing for a man to be in love with; a damfool river in a damfool wilderness. But it's the truth. That's what the damfool Allagash does to a damfool man."

Now it has done it to me.

HERMITS IN THE WILDERNESS

UMSASKIS LAKE—Five hundred feet up over the Maine wilderness, George Later, at the controls of a Cessna 180, tries to punch his way through snow squalls. Thick as wet steam, cold and stinging as the edge of a horsewhip, the squalls rush down from the Canadian border. There is no hole left. And no edge left. "No sense going further up the Allagash," says Later. It is not the storm itself which makes Later swing his plane back toward Churchill Lake, but the fact there is no spot beyond Round Pond (already socked in solid) where he could in an emergency put the plane down.

A mile to the west, Malcolm Maheu's plane comes bouncing into sight again, out of another squall, flying lop-sided on the starboard wing. I mumble something worried-sounding.

"Plane is OK" says George Later. "He's off center because Jack Shaw's 250 pound frame is on the passenger side."

Both planes swing and curve downward through the snow for a float landing on Churchill. No sooner have we dragged the planes and moored them, than a piece of ceiling lifts — and Maheu is flying out, headed for Umsaskis Lake, eight miles away. Over the radio he shouts back "It's open now — but hurry." Moments later we land there and taxi behind him and Jack Shaw, Deputy Chief of Game Wardens, to the float near the newest and plushest wilderness camp, "The Waldorf of the Wardens." By the time our lines are tied, the squall shuts down Umsaskis, this time for the night.

Three hours later, there are a dozen of us in the cabin — all enormously over fed.

Curtis Cooper, Warden Supervisor of District I (a mere two million acres of wilderness responsibility) has cooked the steak and potatoes, helped by Warden Leonard Pelletier (a barrel chested giant who lifted a full drum of aviation gas up onto a bench. That barrel weighs about 450 pounds).

A truth syrup was passed and the doctors in attendance dispensed medicinal rations of Memory Freshener. The talk veered to the old hermits of the Maine Wilderness.

"The hermits are all gone now" said Jack Shaw sounding sad as though he missed their strange ways and leathery faces. And all agree. The wardens bemoan their passing — and acknowledge that no new breed is taking to leading lonely lives deep in the Maine woods. Hermits are extinct.

Jimmy Clarkson was the best known of the hermits. When he died, aged 82, Bangor Hydro established a fund in his memory. On his 80th birthday, in 1952, three plane loads of wardens flew in, other friends came by canoe all along the Allagash. Clarkson spent over 60 years alone in the woods, and was sole resident of Township Nine, Range 14, before he moved to tend Lock Dam. They say Clarkson never shot a deer. But he kept 19 as pets, calling each by name.

"He once had a flaming red beard" recalls George Later "and was a truly magnificent performer with the broad axe. Then, finally, his legs gave out. The man couldn't stand to be helpless or confined. And shot himself."

Ernest Hemingway was an off-beat hermit. By trade, Hemingway was a first rank musician who had played around the world with John Philip Sousa's famous band. Crossed in love, he left the cities and took to the wilderness woods. "I remember he always put a bearskin over his canned goods" recalls Curtis. "His theory was that covered by bearskin, his provisions would never freeze."

And old Joe Klimchook was the Russian Army officer at Russell Stream, near Pittston. "He used to haul a hogshead into the woods, knock out both ends, bait it and use it as a bear trap." Under his cot he kept pictures of himself in full uniform as a Cavalry officer in the Imperial Russian Army.

Bill Gordon holed up by himself at Knowles Brook on the St. John River. He moved camp when a Canadian cruiser and two lumberjacks went through his door yard. "Too darn many people," he griped. And left.

"I used to fly in his winter groceries" recalls George Later. "The whole supply used to cost $47. And he demanded Cream of Tartar in 15 pound boxes and raised hob at the new one pound bags.

"We had to buy a trapping license for him for $15; and then he refused to trap the beaver in his pond because he liked that family. When I flew him to Presque Isle to sign up for Social Security, he refused to sign papers which read William Gordon. Said his name was Bill. And they could keep their money before he would sign William.

"That was the day when he put on a suit! I couldn't recognize him. He said he had bought the suit in 1911, and kept it in cedar for 50 years. And you could smell that he was telling the truth."

When he grew frail and old, a warden with a chain saw offered to cut winter wood for him. Old Bill wouldn't let him use a noisy chain saw. Only a hand axe was permitted on his territory.

Hiram Johnson burned to death at his camp on Chemquassabamticook Lake, where he once kept two baby pigs in bed with him, till they got so big he built them a pen. "Once he floated scrap iron on a raft 22 miles down river. When he didn't like the price they offered, he poled it all the way back 22 miles and sunk it. Finally Hiram had a fight with a man whom he thought had paid him too little and so, at gunpoint, he commandeered his tractor. When the man came to reason Hiram warned him off the porch of the cabin. But the man paid no heed, plunged on, opened Hiram's door—and died of shotgun wounds in the belly. Hiram then burned down the cabin and killed himself in the blaze."

Fred Dushense, once hidden away along the Allagash, would never believe that he had been granted a Presidential pardon as a deserter. Finally in 1958 he agreed, as an old man, to move down to Eagle Lake. Angus McLean, on Indian Pond, holed out there with a nameless partner. The two men would never speak to each other. When a warden came each would refuse to acknowledge that the other existed, even though he was in plain sight.

J AKE DAY AND I FLEW to the North woods with George Later in a light plane. Our assignment was to do a story on Game Wardens in the Maine wilderness. To make it easier for us, the Wardens from the North Woods all gathered at the Wilderness Waldorf, the new cabin built on the shore of Umsaskis Lake.

"The Wardens will be there" said the Commissioner of Inland Fish and Wildlife, "But I can't promise that they will talk".

Talk they did with a vengeance.

By nightfall ten of us were gathered in the Wilderness Waldorf. As each warden arrived, he stripped off his uniform coat as he came through the door. I couldn't figure that out, because it was still chilly in the cabin before the stove got roaring hot. But the reason each warden shed his uniform coat was that rules forbid taking a nip while in uniform.

A roar of greeting welcomed each arrival. A welcome drink was poured all around. Soon we were gathered around the stove, in T-shirts, swapping news and wilderness gossip. As the night progressed, as the steaks were devoured and the drinks were freshened, the volume of talk tripled. I had a tape recorder. But I had to turn it off because too many wardens were talking at once. As each man told a story about poachers, that would trigger a tale to top it from another.

We had a memorable night with memorable men, talking about the north woods, the poachers, the hermits, the animals which they know far better than any other men alive.

But time has passed since that memorable trip. Our pilots, George Later and Malcolm Maheu have retired, but are still flying. George Later spends six months a year flying the back country in Alaska, carrying fishermen and caribou hunters into that wilderness. Dick Varney, bless him, was killed in a crash while flying as a warden. Shaw and Curtis Cooper and Eban Perry are retired but still hunting and fishing. The others are in the Warden service still—a service that makes remarkable men in the Maine wilderness.

THE WILDERNESS WALDORF:

WARDENS & POACHERS

UMSASKIS LAKE — "Five hundred, six hundred, seven hundred, eight, nine hundred dollars . . . "

Out from Gary Pelletier's pocket, a crackling green stream of ten, twenty and fifty dollar bills flows onto the pine table in the warden's wilderness cabin. Birch logs flame in the Franklin stove illuminating the proud young grin, the curly black hair, the violet blue eyes of 25 year old Warden Pelletier. "A thousand bucks — the take from Sunday till Wednesday. Not bad!"

Not bad at all. It's amazing Pelletier is alive to hand over the $1,000 bundle to his boss in the immaculate undershirt and horn rim glasses, white-haired Curtis Cooper, Warden Supervisor of Division I, 3,500 square miles of wooded wilderness in Aroostook County.

Pelletier, wiry, light-boned, collected his $1,000 the hard way — from armed men, lawbreakers all, in the wilderness puckerbrush. He got it from them without a fight, without a gunshot, usually at night, often alone and outnumbered.

The money is forfeit bonds; paid up to Pelletier by poachers after deer and moose; paid by men night hunting with blinding lights, hunting on kill-free Sundays, men hunting without a license, men killing game with snares, even riding them down from aircraft.

Curtis Cooper and his nine wardens in District I alone (there are 10 Districts in Maine) collect forfeit bonds or make arrests and successfully prosecute about 500 cases of poaching a year.

In over 200 cases the lawbreaking hunter will put up his cash bond, hand over to the warden the money which he somehow has on him out in the puckerbrush and never appear in Court. If he has no money, the warden may confiscate his gun, car, chainsaw or snowsled. One warden confiscated so many chain saws, he was nicknamed "Judge Homelite."

Section 2004 of Maine's Inland Fish and Game Laws recognizes it would be impossible for wardens to do their job and at the same time haul violaters before the nearest judge for a hearing. The nearest judge is often 145 miles down the tote road.

Therefore the law provides that any warden making an arrest more than 50 miles distant from the nearest District Court "may accept the personal recognizances of the poacher in the sum of not exceeding $250 for his appearance before the nearest District Court on a specified date." If the prisoner fails to appear, he forfeits his posted bond, his license (if he has one) is revoked and the money goes to Fish and Game to help finance the work of the department.

Back in the early days, the State of Maine budget did not allocate any money from General Fund to pay wardens, buy gas for their planes, ammunition for their weapons or even boots to walk the wilderness beats. So the fines used to go to foot these bills and keep the warden service going. Not so, any longer.

Today 103 wardens in 10 geographical Divisions work under 10 Inspector Wardens. They in turn are supported by five warden pilots, mechanics, radio technicians, supply officers, safety co-ordinators.

Almost all game wardens are Maine-born. Once a warden, always a warden is the rule of thumb. Being a Maine Game Warden is a lifetime career. It is a way of life that runs in families, and is often handed on from father to son. Two Pelletier brothers, Maynard and Leonard, are in the game warden service; and three of Leonard's sons are also game wardens. Five Pelletiers protect the Maine woods.

Life, especially for young wardens with young children, can be isolated and remote. It leads to close-knit families, and to sons who are eager helpers from childhood in their father's outdoor life.

Sometimes it leads to an unhappy wife.

But most 'warden-wives' are either born as outdoor girls; or they become quick learners at a remote do-it-yourself life, where groceries are bought by the truck load, shopping lists look weeks ahead and there is no corner grocery, laundromat or repair man. Even a doctor may pay his calls by plane. Wives keep the cabin, while husbands track armed men in the woods, search for lost persons on mountain tops, become scuba divers, expert at recovering drowned bodies, and develop tremendous appetites, tremendous muscles and tremendous love for animals, wild birds — even wild flowers. Deer, beaver, muskrat, even baby bears join with the raccoons and whiskey-jacks as regular callers in the door yard. And the unexpected dinner guest may be a warden pilot, dropping in out of the skies with a store-bought surprise and tidbits of news from the wilderness network.

But as the children grow up to school age, new wardens with younger wives may move in to use the cookstove, feed the whiskey-jays and nurse next year's motherless fawn — while a new station takes the warden's wife and family closer to town and a school bus. And the tug at leaving the woods, once frightening, is like the tug of leaving very roots behind.

As the bottle emptied, the stories grew. One Sunday, Warden Ted White spotted a Sunday hunter who'd come over the Canadian border to poach Maine deer. The poacher took to his heels, running swiftly as a deer. Ted tracked him. And the hunter, retreating all the time toward the border, raised his gun and fixed Ted in his sights. This put Ted's dander up and he closed in until he was near enough to shout in French that he would arrest the culprit and haul him into jail. "Unless you hand over twenty dollars as a forfeit!" Ted shouted. Keeping his gun bead drawn on Ted White, the poacher pulled out a $20 bill, wrote his name and address on a slip of paper so he could get a mailed receipt; tucked them both under a rock — and fled to safety over the border."

Poachers sell the deer they shoot, getting $100 for a good size buck. Others, noiselessly, stealthily snare deer and moose.

At five mile brook Wardens Gaynol L. Perry, Herbert W. Vernon and Gary Pelletier discover a quartered moose carcass covered by fir boughs near the tote road. Nearby they find the spruce pole and wire, and the wildly trampled underbrush where the snared bull moose had thrashed, pawed and struggled to escape death by hanging, "We lay hidden in the darkness, waiting for the culprits to return to the scene and recover their booty. Soon we saw tractor lights. Waiting in ambush, we watched them load the moose, even to hanging their rifles across his rack; then we jumped them. And handcuffed the two Canadian poachers to each other and drove them into St. Paul. They telegraphed relatives for $400 in bonds, forfeited the money and went back over the border."

Ardent poacher-hunters build high watch towers near the U.S.-Canadian border to spot moose and call them and entice them over the border within range of their rifles.

"I was up to Peaked Mountain in fishing season" says Supervisor Curtis Cooper "when I saw one man climb up a tree, knock the neck off his whiskey bottle and start blowing into it for dear life. Didn't sound to me much like a moose call. But over the hill came a thundering bull moose, galloping hell-bent for the tree. The sight scared the daylights out of the whiskey-bottle-blower's partner, who shimmied up another tree, drew a pistol and shouted "Blow again Jacques! I'll shoot those moose now!"

Blowing into his whiskey bottle, the poacher called a bull moose to full gallop.

"Shoot that moose — and you'll go to the hoosegow" Curtis yelled, unseen behind a stump. Both poachers dropped out of their trees like bolts of lightning, and even the moose turned tail and ran.

Curtis found two airborne hunters from New Jersey in the midst of a dastardly technique. "Four deer were swimming across the lake, and the hunters chased them with the plane, taxiing up behind the deer, trying to force them ashore where a third hunter stood with his gun at the ready."

Others have tried hunting geese from a plane near Chamberlain Lake; have used helicopters to hunt duck; and small aircraft to swoop low over deer herds, firing rifles from windowless planes.

"Warden Pilot Dick Varney spotted a plane crashed near Presley Lake with a pilot waving from the wreckage. Varney radioed for rescuers to approach from the ground. As they drew near, the stranded pilot tried to set fire to his plane. He was a 300 pound man. We used an air force helicopter to lift him out. Found his rifle hidden nearby. The plane had spun in from tree-top height; and the pilot thought his companion had been thrown out and killed. Actually, the companion had walked out of the woods and reported to us that the pilot was dead! We slapped a $400 fine on them!"

At St. Camille, near the Canadian boundary, Gary Pelletier came upon a moose carcass, so freshly killed it was still steaming. "I saw the tail was cut off — perhaps by a hunter who wondered what kind of animal he had shot! I examined the wound, determined it was caused by a .308 shell. I tracked the hunter's footprints from the scene for 1½ miles; and found one man from Vermont, two from Connecticut. One of them had a .308. His boots matched the footprints near the dead moose too. I took his gun and fired two shells. They were scratched in the same way as the shells found near the moose shooting. I told them they were under arrest. Then they ganged up; and refused to let me take the culprit off in my canoe. So I put all of them under arrest. Read the riot act and the law to them. When they heard they could pay a forfeit bond, they were all smiles. One pulled out a roll of a dozen $100 bills. The others had fistfuls of cash money. They paid $700 for one moose. And all they got was the tail."

Warden Eban Perry heard through the wilderness network that "Cappy" Labbe was down over the Canadian border to enjoy some illegal trapping in Maine. Eban set his heart on nabbing this artful dodger and packed a tent into the woods, camping in the wilds on the look-out for three days and nights to catch Cappy red handed at his illegal traps.

At the end of 72 hours watchful work, Eban caught his scoundrel near the edge of a remote lake. Determined now to catch up on needed sleep, but somehow to keep "Cappy" close to heel, Eban stripped "Cappy" of his clothing, took away his boots, then made a bed out of Cappy's belongings and fell sound asleep on them, sure that his prisoner would not leave.

He confiscated the prisoner's clothes — and then slept on them.

From his plane in the air, Warden Pilot Maheu spotted a man waving his underwear as a signal. Thinking it was Eban in distress, Maheu landed. One close look told him the man was not Eban; and he pulled his pistol, fearing Warden Perry had been done for. Then Cappy, unable to speak English, led the pilot to the tent where Warden Perry lay sound asleep upon his prisoner's clothes and boots.

Maheu flew Cappy into Houlton, where he stayed in the jail for 5 days until friends in Canada rushed down his fine and hauled Cappy home.

Among game wardens themselves, and between wardens and hunters, and even the poachers they arrest, there lies a warm and wonderful bond.

Certainly, wardens are police; but that is not the way wilderness people, even the hermits and the outlaws, regard them.

Certainly wardens are of necessity hardy and strong and durable. Yet they are not tough, as a breed. They are strangely gentle, rather quiet and sentimental. Even in the puckerbrush, they are painstakingly well and cleanly dressed, cleanly shaved. And in their wilderness cabins, they are fussy and immaculate housekeepers. Some even make pot holders for their "kitchens" in a wilderness camp. To see the most exotic pair of pot holders in the State of Maine, find your way into the tiny camp on the water thoroughfare between Telos and Chamberlain lakes. But do not dare to pirate them away. They are a treasured landmark, filled with meaning to the wardens of the wilderness.

BANGOR—THANKS TO A HARD-DRINKING CALVINIST

BANGOR — Bangor is a mistake; the name, that is.

This place should have been called "Sunbury", which is a wishy-washy kind of name that better belongs down in Massachusetts.

The reason Bangor is called Bangor instead of Sunbury is that a Calvinist minister cuddled up too closely to the bottle in Boston back in 1791.

Back in 1791 the Reverend Seth Noble was sent from here all the way down to the General Court in Boston to get the name "Sunbury" for this part of Maine.

The Reverend Seth Noble was dispatched on his mission by the 576 inhabitants of Kenduskeag Plantation (fore-runner of Bangor) who wanted their name changed to Sunbury.

But by the time the Reverend Seth Noble, described as a "hard-drinking frontier Calvinist", finally got in front of the Clerk of the

Massachusetts General Court, the proposed name Sunbury came out as Bangor. And Bangor it has been ever since.

Up until that day "Bangor" had been the title of a hymn the hard drinking Calvinist minister was known to sing with special fervor.

Soon after Bangor became Bangor it boasted two taverns, a sure sign of prosperity. But the prosperity and the taverns went up in smoke in 1814, when the British sacked and burned Bangor.

Even then, Bangor citizens were an independent tribe. One of them, Peter Edes started Bangor's first newspaper in 1815, called The Bangor Weekly. And the guts of his editorial policy was to win Maine's independence from Massachusetts — a feat accomplished by 1820.

But they were a go-ahead bunch in Bangor and by 1834 had declared themselves a City instead of a town. No sooner did the City of Bangor reach 8000 population than they set up the first railroad in Maine —and the second railroad in the nation. This train, called the Veazie, ran between Bangor and Old Town.

Then came Bangor's land-and-lumber boom. A courier line ran between Bangor and Boston to handle the wild speculation. Whole townships were bought and sold overnight, sight unseen. Land auctions were held in a hard drinking atmosphere that old hard drinking Calvinist parson, Seth Noble, would have enjoyed. Champagne corks popped by the hundreds until whole wash tubs were filled with French champagne, from which each man at the land auction could help himself at will — and push the bidding higher.

By the 1850's Bangor was the world's biggest lumber port. One section of Bangor — the Devil's Half Acre — where Washington, Hancock and Exchange Streets run, became as brawly and bawdy as San Francisco's waterfront. Here lusty lumberjacks, thirsty and raunchy from months in the woods, quenched mammoth thirsts for wine and women.

The lumber barons cloaked their lustiness with gilded gentility. They built vast mansions, patronized the Arts lavishly, took their wives (and others) to Paris and made Bangor into a cultural Mecca. For example, lumber baron Isaac Farrar built Bangor's famed Symphony House in 1833. To build it, he imported the red brick from

England, insisting each brick be individually wrapped. He imported solid mahogany for the circular room from San Domingo.

Further along Union Street flourished one of the most colorful hotels in all the United States — the Bangor House.

Lick your chops! Steak and chicken for breakfast; Penobscot river salmon, venison and moose for dinner. An open fire in your bedroom . . . all included for $3 a day!

Daniel Webster dined and wined here. So did Presidents Ulysses Grant, Chester Arthur, Benjamin Harrison and Theodore Roosevelt. So did world heavyweight prize-fighter John L. Sullivan and foppish playwright Oscar Wilde. But one famous lady who neither wined nor dined here was Carrie Nation, the prohibitionist.

Instead, Carrie wielded her famous hatchet in the bar until Captain Horace Chapman, the first of the four generations of Chapmans to run the Bangor House, threw the dear lady out.

Maine had prohibition long before the nation went dry. Maine passed prohibition laws in 1846 and again in 1851. However Maine evolved the "Bangor Plan", whereby bar operators paid a standard fine in court twice a year. Then served booze openly for the rest of the year, while police looked the other way.

The liquor question split the Democratic party in Maine wide open. The prohibition law was repealed in 1858 and by 1862 Maine had its first liquor commission.

But that liquor commission did not rake in the millions that today's liquor commission does. During the first 8 months of 1862 official liquor sales in Maine amounted to only $24,607. Today they amount to over $50 million a year. However in the "good old days" most liquor sales went through illegal dram shops.

Moving from booze to battles — Maine made an enormous contribution to President Lincoln's armies in the Civil War. A Maine man, Hannibal Hamlin from Bangor, was Lincoln's vice-president. Maine sent 72,945 men to fight, 7322 of whom died. Maine sent 32 infantry regiments, seven batteries of field artillery, seven sharpshooter companies, 30 infantry companies, 14 companies of coast artillery. And a total of $18 million.

Rangeley

RANGELEY — You can stand on the high ground at Country Club Lodge and look out over some of the most spectacular mountain and lake country in the world.

What's the view worth?

About $24 million a year, according to the state assessor. He has tagged Rangeley itself, where 1,000 people live year round, with this valuation.

About 200 more people live nearby in Rangeley, Dallas and Sandy River Plantations. And the tax assessor likes the view from these places too. He has fixed a value tag on them of $6.7 million, $3.5 million and $5.1 million respectively. Add it all up and you get a year round population of 1,200 and an assessed valuation of $38.9 million.

You can see it is pretty country. And it has been getting about 30 per cent prettier, from the assessor's view, in each recent year.

Next week is one of the biggest weeks of the winter in Rangeley.

I was in Rangeley recently and had a wonderful time, skiing, snowshoeing, riding snowmobiles on the huge frozen lake and doing a few miles of cross country skiing.

You can't ice fish hereabouts: The lakes are too well stocked with trout and salmon, which are protected until the spring fishing starts after ice-out. Then the fishing enthusiasts come in droves to the region. And they keep coming all summer long, filling the camps and inns and motels till the population swells over the 10,000 mark.

Then the crowds stay on to see the magnificence of these mountains in the brilliance of their fall mantles.

Afterwards comes winter—once a lean period, now a money making season, thanks mostly to Saddleback Mountain and its ski trails, and to such events as the sled dog races and the new cross country ski races and the Special Olympics.

I browsed in the old library at the comfortable Country Club Lodge and later talked to some Rangeley history buffs on one snowy night as we sat by huge log fires. I was told that Rangeley got its name from an Englishman named James Rangeley, who inherited 70,000 acres hereabouts.

James Rangeley operated a prosperous tweed mill in Leeds, England, but in 1825 brought his family across to New York with a plan to set up a new home and business as the Squire of Rangeley.

He began by building a two-story house that, in the rough wilderness that was Rangeley in 1825 seemed like a palace. He built it strong. Outside, the house was clapboard over solid brick walls and then the inner walls were plastered. Between the rooms were brick partitions also covered by plaster; and the floors were of half-hewn logs, some measuring 27 inches in diameter.

Squire Rangeley brought most of his materials and tools from England. They came by ocean-going sailing ship to Portland; were transferred to smaller vessels there and sailed as far as Hallowell and from this Kennebec port were carried by horse team to Madrid. From Madrid, everything came through by "the spotted line."

The "spotted line" was a trail, marked with an axe on trees, to show the way through the forest. It continued more than 12 miles to the settlement of Rangeley.

Records show James was liked here. He kept a barrel of West Indies rum on tap for the workmen building his house, then the saw mill and grist mill and dam.

"He paid all wages down in money. He would pay a man $12 a month. My mother, she got 50 cents a week the first year and $1.50 a week the year after," wrote one tenant.

Squire James spent $30,000 to build a road between Rangeley and Madrid, so he could get out his lumber. He shipped pine clapboards to the world at $30 a thousand.

But a daughter died and the winters and the isolation proved too hard on the family. The Rangeleys moved to a large estate they owned in Virginia. There Squire James kept 150 slaves. And he sold his 70,000 acres in Rangeley to a Daniel Burnham of New Hampshire, who was hated here. Burnham lost the $60,000 he paid for his Rangeley tract and ended up serving an 11 year jail sentence in Portland as a debtor.

Jumping ahead to the 1890's, we come to the time when trains brought 200 sports at a time to Bemis station here.

Ruel Taylor, when he was 86, recalled that the station in 1896 was an old log cabin. He sold tickets out of his pocket and lived in the baggage room of the station. His first daughter, Neva, was born in the station. Taylor, according to a newspaper account 20 years ago, said there were only 15 houses in Rangeley in 1896, and one restaurant.

When the sports got off the train, they went aboard Capt. Barker's steamboat, which delivered them to camps around the lake. The area was booming when it was wiped out by a fire in 1921. Then came the depression, followed by floods.

In its heydey, millionaire sportsmen built camps in the region. And three golf courses were built. Summer was the time to make money. Winter was for hibernating or spending the summer's gains in the south.

About 20 years ago, Dr. Paul Fichtner spearheaded a group that envisaged making Rangeley the winter sport capital of the East, with Saddleback Mountain its hub.

Dr. Fichtner, the only medical man in 2500 square miles in 1958, became treasurer of the Rangeley-Saddleback Corporation and Harland Kidder, who was Overseer of the Oquossoc Angling Association, was elected president of the winter sport corporation.

The man who most recently brought most publicity to Rangeley is Jack Douglas, a TV comedy writer.

Douglas, who had summered here as a child, returned to Maine in 1973 and bought a spot overlooking Rangeley which he called Moonlight Mountain Lodge. He moved in with Japanese wife, Reiko, whom everybody grew to love; and with assorted wolves and mountain lions. Reiko acted as barmaid and cooker of Japanese dishes. Douglas acted as a surly man around the place, according to many.

One day, about 18 months after their arrival, the Douglas clan decamped, leaving a trail of feuds and lawsuits. Soon thereafter Douglas recouped his losses by publishing a book titled, "Benedict Arnold Slept Here." It is a scurrilous, funny account of "Granby Lakes" and local personalities.

The Douglas lodge has now been renovated by Bob and Sue Crory, professional innkeepers with many years of Maine experience. Crory hands out the Douglas book as a wry bit of publicity.

The lakes are too lovely, the mountains are too big and too beautiful for men to have made very much dent upon them.

Rangeley is bigger and lovelier than all who come here. That's how it's been for centuries past and hopefully how it will be for hundreds of years to come.

That is the special grace and perpetual attraction of the Rangeley Lakes region of Maine. It is lovelier, bigger, better, stronger and more lasting than anything man can make.

So we come to look and be thankful.

How Amos Begat A Ski Mountain

SUGARLOAF — Amos Winter and Oddman Thompson and Horace Chapman ought to go rummaging in their basements and dig out the old axes, cross saws and bucksaws with which they hand cut Sugarloaf's first trail back in 1951. And tomorrow morning they should carry them to the Base Lodge at Sugarloaf. There, the general manager at the Mountain, should get a display case built, so those old axes and bucksaws and crosscut saws can be on prominent display.

Next winter tens of thousands will drive cars comfortably into Sugarloaf. Millions of dollars worth of equipment and lift facilities will move them easily to the top of 23 manicured trails. But barely a handful of today's "Sugarloafers" know how it all began, 26 years ago.

"Back in 1951" says Amos Winter, now 76, "we'd walk in two miles from the road, carrying our axes and our skis. Up in Bangor, Horace Chapman would walk out of his hotel, the Bangor House; over in Kingfield Fred Morrison would hang up his white coat on a

peg and leave his drug store; and I would play hookey from my general store in Kingfield. With a bunch of local school kids, and maybe some college boys from Farmington or Orono or Bowdoin, we'd go to work, cutting trail on the Mountain."

That Fall of 1951 no one at Sugarloaf had a power chain saw. They used their own muscle to cut a ski trail clear up to the snowfields. "It was only 15 feet wide," says Amos "because we had a long way to cut up, without bothering about cutting sideways".

That trail is still there.

And it is still called "Winter's Way," after Amos Winter.

"To ski down it" says Amos "we first walked two miles in from the road through deep snow. Then put seal skins on over our skis, and began the uphill climb. The bristles from the seal skin faced backward into the snow to give us a grip. The climb took close to 1½ hours. The downhill run took just a few minutes."

Next year, in 1952, these Sugarloaf pioneers horn-swoggled a bulldozer from the Dead River Company and cut a dirt road in from the highway to the base of the mountain.

They formed a Sugarloaf Ski Club with charter memberships selling for $25. Amos Winter turned his timber lease on part of the Mountain over to the club.

"We built a cabin, to have a spot to get in out of the cold, and to sleep overnight," Amos recalls. "In one corner we built one big bunk — big enough for 18 or 20 girls and boys to bunk down, in sleeping bags. Girls one side, boys the other."

By 1953, life was getting softer for the original Sugarloafers. "We had money enough to put in a 1200 foot portable rope tow to pull us up the bottom half of Winter's Way. And we erected an outhouse."

That rope tow and that outhouse are vibrantly alive today in the memories of early Sugarloafers.

Minnette Cummings, the decorative legislator from Newport, remembers both rope and outhouse, acutely.

"The rope tow was always icy and wringing wet from drooping down into the snow" she says. "And unless you endured the frozen rim of those twoholers, and knew Sugarloaf in the days when the paper blew upwards, you are not truly a part of the Mountain." Amos Winter became the first manager.

By 1955, the popularity of skiing was rising, and Sugarloaf moved to meet the demand from more and more Maine people by putting in lifts. To raise money, stock issue was launched, with shares offered at $10 each. The first T-Bar lift was installed, up to Narrow Gauge trail. A second T-Bar went in in 1956, and the price of an all day lift ticket was set at $2.50. In 1960, the Base Lodge was built. In the same year demand grew and more T-Bars were added to Sugarloaf. In 1964 the super-fancy gondola with 50 enclosed cars was put in for half a million dollars. In 1968 came the first chair lift; in 1970 a second chair lift and a double chair lift.

Each year new trails were cut and opened. Amos Winter laid out each and every one, with the exceptions of Tote Road and Narrow Gauge.

Amos Winter at 76 keeps his skis handy still. There is a pair right in the office at the base of the mountain where Amos sells tickets to younger folk, on their way up to ski down Winter's Way. Few know he is the man who fathered Sugarloaf.

I asked Amos for his home telephone number, in case I needed to call him to check details in this story. "Call him here at the office" a lady advised me. "Amos is never home nights, even though he's pushing 76!"

"She's right" admitted Amos. "I play tennis two nights a week, down in Waterville. Two nights I like to go out dancing. And two nights I go to see the new movie down in Farmington. But on Monday nights I am home — mostly."

And so, how about putting up a display case for the axes and saws which cut Sugarloaf's first trail, as a perpetual "Thank you" to Amos Winter, Horace Chapman and Fred Morrison, the grand men who fathered Maine's famous mountain?

———

More lifts were added in 1971, 73, 74 and 75. If all chairs on all lifts were filled a total of 9,000 skiers could be moved up the trails simultaneously.

Season ticket in 1977 was $240 per person, compared to the orignal $25 charter memberships. The first Base Lodge built in 1960 has now expanded to a village; and clusters of "Mountainside" homes and condominiums worth several million dollars now stand where Amos Winter and a couple of helpers began the first ski trail in 1951.

Seeing Sugarloaf today, it is extraordinary to recall that the purchase price for the 1500 acre mountain was $30,690, less than $20 an acre. Its total value by 1977 exceeds $30 million, and an acre or two of prime building land fetches as much today as the entire mountain cost in 1951.

Aroostook

RUTH MRAZ INTRODUCED *us to the wonderful world of
Aroostook — The County, as it is called. (There are 16 counties
in Maine, but "The County" is Aroostook.) Ruth was the Aroos-
took correspondent for the Maine Sunday Telegram in those days.
She was also the lively, beautiful sister of Maine's Governor John
Reed.*

*The Reeds of Fort Fairfield are among the best-known seed
potato growers in The County. The Reeds are also crazy about
trotting horses too, and raise and race them. That combination of
potatoes and horses is The County trademark.*

*The County is almost a nation unto itself. The vast potato fields
are unlike any other countryside in Maine. The men who farm
those huge fields are gamblers rather than cautious farmers. One
year they will make a "killing". The next they will be on the verge
of bankruptcy but you can't see an iota of difference in Aroostook
men, good times or bad.*

*On the Aroostook farms, you find some of the liveliest, most
fashionable women in North America. When they go clothes
shopping in a good year, they may fly over to Paris. In a bad
year, they wear bluejeans but their smile is the same.*

*Freddie Vahlsing drew newspeople to Aroostook often. Vahlsing
was the most colorful, controversial business adventurer to hit
Maine in the 1960's and 1970's. At the start, he was the hero come
to bring Aroostook a money-making second crop of sugar-beets
through his multi-million dollar sugar refinery at Easton. The
dreams of beet crops turned into nightmares. The plant went bank-
rupt and $10 million of loans guaranteed by Maine, and $13
million of federal loans went sour. Freddie became the villain.
And the fate of his white elephant plant drew reporters to Aroostook
time and again.*

"The County", its crops, its men and women, its politicians, its weather of extreme colds and heats, its droughts and its enormous snows, are worthy of books, let alone a few columns.

Aroostook County is unique in these United States.

POTATOES ARE MORE THAN SPUDS

PRESQUE ISLE — In 48 hours in the heart of Maine's fabulous potato country, some of the nicest, most hospitable people in the world stripped this reporter clean of any and all illusions that a potato is a simple, dull, brown vegetable.

Potato farmers like Glenn and George Barnes, Merle Johnston, Wendell Christensen, Glenn Campbell, Glendon Wathen proved in stag sessions that a Maine potato is beautiful; is treacherous; is mercurial; and can bring hair-raising thrills, up and down, to a bank account.

Eating Maine potatoes is a safe and happy occupation. Growing potatoes in Aroostook is a gambler's heaven and hell.

— Potato fields are not simple dirt farms. In full blossom 150,000 acres of Maine potato fields are exciting and beautiful to see. Mile upon mile of rolling green fields, topped by tens of millions of white and purple-tinted blossoms are a breath-taking tribute to God's art and Aroostook men's sweat.

— Fried, baked and boiled, potatoes may be a staple, dull diet. But in the raw and growing, potatoes are a wild-swinging crop; a money-making or money-losing gamble. Aroostook fortunes are made and lost overnight in these fields. A 150 million manhours of toil may either go down the drain or swell up bank accounts, according to whimsical fluctuations of weather and market price. Over these, Aroostook gamblers have no control. But their capital tied up in land and tractors, harvesters, fertilizers, seed and warehouses, adds up to over $200 millions in "The County."

So costly is the overhead and so risky is the gamble that 2,000 Maine potato farmers have gone out of the business in the past 10 years. A small-time gambler, with a 100 acre farm, ties up over $50,000 to get into the game. A big time gambler, with 2,000 acres in potatoes, can have over one million dollars on the line.

— Potato farmers in Aroostook are, as one result, a special breed of men. They are wonderful. But they are totally unlike men of the Maine coast or men of the Maine woods or men of Maine manufacturing towns. If the Aroostook potato farmer is like anyone else in the world (he is not), he lives and acts closer to a Texas rancher or a Southern plantation owner than anybody in Maine.

Aroostook is really a foreign land. If they just spoke a foreign tongue and used a foreign currency, issued visas for passports and set up customs stations, tourists might come by the thousands to enjoy its special magic.

In the potato country around Caribou, Presque Isle and Houlton, the land goes on and on and on — no fences, hardly any hills, scarcely any trees. Just fields so big they seem to have no end. The only interruptions are a few white farmhouses every mile or so, standing there alone, unpretentious, unsoftened by trees and gardens. There is not even a rock in sight.

There is more fertile land, cleared and uncleared, in Aroostook County than in all the rest of New England combined say the experts. The rich silt-loam soil, limestone in origin, is the sediment of a prehistoric lake.

But the potato country is only a small slice of Aroostook's 6,308 square miles. This one county is as big as the states of Connecticut and Rhode Island combined. Its fertile potato strip is about 120 miles long and 30 miles wide. On these acres, there are now about 1,200 farms which raise about 2½ billion pounds of potatoes, or 12 pounds for every man, woman and child in the USA.

An Aroostook potato farmer may make $250,000 one year and be in debt for $300,000 the next — and nobody can see any difference in him. Making big money doesn't seem to make Aroostook people boastful or spendthrift or ostentatious. Losing it doesn't seem to make them surly, afraid or bitter.

To plant one acre of potatoes and take care of it with fertilizer and insecticides may cost $700 or more. So a 100-acre farm means an annual outlay of $70,000 before the uncertain potato money rolls in.

About 800 of these potato farmers work together in a cooperative that should be an inspiration to Maine's fishermen.

This is the 45th year of Maine Potato Growers Inc., a co-op started on a shoestring during the Depression and now worth $4.5 million.

The co-op is primarily a potato marketing arm — in 1976 such sales topped $9 million — but it has many widely divergent and extremely successful sidelines.

For example, it has a fuel and petroleum business that did a volume of 5.6 million gallons last year.

The co-op also runs a dairy operation which last year bought 12 million pounds of milk for $1.1 million from 30 dairy farms.

The co-op owns a factory which makes bags for potatoes. This year the factory made 28 million bags, with sales of $2.3 million. By 1978 the factory will have made one billion bags.

The co-op's other ventures include operating hardware stores and selling grain, fertilizers, farm machinery, sprayers and feed to farmers. It also runs service stations, does furnace and farm machinery repairs and acts as a bank to finance purchases its members must make. And those purchases can be big with a single piece of potato harvesting equipment sometimes costing over $30,000.

All told the co-op does over $21 million worth of business a year. Everything is big in Aroostook. But mostly they keep their bigness a secret from outsiders.

HOW TO PICK A QUEEN

FORT FAIRFIELD — If you are a glutton for hard choices, get named as judge of a beauty contest in Aroostook.

I was. And I lost five pounds. And won a case of schizophrenia (even with ice, you can't swallow it).

Ask me to pick a President. Easy. Choose a Senator. Simple. Or pick a winner in the third. Not hard.

But even Solomon would blow his mind trying to pick a Potato Blossom Queen among 14 Aroostook girls.

The work (in 100 degree heat) would have driven the biblical Solomon to drink. But in Fort Fairfield, judges aren't allowed to touch the stuff in working hours. Judges can't compare notes. Judges can't handle the merchandise. And judges can't show their feelings.

When an absolute knock-out of an Aroostook girl half breaks your

palpitating heart by her lovely smile, her mile-long legs or her dramatic talent, you can't stand up and cheer her, like any ordinary man would. All a judge can do is look bored and noncommittal and make a miserable little mark on a score card. It is a frustration.

Put yourself in the shoes of a judge. A gorgeous 18 year old girl from Presque Isle, or a flaxen haired Juno from Fort Fairfield, or a brown eyed doe from Mars Hill, or a beauty from Madawaska, Bridgewater or Ashland, or a French girl from Houlton, or a heart breaker from Easton or Caribou or Van Buren, Limestone, Mapleton, Washburn or Fort Kent — (that's 14) — comes across stage, walking to you, looking right at you. Try keeping that sour face.

When these beauties reach age 28, 38, 48 years — a circumstance unimaginable to them today — , they will remember that night in Aroostook when they were so tense, so young, competing so hard to win the Queen's crown. And then they will smile with a tender nostalgia, a twinge of amusement at the recollection of themselves at age 17 or 18, on the stage at Fort Fairfield High. And remember the moment when the world stopped still while the judges' scores were counted and the new Queen was named.

Queens who held the title thirty years ago were in the audience. As they were introduced, the beauty still was there. These were the Queens who danced to Glen Miller, and Sammy Kaye, who sipped lemon cokes which cost a nickel and held hands in the movies when tickets cost 35 cents . . . Even then, the finest crop in all Aroostook was the girls they grew . . .

How can the charms and talents of these Maine girls be measured by writing down a miserable number between 1 and 5 on a score-pad? How can a grimy pencil mark on a wrinkled worksheet signify the magic these girls exude?

Judges have short personal interviews with each contestant, getting to know their hopes and ambitions. Then judges have dinner with the girls. There is, I found, a streak of steel in these girls. They are competitors. They are, by instinct and training, people who want to excel.

I asked the six girls I had dinner with one night "How many brothers and sisters do you have?" And the total was 44. The answers ran from a minimum of three to a top of 13 in the family.

More than one contestant runs a big household. Most hold jobs, even those in school or at college. They must make money for them-selves and their families. All had worked in the potato harvests since they were 10 or 12 years old. And everyone had excelled in school — as National Honor Society members, presidents of their class, editors of school papers, and many had starred in athletics.

When you get to know the girl behind the clothes, the mind inside the figure, the business of choosing a winner gets harder instead of easier.

I tried a trick to make it easier. When it came time to mark the score cards. I forgot the names like Cindy and Lori, Heidi and Susan. Sternly I scored by town names. Houlton, Limestone, Mars Hill, Presque Isle. That helped a bit to make it less human.

What wins a title? It is not beauty alone, or curves or those tapering legs that seem to run from heel to shoulder. It is not brains or poise, although without a big dose of both no girl stands much chance of winning.

It is not talent, though these girls had an astonishing variety of dramatic and musical talent . . .

What wins, I think, is a strange alchemy of all these ingredients, and more, working together under alien and stressful conditions of competition and pressure . . . Susan Jean Wanbaugh of Presque Isle won in a close finish with Lori Jean Dodge from Fort Fairfield. But almost any one of these girls would have made a fine queen.

I got a laugh as well as an eyeful in the swimsuit section of judging. This was closed to the public. Only judges, chaperones and family allowed in. This was the first time in many years, a swimsuit division had been included here. There is a strong 'bible belt' in the County. And Women's Libbers also object. So I polled a group of the girls. All but one wanted a big audience, "The more, the better. If I knew admiring boys were out there, I'd welcome that. If we got some applause or even whistles, I'd be encouraged, not embarrassed."

Final observation concerns queens in jeans . . . When it was all over, I saw some of the girls in shirt tails and blue jeans. They looked like every other girl — almost. I wondered: "Could 1400 instead of 14 girls be as poised, as talented, as attractive if they wanted to put out the same effort to act well, look well, dress well?"

The contestants I asked, said scores of others in their towns could match or beat them — if those other girls were encouraged to try.

I am a male who knows nothing of what the girls talk about when they fix their hair or sew their seams. But for four days, these girls were in neck-and-neck competition with each other . . . But instead of clawing at each other in a rivalry to win, they arrived as strangers and left as admiring friends, tearful in their partings and goodbyes.

IV /

Making It in Maine

D*RIVE FIVE MILES in Maine and be nosey about what people do to make a living and you'll find that there is more interesting work going on here in Maine than anywhere you've been.*

Maybe it is because if people stay in Maine or come to live here, they like what they do for a living. In other states, more people work only because the pay is good. In Maine, the pay is seldom good. So maybe the work is more interesting.

Paul Quintal came to cut trees on some land I own. So I worked and talked with him and got fascinated by the way a man on his own, maybe with one helper, makes an independent living cutting trees—sometimes for pulp, sometimes for firewood. Paul has done it for most of a lifetime. The complicated art of selecting, felling, limbing, cutting to size is never realized until you try doing it. Then that leads you into the new world of saw, axes, wedges; then that leads you into the new world of machinery to get the logs out of the woods; machinery to load logs onto special pulp trucks; and the world of bargaining, of making a price with the paper mill.

Jim Brown's wife, on North Haven island, carves sea birds and owls and eagles from balsam, then hand paints them to perfection. She has more orders than she can ever fill. How did she learn? Why? How does she do it with what tools and at what time of day, when running a household of busy men? Dock at Brown's Wharf on the Fox Thorofare and get a lesson in Maine handicrafts. Manley Gilbert builds his lobster traps in New Harbor and as he works in the fish house, he tells me how his grandfather at age 16 skippered a 60-foot lobster smack, sailing between Nova Scotia and Portland. On winter evenings other men, along with their wives, knit the parlors in the traps. Edward Myers and Chester Brown, downriver from me, are aquiculturists. Myers raises mussels and Brown raises oysters in coves by their houses. Millions of each. Myers used to be an official at Princeton University. Brown was a successful, overworked doctor out of state.

Ivan Flye, in Damariscotta-Newcastle, is a worm dealer. He buys and sells millions of blood and sand worms yearly, and has scores of diggers filling orders along the coast. He keeps in contact by radio because his phone bill topped $8,000 a year. Ivan also runs a camera shop and keeps a wonderful collection of the earliest pictures made of this part of Maine a century ago.

Woodworkers, weavers, worm diggers; ambassadors, adzmen, arborists; candlemakers, codliners, coonhunters, college presidents; midwives, mathematicians, musicians, meat packers; sawmill operators or sauerkraut makers. Here in Maine, within a few miles you can find an astonishing variety of interesting people doing work very well that they like to do very much.

Most like to talk about their work, if you come at it slowly and are sincerely interested. As a reporter, I find the two best questions to ask to get people talking are; Tell me what you do for a living? How did you meet your wife (husband)?

Self-employed men in Maine must hustle to make ends meet. Most work at several jobs, swapping as the seasons change. In the woods in winter, fishing in the spring, carpentering in the summer and early fall, for example.

Lots of energetic men make money in Maine in their own business. Always the going is slow and hard at the start. I know successful men here who worked 12 hours a day for six years and hung on by the skin of their teeth. Now they all have a fine business, as an oil dealer, a building contractor, a wholesaler, a hotel man. Lawyers

*and doctors in Maine often do very well. They make a good amount
of money — say $35,000 up to $120,000 in the cities at the top of
their profession. And they have a Maine life to boot.*

*The big city hospitals in Maine are excellent. The law school
and the law courts have talent that rank with the best in the nation.
Maine has more talent per capita than any state in whatever field
you name, outside esoteric research and advanced computers. But
we don't have bigness. No big corporations with big corner offices
and floors filled with vice presidents. There is no space in Maine
for mediocrity to hide in the woodwork. Either you are damned
good or you are damned bad.*

*The very rich are very few in Maine but the comfortably off,
moderately happy man or woman, enjoying life, enjoying Maine,
enjoying being themselves, are plentiful.*

The Old Time Icehouse

SOUTH BRISTOL — Five generations of the Thompson family have been cutting ice from the same one acre pond here for almost 150 years. This may be the last spot in Maine where you can get hand cut blocks of fresh, natural ice. Once Maine used to deliver her natural ice to customers as far away as India and China.

Edgar Thompson, who runs Ed's Gulf station in Damariscotta, cuts the ice from Thompson's Pond here, with an assist from his sons and half a dozen friends.

His father, Herbert Thompson, tried to stay inside this year, in the red clapboard house which he built years ago for $2000, across Route 129 from the tilted, weather beaten Thompson ice house. "I've been 60 years on that pond at ice harvest time, since I was tall enough to hold a horse's bridle. So it was hard to stay away . . But my son Edgar does an expert job. Why not? He started learning how from me 33 years ago, when he was seven."

Lean and blue-eyed, with a slow kind smile, Herbert Thompson has served as County Commissioner of Lincoln County, after being South Bristol's First Selectman, road commissioner and overseer of the poor for more than 20 years. "Melvin Thompson, my grandfather, farmed on this land and cut ice here."

When Napoleon Bonaparte was beaten at the Battle of Waterloo, Thompsons farmed this land. When James Monroe and John Quincy Adams were Presidents of the United States, Thompsons lived here.

Young Melvin Thompson probably stood goggle-eyed on the shore here and watched that famous naval shoot-out between the American ship 'Enterprise' and the British ship 'Boxer' on Sunday September 5, 1813. The Enterprise had lain in Pemaquid over Saturday night. On Sunday she sought out Boxer, who had been raiding the Maine coast. At 3:15 p.m. Sunday she found Boxer. The two ships fought in a 35 minute battle just off shore, between Pemaquid Point and Monhegan Island. And young Melvin Thompson saw it.

"A spring for watering his cattle ran through my grandfather's cow pastures. Melvin Thompson dug down, hit sandy bottom, made a dam, got a clear, clean pond and went into the ice business. Built a little ice house, holding maybe 100 tons."

Bristol had strange weather then. The year 1816 went down as "the freak year without a summer". Frost bit the crops and vegetables every month of that strange summer. On the night of June 6, 1816 snow fell on Bristol.

These were years of hot-and-heavy Town Meetings. At the May Town Meeting, 1816, in Bristol 13 people voted for Maine's separation from Massachusetts and 37 against it. In the September Meeting, the turn-out was bigger. This time 76 voted for separation and 142 against it. Then in 1819 Congress passed a law which permitted vessels to pass from one state to another without paying entry and clearance taxes. This new law completely changed the opinions of the sea-faring people of Bristol about splitting away from Massachusetts and setting up the separate State of Maine. And at Town Meeting on July 26, 1819, 80 people voted for separation and only 50 voted against it. Other Maine towns felt the same way. And on March 15, 1820, Maine became the 23rd State of the Union.

This affected Melvin Thompson's ice business. "An old account book shows that in 1826 my grandfather Melvin Thompson sold most of that year's ice harvest down south. Grandfather took in $700 for that year's ice — a tidy sum 147 years ago."

In Herbert Thompson's living room, his wife Gwendolyn does some figuring about the ice pond. Gwen's figuring is good. She taught school in Massachusetts for 17 years and for 23 more years in South Bristol where she was principal. "I figure that over 150 years Thompsons have cut close to 120,000 tons of ice from that one acre pond." That is a lot of ice from a one acre plot. . . 240 million pounds of ice.

"When my grandfather died, he left the pond to sons Walter and Edgar. Edgar chose to go lobstering. So it became the W. W. Thompson Ice Co." says Herbert. "We used covered wagons and horses to deliver ice to cottages 'round South Bristol and Christmas Cove. Then we went to a Model T truck. Price was 75 cents per 100 pounds retail, 45 cents wholesale. But I'd fill a customer's ice box for 50 cents, never bothering to weigh." That was back in the days of Herbert Hoover and FDR.

More recently, Herbert Thompson hauled ice down to the gut at South Bristol to ice the fish trucks heading for New York. "They all said that with my natural ice, they could run right into New York and never need to stop for re-icing. Artificial ice melts faster. Trucks with man-made ice had to stop and buy more. When my Maine ice arrived in New York, it stayed so good that the kids would take chunks home to eat."

Gwen Thompson knew nothing about cutting ice when she came to South Bristol for a visit in 1946. "I just landed here for a visit after New Year's when Herbert said he was going to cut ice next day. I didn't really know what he meant. But he told me to ready dinner for 25 men," says Gwen. "A blizzard blocked the roads to stores in Damariscotta. So I rustled up cans of tuna fish and boxes of noodles and made apple dumplings and fed 'em all. When it was over Herb said to me "For a school marm, you cook pretty good. They'll be 25 more for dinner tomorrow. And the next day too. . ."

Herbert Thompson proposed marriage, after the ice was in. The

schoolmarm-cook soon became Mrs. Thompson. Ever since she has been chief bookkeeper for the ice business.

Cutting ice from a pond is an art. Herbert likes to cut his pond when ice is about 17 inches thick, usually about the second or third week in January. Best temperature for cutting is around 28 degrees. If it is colder, the ice sticks and won't slide; warmer it melts. Harvest requires fair weather for three good working days, when work starts before day break and lasts till sundown.

"First, we sweep off all snow. Next, we mark out the cutting lines. Use a 30 foot straight edge, sight up the pond and run a line straight as you can. Then do the same thing but across the pond. Working from these guide lines, we start cutting.

"First we cut a channel two feet wide, to float the other blocks in open water. Then men using a gas driven saw cut blocks 22 inches by 33 inches and 17 inches thick. Those weigh about 500 pounds each. We don't cut 17 inches deep — else the block might sink. Cut down only 12 inches, and knock the last five inches out with needle bars and busting bars. Those tools have gotta be sharp. That's one reason I won't allow any liquor on the pond, no matter how much a fellow might want a nip to keep warm."

"We use a handsaw to cut out the headers. Then cut out a raft — about 60 blocks of ice; and float the raft up to the head of the two foot channel, guiding it with long handled picks. Then we use tool bars to break the big float down into chunk-blocks; swing 'em onto the hoist for lifting onto the chute into the ice house. Gwen runs the hoist from a truck. Lifts two blocks at a time, weighing about 500 pounds each. Once off the chute the blocks slide down fast into the ice house."

Inside the ice house men expert with tongs swing fast sliding ice into tight packed rows. When they have the bottom tier packed, the chute is raised, and the next tier is filled. So it goes until the ice is packed seven tiers high inside the ice house.

"To keep the ice from melting, we crush up a few blocks, and use the loose stuff in the cracks, to ice the ice. When it is all in, I get special meadow hay to spread over the top layer. Meadow hay is light and fluffy and doesn't pack down like cattle hay."

The Old Time Ice House / 141

Tools for cutting and handling big blocks of natural ice are hard and expensive to get these days, and Thompson treasures his inventory of them. Thompson's ice house is double walled, and the space between walls is packed with sawdust. The doors are boarded over. And there the ice keeps till summer. "But foggy days melt it. Fog is worse than sun for melting ice. Most always you lose at least one tier to melt. In a foggy spring you might lose two tiers."

A tier of ice amounts to 280 blocks, each block weighing 300 pounds. So a melt of just one tier represents 42 tons of ice.

When it is time to move out the ice, this too must be done with skill, tier by tier, to reduce the unavoidable melt. "Working inside an ice house is hot work. Summer people say 'you must be nice and cool in there.' But if you are working inside the ice house it is hot and you sweat. There is not much air inside.

Clean, clear spring fed water is the secret of the high quality of Thompson's ice. So on a summer day, you can find Herbert Thompson paddling round his open pond, dragging a big chain behind him, along the bottom. "That's to stop weeds growing. A clean bottom makes clean ice."

The Thompson Ice House is now listed on the National Register of Historic Places.

WORM DIGGERS AT WISCASSET

WISCASSET — I could hear a duck breathing. That is how quiet the night was. Stars were brilliant and the Milky Way a wide bright band running across the sky. The sea was dead calm, a mirror in which every star scintillated, winking at itself back in the sky.

It was 3 a.m. and I was out on deck, reveling in the silence and loneliness of the night. Our anchor was down in a place wonderfully called "The Oven's Mouth," remote from any human habitation.

Then came the roar of outboards. In the black silence of night— two boats came blasting into The Oven's Mouth. It was coming to low tide, and the men drove their boats hard into the mud where the water had already drained out. They were not 100 yards from me.

I had been hearing tales enough of housebreaking from boats in the nighttime that I wondered for a second if I was to witness a heist.

They shut off the motors. I now could hear voices but could not distinguish words. Then two lights flashed on, and the lights began darting over the mud flats, close to the ground. I heard the suck of thick oozy mud, sucking at boots. And then I knew I was watching not thieves, but the hardest-working men in Maine — worm diggers.

Two worm diggers had come to work the early tide on the buddy system. They watch each other because hereabouts are "honey pots," as they call sudden patches of quicksand. Some honey pots just scare you half to death when you feel yourself sinking. Others can kill a man, either by sucking him down, inch by inch, or by driving him to such wild terror that he works himself to exhaustion, collapses facedown into the sucking mud and suffocates.

These guys waste no time. No sooner are their engines cut than they are in the mud, flailing their deadly looking worm rakes into the ooze, turning up bloodworms or sandworms, which will be shipped today to fishermen from New Jersey to Florida.

The lights I see bobbing are lamps strapped to their heads or hard hats, used like miner's lamps to light up the area where they are digging.

They dug for three hours, backs bent, legs wide apart, high-booted feet planted deep in the mud. Then as the tide rolled in and daylight broke in the east, the men washed off the mud and climbed into their boats with their worms. The outboards exploded and they roared off to sell their catch to a worm dealer.

A good part-time digger of worms may make $6,000 to $8,000 a year. A real workhorse who digs two tides a day, rising some days before 3 a.m., and digging by flashlight, can make as much as $15,-000. A 20-acre mud flat produces $75,000 worth of worms yearly.

Maine's bigger worm dealers will ship millions of worms a month. In special boxes, looking like flower-boxes, Maine worms travel by plane, bus and refrigerated truck to distant fishermen who swear Maine bloodworms and sandworms are the finest bait a fish can take. The worm crop in Maine has a cash value of around $3 million.

Don't scoff at worms.

One pound of good Maine bloodworms fetches a far higher price than a pound of Maine lobster. Worms are many times more expensive than the best steak you can buy.

Maine Blueberry King, Senator Wyman

MILBRIDGE — Eighty million bees from New York are pollinating the blueberry crop on some 2000 acres of Senator Hollis Wyman's blueberry barrens outside Milbridge, Washington County.

Norman Sharp, who hauls the 80 million bees in 1600 double hives on open trailer trucks (covered with protective nets) from Rochester, N.Y., is a sunburned, blue-eyed, laughing bee-man who began in the bee business as a 17 year-old lad working on a 4-H project. Sharp's 80 million bees have been coming to Maine each June to pollinate the blueberry crop of Jasper Wyman & Son, largest and one of the oldest growers and processors of Maine's famous wild blueberry harvest. Last year Maine's crop totalled 29 million pounds.

"People have a mistaken idea" says Hollis Wyman (77 years old, Harvard graduate and 9 times Maine senator) "that to raise blueberries you just burn off some wild land, wait a year, and then rake in a blueberry crop. Truth is that to raise a good commercial crop today a grower uses low - flying planes to fertilize and dust his fields, jet flame throwers to prune the crop, millions of bees to pollinate it, irrigation systems to water it, and spray machines to kill off choking weeds. On top of this he must fight winter - kill, cut worms, beetles, blossom blight, late frosts, drought, high winds and finally an inefficient blueberry rake."

Wyman should know. His family has been in the blueberry business for 104 years and the Wyman blueberry fields lie in a 36,000 acre block of land north of Cherryfield, known as the "blueberry barrens". From this glacial plain, once covered with pine, Jasper Wyman and Son today harvest the largest single blueberry crop in the world, raking in as many as 4000 bushels in a single day. Wyman actually harvests only about 2000 acres a year out of the 36,000 acres of barrens. He needs 100,000 gallons of oil just to fuel his flame throwers, and the largest of his eight irrigation ponds covers 90 acres, with water depths running from six to twelve feet.

Bees, millions of hard working bees, are a key factor to a rich blueberry harvest. "When the job of pollination is left to the local bumble bees doing what comes naturally, only about 10 per cent of the blueberry bushes are effectively pollinated" says the young botanist on the Jasper Wyman & Son staff. "By bringing in up to 80 million 'social' bees, (50,000 to each of 1600 double hives) we increase pollination to over 40 per cent."

Hard working hive bees work themselves to death in about 5 or 6 weeks of life during the summer. "For the first two weeks of its life" says bee-man Sharp "the young bee works inside the hive, cleaning it, feeding the young and acting as a guard bee. Then for three weeks it goes to work outside the hive, nectaring and pollinating and bringing honey back to the hive. In these three weeks a bee may fly 250 miles, back and forth to the hive, though seldom travelling more than one mile from the hive. Then it dies from overwork."

KCM

PAWS OFF!

In the Wyman barrens, bee hives are ganged-up in groups of four or so, for mutual protection against bears. "Bears love honey," says Norman Sharp. "And a solitary hive is no match for a huge bear with a sweet tooth and honey on his brain. But when the bear must risk the sting of 200,000 bees in four hives to get his honey, his passion for honey is apt to cool off."

"When we used to set hives out singly, we lost 50 hives or so to bears each June. Now bears destroy only one or two a season."

Bees don't work just for the fun of buzzing over Maine's blueberries. Rental costs alone for 1600 active hives therefore amount to $30,400. The honey which the bees make is sold to local bakeries, which further sweetens the bee-keeper's lot. But honey comes hard. Experts estimate that if one bee were to gather in one pound of honey, he would have to fly the equivalent of a journey around the world in search of nectar.

Bees carry the blueberry pollen on the tips of their tongues and also in the hairs of their hind legs. When they suck nectar from a plant they leave behind much of this pollen taken from another. Pollen makes up the protein in a bee's diet and the nectar provides the carbohydrates needed by a busy bee.

Bees are fussy about weather conditions. They won't work outdoors until the temperature reaches 55 degrees. They won't work in the rain. They won't work if the wind blows over 15 miles an hour. Come dusk, they quit and fly home to the hive.

Each August some 300 pickers, many Canadian Indians, have converged on Wyman's barrens to harvest millions of pounds of prime Maine low-bush blueberries. "If everybody in the United States ate just two slices of blueberry pie a year" says Hollis Wyman "that appetite would use up almost the entire U.S. crop which last year totalled almost 100 million pounds."

As a good Maine trencherman, how many slices do you eat in a year? Twenty-five or fifty? If so, remember the hard working honey bee who may have worked himself to death getting the pollen to put that fine pie on your table.

CAPTAIN GUILD OF 'VICTORY CHIMES'

ROCKLAND — Victory Chimes of Rockland is the very last three-masted schooner left working the coast of Maine, and the last in the nation, I am told, still carrying passengers.

Not too long ago Maine's fame and our fortune hinged upon such vessels. We built hundreds of them. They sailed well, but they sailed into gradual oblivion after the advent of power.

Victory Chimes itself is not a Maine built schooner — we don't have any of those left, despite the fleets that were launched here. She was built in 1900 at Bethel, Va., 170 feet long, masts 80 feet high, and for the first half century of her life was a merchantman, mostly hauling lumber, Georgia pine, to the West Indies, to New York and Philadelphia.

She came in Maine as a windjammer cruise ship in the 50s. Frederick B. Guild was her skipper then, and in 1959 he bought the Chimes and has sailed and cherished her ever since.

I went to see him in May, when he was getting the ship ready for its annual 17 weeks of cruising the Maine coast. He is 64, his ship is 78. Both looked sound, solid and seaworthy. Guild, one could say, is ruggedly handsome; but his ship, even swathed in a cocoon of plastic to protect work and workmen from the weather, is beautiful.

Sitting on the rails at her berth in Rockland harbor, Guild talked about the upcoming summer. "We'll make 17 cruises, each a week long, starting early June, finish in early October," he said. "Each cruise is different because of differing weather. But we sail around 200 miles each trip."

"My best helmsman," says Guild proudly, "is my wife. She steers better than anyone. Holds a tighter course. In fog especially I always put Mrs. Guild at the wheel."

Janet Guild is also an expert weaver, needle pointer, photographer, raiser of orchids, breeder of horses, mother of four, grandmother of eight and restorer of a 200-year-old glorious yellow house at Castine.

She sails every cruise on Victory Chimes, greets every guest, orders a thousand dollars worth of groceries a week — and does her full stint at the ship's wheel.

Talk of the handsome wheel brings up the whole subject of the brightwork on Victory Chimes.

Few words spell work better than brightwork: Hand-sand down the old varnish; re-apply the new. Flow it on. Sand that down, flow it on again. And Victory Chimes is famous for her masses of gleaming brightwork.

"I have a shed on shore exclusively for brightwork," says Guild. "The big binnacle, the wheel, the teak gratings, the skylights, the wheel boxes and the doors and quarterboards are all ashore now being hand sanded and varnished. I used to do it all myself — took three weeks. Rub, rub, rub. Somebody else does it for me now. But let me show you the decks."

Captain Guild pulls back tarpaulins which protect his pride and joy. "These decks are 90 per cent original wood, and look at the job we've just done." The decks gleam, the captain beams and talks about them.

"The decks are 132 feet long, 24 feet wide midships."

"First, we routed out the old putty between planks — that's more than half a mile of seams. Then we horsed in oakum with a horsing iron and forced caulking on top. Of course, the whole deck had to be sanded down — that took a week with big machine sanders. Then seams had to be taped on both sides, a mile of taping. We used air guns to blow deck compound into the seams. Then we took up the tape and recleaned all the decks.

"Afterwards we applied two coats of sealer, then a coat of varnish, then a light sanding, then another varnish. With luck, we'll get a third varnish coat on before we sail."

Meanwhile, up above, Bill Brown, six feet six inches of skinny sailor, is in the rigging with a bucket at his waist and thick glove in his hand, tarring and oiling the rigging. "We tar the rigging, oil the masts," explains Guild.

Suddenly the skipper lets out a blast of salty language. Wind gusts are blowing a duststorm off the city of Rockland's mammoth sand pile. The sand is part of a sewer system. Demanded by the Environmental Protection Agency, it now is causing the worst environmental disaster imaginable to a skipper with newly oiled masts, rigging and decks.

The final job will be to paint the hull and topsides, two thin coats of green on the hull, and white above. Then Chimes' bottom will be coppered, for which she has to come out of the water.

Copper paint for bottoming can go up as much as $70 a gallon and it takes 30 gallons to do the job, says Guild.

Ashore in the paint sheds, 110 blocks — the heavy wooden tackle for hoisting sail — hang from the rafters, drying. Every block has been dismantled, the pins and shivs inside removed, inspected, oiled and greased. Each block gets two coats of glossy white. The new iceboxes, the enormous lockers, the long boats, even the life rings are all being freshly painted and spruced up.

"We start winter maintenance in October, the day after the last cruise ends," says Guild. "We pray for dry weather those final days. And you know, the only time it's rained was 1975. We came in with wet sails. And you can't store wet sails. Try and find space ashore to dry 6,000 square feet of canvas."

Once the sail and ropes — a mile of manila — are dry, the sails are folded expertly, the lines are coiled, and they're all stowed in a cool, dry loft. "We take utmost care of our sails," says Guild, which is not surprising: A new suit of sails for the Victory Chimes would cost about $12,000.

At least a dozen windjammer schooners now offer vacation cruises in Maine waters.

The cost is about $225 a week per head on most schooners.

Schooner cruising is becoming a highly popular vacation idea and a not inconsequential source of revenue for Maine.

The weekly grocery bill for provisioning the windjammer fleet is over $10,000.

Young men are rebuilding some of the famous old Maine vessels into modern windjammers. But don't think you can rush out and buy a good sailable ship easily now.

Over 20 years ago, Captain Frank Elliott of Owls Head paid just $21,000 for Victory Chimes from Hosmer Phillips, a General Motors executive of Ellsworth and New York.

Three years later Guild bought her, for a little more. He figures he has spent $250,000 on improving her.

What would Victory Chimes cost today to buy? Well, this past year, says Guild, two bidders each offered about $350,000; which he rejected.

So what is the value of these wonderful, beautiful windjammers?

Perhaps the best yardstick may be the happiness they bring — if happiness can be measured.

How does a city dweller measure the value of standing on a schooner deck at dawn, watching the New World come to life as the first sun touches America?

Making it as a Country Boy

DAMARISCOTTA — The man who is his own boss, running a business he built in a small town in Maine, is the envy of thousands.

How does a guy make it?

Take the case of Gary Pinkham. Gary, who is 35 now, quit his job with Central Maine Power and struck out on his own six years ago.

"I had $150 in a checking account. I was paying the bank each month for my house and car and I had a $16,000 skidder on which the payments were $100 a week. And I was married. I had to hustle," says Pinkham.

I had known Gary a few years. He plows my garden in the spring and mows my fields in summer. Atop his high-wheeled tractors, he smiles his slow smile and doesn't look like a capitalist or a driving entrepreneur.

But that's what he is. Thousands like Gary in Maine are—those quiet, competent, independent men who run their own fishing boats or their own woods operation or their own sawmill or their own farm or their own construction business. Work shirts and lace-up boots kid you into thinking they know less about the ways of money than the white collar banker inside an office.

That's part of the camouflage.

Gary Pinkham hustles all the time. He has so many different jobs going, winter and summer, that he seems like a one-man conglomerate.

One day after it had been raining hard for six hours straight, and the ground was so soaked that no one could move earth or mow fields, I phoned Gary Pinkham, expecting to find him home.

His wife, Patsy from Texas, whom he married while out there in the Air Force, answered the phone. "Gary home at four in the afternoon? No way. He's down at his sawmill, trying out the new machinery."

"A sawmill? Where is it?"

"You know the Lakehurst dance hall?" said Patsy "Well, it's just half way between the dance hall and the cottages."

Down at the sawmill, Gary, soaking wet but proud, points to a machine. "New today," he says.

"It's harder than you think to make a flat rectangle out of a round log. But we cut so much lumber, it's time we had a sawmill. So we got one."

Gary agrees to come out of the rain and answer some questions. He takes me to his Lakehurst dance hall. And the world of Gary Pinkham, which I had thought to be a tractor only, begins to open up.

"My father began this dance hall back in the Depression, in '32. Prices were something else, then. That stone chimney, 30 feet high, with a 12 foot fireplace cost him $289 to build then. This great barn was filled with dancers. I remember after World War II, we had 800 dancers here of a night. And the same bands, season after season for 35 years.

"There was Lloyd Rafnell's band from Auburn, Joe Avery's from Bath — they're in the 70's now. But they played up until a few years back.

"People would come from Fryeburg and Bangor to dance here. Back in those days, it used to be 60 cents a ticket. Now we play Country and Western and it's $6 a couple."

Gary talks about the cottages by Lake Pemaquid which he runs summertimes. "Five, booked solid. Same families back year after year." Gary is the Mr. Fix-it. He worked a few years as a youngster as a plumber's helper, later became a mechanic in the Air Force and put in three years at Bath Iron Works before going to Central Maine Power Co. "I can do the wiring, the plumbing, cut the firewood and, with my graders, keep those roads into the cottages in good shape.

"My father taught me how to work the woods. When my brother and I got to be 10, he gave us each an acre of woodlot to take care of. We started learning how to use an axe. Then got a cross saw. When we were 14, we'd saved the $170 we needed to buy our first chain saw. I've got it still, in my basement."

Gary leads the way to his yard to show his equipment.

"This skidder is $30,000 new, and the crawler $3,000. So we have to hustle to make it pay for itself. Thanks to my top helper, Donald Eugley, we cut 105,000 board feet of good wood last year, plus 300 cords of pulpwood and 50 cords of firewood."

Gary has about 100 acres of wood at Lakehurst to cut. But haying and mowing and plowing and tree planting are his business, too.

"These three tractors today cost about $13,000 each. The two rototillers are $2,500 each, two rotary mowers $1000 each. These four pieces of haying gear together are close to $10,000."

Gary pounds the tire on a skidder. "Just one of these new is $450. And one tire for a tractor is $290."

To keep this expensive gear working hard enough long enough to show a profit, Gary Pinkham must hustle as few office workers ever do. The small town, independent man who is his own boss is maybe the hardest working man in the nation.

"In winter, before I go to do the woods, I plow driveways. After a snowstorm, I have 60 driveways to plow. In spring, I turn over, plow and harrow 300 gardens. In summer I mow fields for 250 customers — last year I put up 16,000 bales of hay. And then we do tree planting. In 1974, I planted 75,000 trees for the state. Last year it was over 50,000."

Before his working day even starts, Gary takes a plow over to the town dump. "I have a contract to keep it neat, and the accumulation of junk and garbage has to be plowed off each morning, early."

We leave Lakehurst and the dance hall and sawmill and cottages and equipment and travel back to Gary's house. Next to it is a nursery for plants and trees. "Oh, yes, we started in this nursery business four years back. Went into partnership with an ex-marine, Doug Leavitt. Last year, we sold over 5,000 plants and bushes here. It's going up this year."

Is the endless work, the hustling from season to season, worth it?

Gary smiles slowly. "Well, I got my house. I put food on the table for my wife and kids. I pay my bills. And I'm my own boss."

Across Maine there are thousands of men who are their own bosses, making it in Maine in their own hard working way. I've seen the others, high in the skyscrapers of New York, making it too, in a different way. But the men in Maine's small towns are more self-reliant, more self-confident, harder working. And a lot happier. And if that's not richer — then what's rich?

JOHN UPTON, EAGLE CARVER

DAMARISCOTTA — Meet the man with an un-pinched soul who carves eagles.

His name is John Upton, wood carver extraordinary, of Damariscotta, Maine.

"I am working on my 506th wood-carving" says lean, lanky Upton, peering through gold-rimmed glasses. "And more than 300 of them have been eagles."

One of the most famous eagles Upton carved was given to President Eisenhower by Governor Muskie, when Ike visited Maine back in 1955, when Muskie was governor.

"I really hustled my butt over that job!" Upton recalls. "On a Monday afternoon, Muskie's press secretary, drove down from Augusta to my workshop. He said the Governor wanted a 32 inch Salem Eagle by Sunday afternoon to present to the President. I went into the barn at five each morning, locked the door and worked till dark. By Sunday afternoon I was finished. I called up my neighbor, Harry Marble, the TV man, and together we drove the eagle up to the Blaine House and handed her over to Governor Muskie."

As a young man, John Upton, aged 17, sailed the sea in square-riggers. In World Wars I and II, he served in the Navy, got "banged about" in the Pacific, and was retired in 1946.

"I went back to my old job in Cambridge, Mass., as a design engineer in a machine shop. Couldn't stand it! So when I was 50, in 1947 the Uptons moved to Maine. I'd learned to handle wood tools from my father. He taught me to carve wood when I was knee high to a hop toad. And so I turned to wood carving to make a living in Maine."

That March of 1949 Upton ran a one-inch advertisement in the New Yorker magaizne. "John Upton, woodcarver, Broad Cove, Waldoboro, Maine. Specialty Eagles" is all it said. "That ad pulled 22 letters for wood carvings. And the New Yorker Magazine has been my bread and butter for 22 years since then," says Upton.

"I remember my first order. It was for a bread board, to be inscribed with "Give us our daily bread," in French. I didn't know any French. So I called up the most bookish man I knew — author Henry Beston, who lived nearby. Henry looked up the Lord's Prayer in his mother's French language prayer book. I carved the board, carved the French prayer around it. Gave it to my wife Eleanor to look over before I mailed it. Eleanor found I had left out the most important word! So I had to start again from scratch. Now, I do a tracing of everything first; only after she approves it as correct do I start carving."

In his small workshop, part of his garage on Church Street, Damariscotta, Upton has 73 wood working tools and a power saw. And piles of fine woods. From this combination emerge Great Seals of the United States, State Seals of Maine and Pennsylvania; and dolphins leaping in the ocean, partridges running in the woods, whales blowing in the Seven Seas. But above all else, hundreds of eagles from Upton's hands. Eagles in all positions, in all sizes, in every wood.

Upton's work is treasured in 47 of the 50 states. He has filled orders from Venezuela, France, Italy, the Philippines, Great Britain and the Far East.

Upton's prices depend, of course, upon the complexity and size of each carving. His least expensive work is priced at $100. His largest pieces, beautifully finished and gilded, cost up to $2500.

In 1950 Upton was urged by a publisher to produce an illustrated book about "The Art of Wood Carving." For two hours early each morning, Upton wrote. Then, he says, his wife translated it into good English. Then his neighbor, Ivan Flye made the necessary photographs to illustrate the text.

The slim, definitive volume is now in its fifth printing. It is a classic of its kind and still in constant demand, producing a sizable royalty check each year.

Biggest collector of Upton's work is a Philadelphia realtor, Edmund C. Geatens, who has a summer cottage in Boothbay Harbor. "Geatens has bought 13 carvings from me, all of eagles. He is a tremendous collector of eagles. In his cottage at Boothbay alone, he has more than 104 eagles — collected from everywhere."

The eagle most admired by eagle-carver Upton is a white-painted carving which hangs over a doorway in Upton's study: "That was carved by the master of us all — John Bellamy, of Kittery. Bellamy used to carve his eagles at Kittery, then load them on a wagon and peddle them across New England, door to door, at $4. My sister picked this masterpiece up for $2 at some auction. I would not part with it today for $2000" says Upton.

Bellamy, who was in his heyday in the 1880's, died at Kittery in 1914, aged 78. His most massive eagle — standing 18 feet high — was on the bowsprit on the U. S. frigate Lancaster. It is now on exhibit at the Maritime Museum in Norfolk.

"I learned about eagles from watching them" says Upton. "It was a rare day when we did not see an eagle down at Broad Cove, Waldoboro, where we used to live. But my eagles don't pretend to be ornithologically correct. I couldn't care less about that. My eagles are symbols — I carve them the way I see them in my mind's eye."

"I have plently of work on order, thanks to the small advertisements I run three times a year in the New Yorker. I may not make much money carving, but I feel far richer than most of those $60,-000-a-year men from the cities. They come here, with full pockets. But with pinched souls."

Spot an eagle, haughty and spirited, guarding a Maine house, decorating the transom of a Maine boat, and chances are you have spotted the proud owner of an Upton eagle. Upton eagles are standouts. Plainly, they are carved by a man whose soul is far from pinched.

How an Air Force Major Started
Maine Antiques Digest

WALDOBORO — If you like success stories in Maine, here's one for the books.

It's the story of how a B-52 navigator with Strategic Air Command and a Texas schoolteacher who shared a yen for early American antiques retired from flying and schoolteaching, came to Waldoboro and began publishing a monthly newspaper called Maine Antiques Digest.

Sam Pennington retired from the U.S. Air Force in 1973 after 21 years of service.

Sally Pennington is the Texas school teacher he married when he was stationed at Carswell Air Force Base, near Forth Worth, back in 1958.

Together they launched the first issue of Maine Antiques Digest in November 1973. In three years it grew up to one of the fattest and bounciest babies in American publishing.

Neither of them knew anything about newspapering, says Sally. "We put out the first three issues with one portable typewriter, using the kitchen for an office. We got our five kids and their school friends to do the wrapping, addressing and mailing."

Together the group wrote 6,000 addresses by hand to send out sample copies of the first issue.

Sitting in the Maine Antiques Digest office building in Waldoboro, Sally Pennington proudly holds up the November, 1976 issue. A bumper 122 pages, it now has 8,000 subscribers and about 2,000 people who buy it at the newsstand. The current issue includes 84 pages of advertising at $132 a page — all of it unsolicited.

How did an Air Force flier and a Texas school teacher ever start a newspaper about antiques? And why did they start publishing it in Waldoboro, Maine?

These were questions which came to mind when Patricia Reed, an antique dealer in Newcastle, who buys a page of advertising in nearly every issue, waved a copy of Maine Antiques Digest under my nose and said "I swear by this paper. The day it comes out, my phone starts ringing. People call from all around the country."

The day I drove over to Waldoboro Sam Pennington was out. Sally Pennington was running the office.

Dressed in white turtle neck, blue stretch pants and blue sneakers, she welcomed me with a beguiling smile and an editor's pencil clutched in her fist.

Sam, she said, was up at Loring Air Force Base, which was where he fell in love with Maine, "long before he fell in love with me."

When they were married in Texas, Sally said, she had never been north of the Mason-Dixon line. "So Sam took me to see Maine, and while we were driving around we asked a realtor here in Waldoboro to show us a few houses. He showed us the old Waterman house. At first sight we loved it and we bought it. You know, Watermans had lived in that house from 1775 until 1932; we are only the third family to live in it in 200 years. To a Texas girl, that's incredible."

But the Penningtons couldn't come to live in Waldoboro then. "Having babies in the Air Force is cheap, we stayed in and I had five," says Sally.

Working on and furnishing the old Waterman house got them started on antiques and when Sam got transferred to Dow Air Force Base near Bangor in 1965 they started scouring Maine auctions and antique dealers looking for appropriate pieces.

"Well, in next to no time we had too much, so Sam began selling stuff from a barn, and talking about going into the antique business when he retired.

"I couldn't see hustling out to wait on tourists every time a car came up the drive and blew its horn. So I said 'No' to that."

Sam, she said, got his idea for the newspaper during a long night flight to Goose Bay, sitting over his navigation table. "This way he could put his hobby of photography into harness with his new hobby, which was antiquing. He came home from that flight bubbling with excitement, ready to retire and start a paper."

Every Maine expert on antiques or on publishing whose advice Pennington asked told him to forget the idea.

But in October, 1973, Sam retired and started work on the first issue.

"We got a lawyer to draw up the papers," says Sally. "Sam haunted the auctions, taking pictures of what was selling, reporting the prices fetched. I typed and edited. The Coastal Journal in Bath did paste-up, the Courier-Gazette in Rockland did the printing.

"Sam knocked on doors and persuaded dealers and other people to take six pages of ads. Oh yes, we were soliciting then.

"By the end of five issues, we had 1,000 subscribers, by the end of a year, 2,000. Now we sell around 10,000 copies and the advertising comes in unsolicited.

"We aren't getting rich. But we have created a going business and we have great fun and lots of satisfaction.

Sally Pennington thinks Maine is full of good business opportunities. "But you've got to be willing to grub it at the start and work round the clock, seven days for the first few years — Sam and I reckon we still put in about 80 hours a week.

"Our advice would be to go slow and start small. We started with $2,500 and we've never gone into debt for long. What we've made, we've ploughed back.

"But that's the joy of Maine: It doesn't cost much to get started here. And if you make it in Maine, you get noticed. In other states, you'd be lost.

"Nobody in Maine looks down because you pinch pennies getting started. Here it's fine for the boss to sweep out, carry sacks to the post office. Every person we and our five kids know works at something, digging clams, managing the bank. I like that. What's more — my kids like that."

Would You Buy an Old Snowball from Eddy Noessel?

BROOKSVILLE — Maine towns don't get much smaller or much nicer than Brooksville. Begin with the harbor, called Buck Harbor by the natives and Bucks Harbor by chart makers. It is horseshoe shaped and is entered from either side of a little island which protects the main anchorage. To the east there is the protecting shoulder of a mountain; to the west, the lovely farm of Archibald Cox, special prosecutor in the Watergate affair.

Ashore, a path leads by Bucks Harbor Yacht Club, a one-room Victorian building that is mostly porch lined with well used rocking chairs. It teems with kids who at 10 are already expert dinghy sailors. Then past a tennis court and along a tree shaded street to the cross roads of downtown Brooksville and the shopping center.

The shopping center consists of Condon's garage to the right of the crossroads, and to the left a single building which houses the post office and yarn shop and a special kind of library. Yachtsmen can take paperbacks they've read and swap them for paperbacks they haven't read.

Eddy's Market is the commercial hub, the news center, the meeting place of Brooksville. It is the stocking-up spot for all boatsmen sailing the Eggemoggin Reach.

Eddy's is famous as the place where you can buy Maine snowballs in July and August at 69 cents a bag of five. "I sell out before August ends" says Eddy.

When yachtsmen come in for supplies and ice, Eddy asks if they want snowballs too. They think he's crazy until he shows them the bags of snowballs. Then they buy, at 69 cents for five.

It all began one winter, says Eddy, when he worked all morning shovelling snow three feet deep from in front of his store.

"Every muscle ached and I hadn't a penny to show for it," he says. "Then my brain lit up. Make snowballs, it said. Freeze them.

Eddie Noessel / 161

Sell them in mid summer . . . I've been selling them in July ever since, at the highest profit in the store."

Eddy Noessel from the Bronx in New York City, has found a wife, prosperity and happiness in small town Maine.

More than that, he is doing something to help senior citizens and shut-ins for miles around Brooksville — more, possibly, than some costly government programs.

Eddy runs a "store-to-door" service. Two refrigerator trucks from his market sell groceries, milk, sundries, vegetables and meats to more than 1,000 customers a week. The trucks go right to the homes of rural customers in Castine, Penobscot, Brooksville, Cape Rosier, Blue Hill, East Blue Hill, Sedgwick, Surry, Stonington, Burnt Cove and Brooklin.

Store-to-door is a boon to senior citizens and a profitmaker to Eddy, who was a meat cutter in the Bronx when Marguerite Farnham from Brooksville went visiting there in 1933.

They fell in love, married in 1935 and spent their vacations in Maine until 1940, when they moved here permanently.

Looking around for a way to make a living, Eddy spotted the need of home delivery and bought a truck from which he sold groceries and meat.

Most roads in the vicinity then were dirt and potholed and it was tough going even for families with cars to get into town. He was 25 then and he worked long hours to build his business up. Now his store and delivery business employs seven people and grosses more than $250,000 annually — a long way from 36 years ago when his $28.50 monthly truck payment "seemed like the national debt."

During World War II Eddy joined the Navy "to see the world" and "got stuck on Pier 6 in New York cutting meat for the troops."

He and Marguerite bought R. C. Gray's store — now Eddy's Market — in 1951.

Eddy's drivers, Arthur Cousins and Archie Black, are trusted friends of most families on their routes. When customers are not home, Cousins and Black are welcome to walk in the kitchen, put the meat and milk into the refrigerator and pick up next week's order, which is usually written out and waiting on the kitchen table.

"Arthur and Archie are members of a thousand families, says Eddy. "For instance, Archie has an old lady who's sick on his route. When she can't get out of bed, Archie empties her slops.

"Arthur has a man crippled with arthritis. When the pain is bad in winter, Arthur takes the coal hod down to the cellar, fills it up and brings in a pile of wood. Things like that are part of my 'store-to-door' service."

A nasty thing happened in Brooksville while we were in harbor. Thieves broke into the farmhouse of Archibald Cox and stole his most precious belongings. Natives say that such breaks are frequent and are obviously perpetrated by experts. "I don't dare leave my place empty," said one modest homeowner. "If we go off even for a single night, we hire a house sitter."

Yet Eddy's store-to-door people are wholly trusted. In fact, say local law authorities, these drivers know more about what goes on and who goes where than anybody. And if they see something or somebody strange, they pass the word to the police.

Even before Eddy took over, the old Ray C. Gray general store was famous as a yachtsmen's cooling place. Gray's produced home-made ice cream. Yachtsmen from Boston and New York would sail out of their way to buy it in Brooksville. Perhaps the most famous incident happened early in World War II.

President Franklin D. Roosevelt, on his way home with the US Navy from signing the Atlantic Charter with Winston Churchill, was off the coast of Maine when he ordered the ship stopped: He was hankering after Gray's home made ice cream.

A launch was sent ashore and Gray routed out of bed. The officer and sailors explained they had been sent to buy several gallons of ice cream for the President of the United States. They swore Gray to secrecy until after FDR was safely home and away from the threat of German U-boats.

This 28 year old launched "Woodenboat" magazine

BROOKSVILLE — We are constantly hearing about young people forced to move away because they can't make a living in Maine.

Well, this is the story of a young couple who came here before they were 25 and who are risking all their money, talents and prime years to start an enterprise they love in Maine. And they are succeeding, although so far only barely.

Their names are Jonathan A. and Susie Wilson. Their enterprise is a new magazine called "The Woodenboat," a beautifully illustrated bi-monthly devoted to the design, building, exploits and tender loving care of wooden boats.

"We launched it in 1974 with only two paid subscribers" says editor-publisher Jon Wilson. "Now in 1977 we are about to 20,000 paid circulation. We hope to reach 50,000 eventually."

Woodenboat's office is a small wooden house in Brooksville, very close to Buck Harbor, favorite of cruising boats, wooden, fiberglass and aluminum. "For the first two years, the office was in our home" says Wilson. "But that's no more than a cabin in the woods, which Susie and I built. It measures 24 by 30 feet and the office took up 10 by 24 feet of that space."

Which left the Wilsons and their two sons, 4½ and two, very little space. "And mind you," says Wilson, "we had no electricity or running water there and our only heat came from a wood stove."

Today, the staff comprises six people plus two part-timers. All are young, underpaid and happily overworked.

Mary Jo Davies, the circulation manager, must enter about 100 new subscriptions every day. The magazine, she says proudly, now goes to 20 countries.

Then there is Mary Page, from Vermont, who pasted up every page of the early issues by the light of kerosene lanterns in the Wilson cabin. And Jacqueline Michaud, who is managing editor, secretary and production boss. Steve Ward, 23, from Brewer does the lively graphics which distinguish The Woodenboat.

This team, all in their 20's, had just put into the mails Woodenboat number 12, an issue of 88 pages, 17 of them advertising. The print order, says Wilson, is 20,000 copies, cost $1.05 each. "And thank God, we're breaking even now," he says. The magazine retails at $1.75 per single issue or $9 annually mailed.

Susie and Jon Wilson came to Maine from Rhode Island in 1970 to work for the Outward Bound School on Hurricane Island. Their jobs were to repair and maintain the school's 30-foot double-ender whale boats.

"We'll never forget that first, wonderful winter," says Wilson. "We spent it out on Hurricane Island, November till May, alone except for two other boat builders. It was the first time in 50 years anybody had lived all winter out on the island.

"But my trade was building small boats and I wanted to get back to designing and building my own. So that took us to Pembroke, near Eastport — it was the only place in Maine I could buy the waterfront I had to have at a price we could possibly pay. And it was the isolation I felt up there as a wooden boat builder that eventually led to our starting the magazine."

To get $10,000 to print the first issue, the Wilsons sold their own 35 foot Alden ketch. They are still without a boat, a fact that bothers them "acutely." Soon, however, they hope that the magazine itself will be able to undertake experimental projects in wooden boat building. And this will finance a boat.

Wilson says he managed to survive the economic disaster of the first issue by taking copies to the boat show in Newport, R.I., where he was known. He sold over 200 subscriptions there. "I guess those 200 showed their copies around a lot, because soon we got 1,000 more through the mail. Even so, it took me eight months to sell all 12,000 copies of that first issue. Now they're collector's items. In fact, we've had to reprint the first and second issues."

Of course, the going has been hard, the money worries constant, the work seven days a week. And Wilson admits there were some moments when he and Susie "felt like sinking Woodenboat." But now all signs are for smooth sailing. "I've promised Susie that with the first profits, I'll put running water and a bathroom into the cabin. After that, maybe we'll even swing electricity and oil heat."

Sitting on a packing crate in his half-furnished office, Wilson was optimistic. "I think we can go to 50,000 circulation. I think we're answering a real hunger out there. We get hundreds more letters than we can answer. But we use them in the magazine and they inspire us in black moments.

"Now over here" he says pulling out other boxes, "are manuscripts. Over 75 have come in, unsolicited.

"We can afford to pay only four cents a word and $5 a picture. But we've been sent great pictures by some of the best marine photographers. Half these manuscripts are from expert boat builders or professional writers. And the letters we get are from all over the world. — the Soviet Union, Fiji, Japan, throughout Europe. Our subscribers take issues of The Woodenboat cruising with them and that's how we extend overseas. We just seem to answer a need felt by people who own wooden boats. The language barrier is not insurmountable, apparently."

Wilson is a dreamer, otherwise he and Susie would never have gambled their savings and their own ketch to launch Woodenboat. He thinks, however, that there are many other aspects of our culture that offer similar opportunities to that being explored by Woodenboat.

"And what place could be more suited than Maine to publish a magazine with this kind of philosophy about craftsmanship and excellence."

Across Maine today, scores of young people like the Wilsons are launching their own new enterprises. Many will work their fingers to the bone barely surviving during the starting years and then, if they're lucky, blossom into hard earned success.

Many will never make it; some no doubt should never have started. But what is most important is not the success story, but the dream and the gumption that gets even the lost causes fired up and off the ground.

There ought to be some kind of clearing house for sharing and exchanging their experiences. Maybe they need not just help but recognition of the value of what they are trying to do. For these young people are the yeast that will liven and richen Maine's future.

Fire devastated the offices of the Woodenboat Magazine in March 1977. But out of the ashes the "Woodenboat" is sailing again, without skipping an issue.

MR. REPUBLICAN GROWS CHRISTMAS TREES FOR A LIVING

NOBLEBORO — Could there be a happier job in Maine than loading a thousand of your home-grown Christmas trees on a snappy, sunny, peacock blue December morning?

And then to pocket $7,000 for those 1,000 trees which cost you one dollar each to grow. That makes a gorgeous morning even more beautiful.

The man who has such a job is Linwood E. Palmer Jr., of Nobleboro — a man, incidentally, who hopes to be Maine's Governor.

Lin Palmer was born in Maine but left these parts to do well for himself in the steel business. He came home in 1972 to grow Christmas trees and work at politics. Quickly he was re-elected to the House of Representatives in Augusta (he'd been elected first when he just turned 21 — but that was over 30 years ago). By 1975 he was elected Republican leader in the House.

In December, Palmer is busy harvesting and selling Christmas trees. Politics, he says, can wait.

I watched Lin Palmer and Harold Stevens, his helper from Wiscasset, load a thousand trees onto a trailer-truck headed for Massachusetts. Palmer sells primarily to Pepperidge Farms, which was bought by Campbell Soups, which owns nurseries called Lexington

Gardens, which has outlets in Massachusetts, Connecticut and New York.

Well-to-do suburban families there will pay $12 to $20 for Christmas trees which Palmer raised and sold wholesale for $6 to $10 each. It cost Palmer about one dollar to plant and grow each tree — plus his labor, plus his land.

These trees fetch a premium price because they are hand raised, perfectly shaped and symmetrical. "Cultured" is the trade word for them, as contrasted to "wild" trees, cut from the woods.

Each cut tree is gift-wrapped. Palmer thrusts the butt end of each into a home-made contraption which looks like a Rube Goldberg wind tunnel, and Stevens pulls the tree through it. When it comes out at the other end of the funnel, its spreading branches have been neatly compressed, and the tree is temporarily shaped like a slim torpedo and wrapped in white plastic which looks like chicken wire but has no sharp edges.

At a lunch break, we go inside Palmer's handsomely restored farmhouse which dates to Revolutionary times. Over soup and sandwiches, we look out on the fields Palmer has planted with 1600 trees to the acre and at the ice-coated farm pond which holds a million gallons of water and a few hundred trout.

Below the woods is the beautiful Damariscotta Lake where Palmer has a swimming dock. On the high ground across the valley is Bunker Hill, resplendent with red barns and white farmhouses.

Growing Christmas trees is profitable and fun, says Palmer. "You can cut about 125 market-ready trees, six to ten feet tall, from each acre each year. If you get $6 a tree, that comes to over $700 an acre. Deduct the costs of growing, trimming, fertilizing and you can clear over $300 an acre, provided you do the labor yourself. Now compare that to the half-cord of wood you can harvest, on average, from a woodlot per year. A half cord of wood fetches about $20."

Palmer staggers his cutting and planting in most fields. "Some trees grow faster, same as people. When they're big enough for market, I cut them." In the spring, he plants a new tree wherever he cut an old tree and he fertilizes with Magamp, which he says releases its nourishment over two or three years.

To keep the grass down, he mows or uses herbicides. And to give trees a fine green color, he uses 10 ounces of urea per tree — "that's a high nitrogen fertilizer." Then in April and September, he sprays against white pine weevil and cuts out any diseased fir. By July all the trees that will be ready for Christmas are sold.

Usually it takes 8 to 10 years for a tree to grow to market size. But the University of Maine has developed methods allowing tree farmers to get them to market size in six or seven years, says Palmer.

Robert Umberger, a Christmas tree specialist with the state forestry department, says quality is the prerequisite for success in growing Christmas trees for profit.

"Back in the 1950's," says Umberger, "Maine sent a million trees to market. Half of them were junk and they ended up unsold and were taken to city dumps. They'd been cut wild, from the woods. Now we send about 250,000 cultured trees to market. But they make more money than a million wild trees."

Umberger says that for top quality trees and wreaths, the city demand still far exceeds the supply from Maine.

About 150 Maine Christmas Tree growers support a statewide organization to bring about improvements in growing and marketing.

The biggest grower of Christmas trees in Maine is Carlton H. Hodges of Skowhegan, who sells close to 15,000 trees a season.

Balsom fir, scotch pine, douglas fir and white spruce are the leading types of Christmas trees grown in Maine. But Maine is still only a small fish in the national Christmas tree picture.

Americans will pay more than $400 million for some 27 million trees this season. The big producing states are Pennsylvania, Wisconsin and Michigan. It's a big business whose star performer is a little town called Indiana, about 45 miles from Pittsburgh. This hamlet is sending 3½ million Christmas trees to market — about six times as many as the entire state of Maine.

Experts say there is great opportunity in Maine for more development of high quality trees for near-by markets. Maine is ideally suited because of soil and climate. What it takes is the right land, about $225 to buy some 1200 seedlings per acre, some tender loving care — and the patience to wait for 10 years for the first harvest.

How a super-salesman finds
happiness in Maine

CHAMBERLAIN — "Can a high-powered super-salesman from the city retire and find happiness in a Maine fishing village?"

Jefferson Davis Bates, is proof positive the answer can be "yes", provided the super-salesman keeps selling.

Retired supersalesman Bates, freckled, heavy, laughing, talking, making sales, swapping stories at age 75, was born the son of a salesman in a Boston suburb.

"My father was New England sales manager for the old Fairmore ranges and the first Leonard iceboxes. When I was 18, I started selling Kelvinator refrigerators, a new competitor, in 1916. I got my hands on the list of my father's Leonard icebox customers. Proved the hottest leads a fellow could get."

Soon young Jeff Bates was Kelvinator's top salesman, breaking national records. He was made sales manager, on the road everywhere.

"Then, when I was in Europe, American Motors bought out Kelvinator. And after 27 years at the top, I found myself out of a job."

Bates sold himself to Bendix, becoming sales manager there in time to introduce the new line of automatic clothes washers and dryers. "I went out to demonstrate the new washer to a theater full of people in Detroit. Threw in the same cupful of soap powder I used to demonstrate in New England. But Detroit water is different. Soon the stage was filled with foam overflowing from the machine and I was wading half to my knees in soap suds. But we sold 'em by the carload."

The first automatic dryers bounced enough to rock a small house when they went into their spin-dry cycle, Bates recalls. "I was demonstrating the line out in Cleveland or Cincinnati, and the thing shook so much it busted loose from the floor and agitated itself clear across the stage, crashing into the orchestra pit before we could turn it off . . . But we sold 'em by the trainload!"

Merger again put Bates out of a job. "One day, Philco bought out Bendix, and out I went again," he laughs.

Fifteen years ago Jeff Bates and his wife Marion built and moved into their retirement home on the ocean here. "We'd been coming to this part of Maine 27 years on vacation."

"Now," says Bates, "I wake up each morning with nothing to do except look at the sea and walk to the wharf and swap stories that I had already swapped sixteen times. So I went back to selling."

This time it was barbecue machines.

Loading barbecue machines into his station wagon, Bates travelled Maine and New England. Before long he had 1,000 customers barbecuing chickens in local restaurants and local grocery stores. And he was happy again. In 'retirement' Bates sold more commercial barbecue machines than any man in New England.

"I even put an $800 machine on my lobster boat and hauled it out to Monhegan Island, 14 miles out in the Atlantic Ocean to make a sale," he laughs.

When Douglas Odum, the only big storekeeper on Monhegan protested he didn't have enough home-generated electricity to operate it, Bates sold him a machine that operates on bottled gas.

Fine as the chicken barbecue business was, Bates believed it would be still better if the chickens had more flavor. "We raise broilers so fast in Maine these days, we feed 'em dynamite to speed 'em along," jokes Bates. "They are fine birds, but they don't have as much flavor as the old time chicken that had to go out and scratch for his dinner."

So Bates decided to sell flavor right along with machines. In the cellar of his home in Chamberlain, Maine he began bottling flavoring salt to put on the chickens cooked on his machines. But on his label he called it "Texas Bar-B-Q," and decorated it with a big Lone Star.

Everywhere he travelled, he carried samples. Soon he was spending nights in his basement filling little jars with his seasoned salt. "I was dizzy slapping on Texas labels at two in the morning. It dawned on me this was crazy for a retired man to spend his nights this way. So now I sell only big bulk orders."

Scores of his barbecue machine customers now have standing orders in 100 pound lots for Bates' Texas Bar-B-Q salt.. "If I wasn't 70, and didn't like my lobster boat so much, I could do 50,000 gross on that item alone," says Bates a bit mournfully. "You can't find real salesmen anymore!"

Bates could not stand seeing tourists pouring down to his seacoast village with money to spend and too few chances to spend it.

So he started a catch-all store, stocked it with 2,000 items, and hung out a sign "Elegant Junk . . . We Buy, Sell or Swap Anything . . . Trading with or without Conversation."

If Jeff Bates was doing the selling, there was conversation. Lots of it, together with lots of turnover and plenty of mark-up.

He bought old traps from local lobstermen, for example, for a buck or two apiece, and sold them to tourists by the hundreds for four times what he paid. He bought discarded lobster buoys for 25 cents and sold them to folks from New York for $2.50.

"After Labor Day, I had fifty of each left over. So I combined them into a real bargain. Put the buoy inside the trap, and offered tourists an end-of-season bargain at $5 for both. I sold them all in a day."

Bates chuckles. "The fishermen thought I was nuts paying them 25 cents for a beat-up trap and a worn-out buoy. Junk, they called it. But those city folk just loved to pay me $5 for each piece of that junk. Everyone was happy."

Bates loves to tell the story of an Italian storekeeper in Boston, where he sold a $500 barbecue machine. "I commiserated with him because his storeroom was jammed with old green wine bottles. I offered to help him out by taking them away. Gratefully he filled my station wagon with them. I brought them back to Maine, wrapped their nice green shapes in netting used in lobster traps and sold 300 of them for $5 apiece . . . ."

That is Jeff Bates on his lobster boat pictured on page 134.

V /

Along the Coast

Y OU LOVE MOST *what you know best.*

We have come to know the coast of Maine better than the rest of this lovely state, simply because we live near the coast, and we keep a cruising boat in New Harbor. It is on that boat, cruising this coast, that we spend 20 weekends a year and all our vacation time. After 12 years, we are getting to know the little islands, the remote coves, the small harbors and the men on the wharves at the fishing ports.

If you come to a town by boat you see it differently. You get treated differently, and you probably meet a different kind of people than if you came to the same place by car.

It is harder, very often, to get to places by boat, and that helps. If you have had to work your way through fog or stormy seas to get to a harbor, then you have a special feeling in your heart when you come alongside safely to the dock. Sometimes you come in under blue skies and flat seas, but later fog or bad weather catch you in harbor. So you stay and sit it out. This waiting too gives you a different link to the people, the harbors, the towns where you go by boat.

After a few years this results in slow cruises.

Nowadays on our cruises we enjoy many home-comings in so

many harbors. We zig-zag to see mechanics, storekeepers, lobster dealers, fishermen we met in earlier years.

For instance, it is only two hours at most from New Harbor to Pleasant Point Gut. But whenever we head east we decide at Franklin Light to make a turn and come in to spend the night at Pleasant Point Gut.

Well, there is a special feeling of envy when we come past the Caldwell Islands, just outside of Port Clyde. Soon after, we turn into Pleasant Point Gut and the home-coming feeling comes on stronger. We come in past Flea Island, very slow, skirting the shallows while our eyes scan the harbor for that raked mast, perky little schooner "Samantha" we admire so much. Then we look for the lobster boats we know, to see who is "in". We smile a private smile to each other as our eyes swing to look at the red privy on the shore at Flea Island. We see again the funny afternoon years back when we watched them load that mainland privy and float it across the Gut and set her in place where she was needed on Flea Island. We never before, or since, saw a privy underway across a stretch of salt water.

In harbor now, we steer over by the lobster wharf. We have to check in with Lester Young, always there in his high boots, working. We come slowly by, swap a wave and a shout. Took three years of coming in here to get that close to Lester. Then we wave a long hand-flagging wave to the Robinsons in the white house overlooking the harbor where he sits watching his harbor from the picture window, in a wheelchair since his stroke. He loves this harbor. And it loves him. He is a big warm-hearted friend with a little, gracious and warm-hearted wife.

Thanks to Al Elliot, we have a mooring here to use. Al Elliot's family have sent ships to sea from Thomaston, for about 150 years. Now a destroyer is named after his son, a navyman killed in Vietnam.

When we are secure and shipshape, we climb into the dinghy and row ashore to Gay Island, supposedly to take our Dalmatian, Piper, for a walk. But that is our excuse to go calling at "Tide's Way", the old white farm where two fine writers and two great women live—Elizabeth Ogilvie and Dot Simpson. Between them they know these Maine islands and island people as well as any writers. We visit them, admire Elizabeth's ability to produce a good book every nine months, get the winter's news, fuss with their pets and then walk through the woods and along the shore to the Andrews cottage for another bit of homecoming. Here Ed Andrews is a persistent clam digger and mackerel fisherman. On the mainland, during the week, Dr. Andrews is president of Maine Medical Center in Portland. Back to the boat.

When the dinner dishes are done and the moon is up, we sit on deck, hearing the night noises. A loon cries. Always we hear loons here. We hear fish jump and plop, and kids voices shout from cottages where they are visiting.

In the morning we share doughnuts with our friend the harbormaster. Then after a leisurely visit, we head east. But not far. In 20 minutes we drop anchor at the Caldwell Islands. Just for a swim, a walk to the top, a look at the view—a quick hello. Then we head through the channel at Port Clyde. Bill Thon's Friendship sloop is on her mooring. He is one of Maine's best painters and nicest men. Who can pass by without saying hello?

It is the same all along the coast. There are so many places and people we love to revisit. Some days we don't budge. Some days we cruise only three hours, then swim and snooze at a lunchstop island, then maybe. just maybe, we get underway by two o'clock.

I keep a small typewriter aboard. That machine, a very light portable in a thin steel case, has been around the world with me five times. I bought it during the first Eisenhower presidential campaign so I could fly, writing on my lap in the plane. It has been to Korea, Vietnam, to wars in Israel and to coronations and royal weddings, to bullfights and to space shots from Canaveral. It is an old, loyal friend. Now, lucky typewriter, it is spending its old age on a small boat cruising the Maine Coast.

I use it now to write pieces about the coast from the boat. The cockpit of Steer Clear is the best place in the world to have a summer office. What better spot to work than anchored in a small cove by a little uninhabited Maine island, with salt on the keys?

Seagulls are really Landlubbers

CAPE ELIZABETH — Seagulls and the Maine coast go together. But the real bird watchers get upset when we amateurs talk about "seagulls." The experts insist that gulls are not seagoing.

They say gulls are mostly land birds, scavengers, which sometimes spend their lives along the coast, but prefer the easy pickings of a town dump.

Watch a fishboat coming home, cleaning fish on the way and 5,000 gulls seem to surround it diving for scraps. Or as you eat dinner in a harbor restaurant, try throwing crusts of bread or necks of clams, in the air and let them drop toward the water, then see the gulls swarm in to feed, often snatching the food in mid air.

Scavengers? Or fliers of fantastic grace, skill and beauty? Are they greedy tramps or Jonathan Livingston Seagulls?

Experts insist there are 44 different types of gulls, each with different specific personalities, shapes, quirks. But when it comes to gull watching along the Maine coast, we see three types mostly—the herring gull, the black back and the laughing gull.

The herring gull is the one which sits on boats and messes up the roofs and decks to the fury of boatsmen. It is the commonest hereabouts, with a white neck, white back and mostly gray wings.

The black back is the biggest, fiercest and meanest gull. They will swoop down on a raft of new born eiders and gobble the young, taking three or four babies in a series of killing swoops. Some of the lobstermen who hate to see kidnaping and murder in daylight carry shotguns and shoot the black-backed gulls in the act.

You can spot them by the fact they are largest of the gulls and their backs and wings are strong black. Other gulls are frightened by them. They will force herring and laughing gulls to drop their food in midair by swooping down on them, claws extended. Then when the food is dropped, the black back will execute a marvelous feat of aerodynamics and make a swift turn and faster dive and catch the food even before it hits the water.

Laughing gulls don't breed in Maine any more, at least not in sizeable numbers. You can tell them by their black heads. It looks as if they were wearing a small black watch cap. The black backs and the herring gulls are getting all the best nesting places first. If laughing gulls nest and hatch eggs later in the season, then the others are apt to fly in and eat the eggs.

Another gull common in the southern harbors of Maine in summer is the ring billed gull, smaller than the herring gull. Smaller still is the Bonaparte gull, just bigger than a tern and here only in late summer.

I have a hard time telling gull species apart. This is because they change a lot as they grow up. And gulls live far longer than most people think they do. Herring gulls live as long as 15 years. They don't breed until they are five or six.

You can easily tell the young gulls. First, their plummage is brown, a speckled grayish-brown. Second, they cry like babies even when they are physically big. It is a dreadful noise, the never ending, petulant, irritating cry of a young gull begging to be fed. Young gulls look big but they squawk, squawk and open wide their mouths, begging parents to stuff them.

Gulls nest mostly on small islands and ledges. If you go ashore in early summer, clouds of gulls rise up and circle furiously. Their nests are mostly on the ground in the grass. The eggs are speckled, hard to see, easy to tread upon. For a good many years, State Wardens used to poison the eggs to keep down the growing gull population because they were killing off other birds.

It's hard to believe today, but not so long ago gulls almost died out.

"Egging" used to be a livelihood. "Eggers" would row or sail out to an island where there were hundreds of nests. They'd go ashore and smash all the eggs. A few days later they would return to collect thousands of newly laid fresh eggs and then sell them by the barrel load.

But worse than "egging" was "gunning."

When ladies wanted feathers in their hats, the New York millinery trade paid gunners in Maine 40 cents apiece for white adult gulls and 20 cents for the immature brown gulls. That was good money in 1890 or so.

Fleets would go out to the islands and slaughter thousands in a daylong hunt. In 1899 a New York milliner even furnished the guns and ammunition to Maine's Passamaquoddy Indians to kill gulls.

The slaughter helped stimulate the formation of the first Audubon Society, which launched a crusade to stop it. Now there is a $50 fine for shooting gulls, even though they have overpopulated the skies, even though they now pollute reservoirs.

The cries of gulls on a foggy day, the sight of gulls arching white and graceful against a clear blue sky—these are the sounds and sights of Maine's coast.

MYSTERY OF THE TIDES

PORTLAND HEAD — Stand on a Maine beach and watch the tide rise. Then marvel at the mystery that the moon, 225,000 miles away, is causing it.

Wonder at the magnificent fact that the pulse pushing up the tide at Portland Head began in the deepest part of the Southwest Pacific Ocean. It swelled through the Indian Ocean, on into our Atlantic, and from us it will pulse north into the iceflows of the Arctic. Eskimos will watch the same tide rise that you watched rising here in Maine; and Fiji islanders saw the same rising tide lap the beach at Suva.

Tomorrow, high tide will top Maine beaches 50 minutes later than it did today. For the Eskimos and the Fiji islander high tide will be 50 minutes later too. Why 50 minutes?

The reason is that since the moon rotates around the earth in about 29 days, that moon is 50 minutes later every day reaching the same position over Maine. The pull of the moon when it lines up with the sea twice a day is what causes the pulse in the ocean which we call a tide.

Walk any beach in Maine and be fascinated and perplexed by its multitude of special wonders. Here are just two more:

The phosphorescence in the ocean on a dark and moonless night is a thrilling phenomenon.

Row a skiff across a cove when the moon is dark, and see each stroke of your oars create a glorious display of underwater fireworks. The pools where your oars dip explode with a galaxy of golden light. Swim through the ocean water on a dark night and your body blazes a trail of tumbling yellow light.

This is phosphorescence, and it is caused by millions of minute organisms, part plant, part animal. They are too small to see. But when you swim through them or dip an oar among them, they throw off pinpoints of light by the millions.

They have a beautiful Latin name — Notiluca, which means night light. In a quart of sea water which looks clean and clear, three million Notiluca may be swimming.

Another special wonder . . . What makes the ocean change color? Why is it blue one day and pea green or grey another?

The answer, I have found, is that the blue color is caused by a scattering of light among molecules of water. The same scattering that makes the sea seem blue also makes the sky seem blue.

But the bluest water is the barrenest water. Don Dorsey, a marine biologist at University of Maine, Portland-Gorham, took samples of the bluest waters of the Gulf Stream when we were sailing with the Tall Ships from Bermuda to Newport. Where the water seemed bluest and most inviting, it was in fact a watery desert, almost devoid of life. But the less lovely looking, greener-gray ocean teems with diatoms, the prime nutrient in sea water.

To the naked eye, a million diatoms look like a spot of greenish-brown scum. But when Dr. Dorsey put them under a microscope, men would rave for hours about their beauty and function. They are the meat and potatoes of the ocean world. Their abundance in summer makes our sea look greenish. Without them, there might be no fish life in our teeming seas.

WOMEN SKIPPERS OF MAINE SHIPS

ROCKLAND — Maine has chalked up more "firsts" than most states. But the Maine tradition has been to do it, and say nothing. Maine does not blow her horn, traditionally; but maybe even that is changing.

In April 1976, Maine newspapers tooted their horns over Deborah Doane. Debbie Doane was news across the nation because she was the first woman to graduate from the Maine Maritime Academy, or for that matter, any American maritime academy.

She was news because she was the first woman to win third mate's papers in the United States Merchant Marine.

Debbie Doane graduated at the head of her class. Shipping lines vied to hire her. One reason may be that the first line to name the first woman captain of an American merchant ship will get millions of dollars worth of free publicity.

And, as she said to me on graduation day, Debbie Doane is ambitious to be the first woman skipper of the fleet.

I hope she makes it. All Maine hopes a Maine-trained woman becomes the first woman to command an American ship.

But will this really be a new role for Maine women? Here, as in scores of fields, Maine led the nation long, long ago. But we never blew our horn.

A woman writer, Liza Graves, has done some fascinating research into how Maine women long ago commanded ships at sea.

More than 150 years ago Maine women by the scores went to sea, on voyages lasting two years and more, as the wives of Maine sea captains.

Because of their ability to read and write well, they often became keepers of the ship's log, and handled all the ship's correspondence.

Mary A. Brown married Capt. John A. Patten of Rockland when she was 19. For her honeymoon she sailed aboard his vessel, "Neptune's Car," out of Rockland bound for San Francisco in the year 1855.

Capt. Patten taught his bride how to read a chart and how to plot a course and how to take bearings on the sun and stars. In his journal that male chauvinist wrote, "Mrs. Patten is uncommon handy about the ship and would doubtless be of service, if a man."

Two years later, again bound from Rockland to San Francisco, disaster struck "Neptune's Car."

First, the chief mate stirred up so much trouble with the crew that Capt. Patten had him thrown in irons. Then Capt. Patten fell sick of "brain fever." He lost hearing, sight and sometimes consciousness.

So Mary Patten, aged 21, took command. On the bridge, she skippered the ship, doing the navigation, giving the orders.

In the cabin below, she nursed her husband. For 40 days and nights, Mary Patten was so frantically busy in both places that she never took off her clothes.

She refused to let the mutinous first mate out of irons. "If my husband could not trust him when he was well, I certainly shall not trust him when the Captain lies ill."

Mary Patten took the ship around the dreaded stormy seas of Cape Horn and up the coast of South America to San Francisco. After 136 days she brought her vessel safely to anchor in San Francisco harbor.

But Mary Patten proved herself very much a woman as well as a skipper.

Once her ship was safely battened down and shipshape, Mary Patten announced she was over six months pregnant.

LIGHTHOUSES, STRONG SENTINELS
IN HEAVY GALES

BLUE HILL BAY — My wife has an ancestor who was keeper of the Blue Hill Light. She recalls him with so much pride that every time we cruise by that light, she lets go with three blasts on our boat's foghorn, as a salute.

Thanks to this connection we collect books about lighthouses and lightkeepers.

In a living gale on a recent winter night, I lay awake in bed watching flashes in the sky from the lighthouse on The Cuckolds. And I took down a few favorite books on lighthouses and read from them during the stormy night. I was filled again with admiration for those men and women who kept the lights burning amid terrible storms and terrifying seas all along our coast.

Begin where Maine begins, with the Isle of Shoals Light, six miles out to sea, set among five rock ledge islands. Capt John Smith (whom Pocahontas loved) wrote of them in 1614. Soon 40 families, mostly from Wales, settled on Hog Island (later beautified to Appledore). On these four seabound acres fishermen built the first church in the Province of Maine. The pirate Capt. Kidd buried treasure nearby, on Star Island. Then Indians swept down upon the 40 families and kidnapped or killed all except a Mrs. Moody. She hid herself and her two children under rocks. But the scared children cried out, and Mrs. Moody drew a knife she carried and killed them lest they be captured. The spot still is called Betty's Cove.

In 1821, the year after Maine became a state, the first Isle of Shoals Light was built, a 90-foot tower with a lantern. I figure politics was soon mixed up with the keeping of the light. For when Thomas B. Laighton was beaten in 1839 in his race to be governor of New Hampshire, he sold his business in Portsmouth and went offshore, having been appointed keeper of the light at Isle of Shoals.

Sail along the coast to Boon Island Light, one of the most isolated, dangerous lights along the coast, six and a half miles to sea. Built in the War of 1812 at the order of President James Monroe, Boon seems to rise right out of the sea. The first keepers had no place to shelter except the light tower and a crawl-hole. Capt. William W. Williams was keeper of the Boon Island light for 27 years about 100 years ago. When he was 90, in 1935, he told about the wreck of the schooner Goldhunter. "When the thermometer was four below zero; it was a thick sea vapor and blowing a gale of wind from the northwest."

"The schooner struck Boon Island Ledge three miles from the light. The crew made it off in lifeboats — a six hour row at 1:30 in the morning . . . They were frozen to the thwarts and almost helpless. One of the sufferers was a negro boy 14 years old . . . "

Williams said "Boon Island" derived its name from a "boon" in the form of a barrel of food always kept on the rock from the 1600s until the new light was established in 1854. Local fishermen from York put out the food year after year for 200 years to help shipwrecked sailors.

Remember that stormy, icy night of Jan. 28, 1977? Well the same icy, stormy weather hit 100 years ago, and drove the schooner "Australia" aground near the Cape Elizabeth Light. The skipper and most of the crew were washed overboard into the icy sea amid a gale. But keeper of the light Marcus A. Hanna spotted two sailors clinging high in the rigging. Their bodies were sheathed in ice. They were unable to move. Hanna hurled a stout line with a great iron spike noosed in its end. The spike broke the ice sheathing from one sailor enough so he could bend the line around his waist, and he jumped into the raging sea. The keeper hauled him up across the rocks. More throwing, and the second ice-sheathed seaman was hauled ashore.

Lying abed safe and dry in raging storms these nights, I recite like a litany those magic names of Maine's offshore lighthouses which suffer most in storms . . . Isle of Shoals, Libby Island, Mount Desert Rock, Petit Manan, Great Duck Island, Boon Island, Matinicus Rock, Seguin, Halfway Rock, Wood Island. May they keep living through the worst the Atlantic can throw at 'em!

TRAP DAY ON MONHEGAN

MONHEGAN ISLAND — Trap Day out here ranks right up there with Christmas and July Fourth. It is the day lobstering begins, the day traps are set out here. But few outsiders see it celebrated, because Trap Day falls in January.

Monhegan Island is a spell-binding, fearsome, wonderful, magical and lonely place in winter.

An hour's run southward to sea out of Port Clyde on the three-times-a-week mail boat, or nine miles southeast of Pemaquid Light, Monhegan is where Capt. John Smith (of Pocahontas fame) fished 354 years ago.

Monhegan still has the world's best lobster fishing grounds.

But woe betide anyone who is not a Moheganer who dares to set traps within two miles of Monhegan's shore!

One recent year 17 Monhegan lobstermen caught better than 170,000 pounds of lobsters during Monhegan's special short six month lobster season. Or an average of 10,000 pounds a man, with prices often over the $2 a pound mark.

Compare this to the catch of 3,000 pounds for the average Maine lobsterman. Maine's 6,000 licensed lobstermen in 12 months of fishing catch about 18 million pounds between them.

Out of all the lobstering communities along Maine's 2,500 miles of coast, only Monhegan has imposed a "closed season" which lasts half the year, from June 25 until January 1st.

By common consent, Monhegan's 100 families have decreed since 1909 that no lobsters shall be trapped there from sunset June 25 till dawn of January 1.

All lobstering must be done in the rugged winter months when icy winds, snow, and fog test a man's endurance. Come January 1st those biting northwesters make the Atlantic so cold, the ocean smokes with sea vapor. But these are the months when lobsters are plentiful, when their shells are all hard and when the prices are highest. By sunset June 25 all Monhegan traps are up and lobstering stops.

After Labor Day, Monhegan's population shrinks down from thousands to a mere one hundred. For a few weeks, Monhegan men may make their living "winterizing," closing summer cottages, boarding up picture windows against the rough Atlantic blows, taking up water supply lines.

By October, they haul their lobster boats ashore, scrape, caulk and paint them for the winter's work ahead. Moorings are brought up and checked to see that the chain and granite are shipshape enough to hold fast through the storms ahead.

Sounds of hammering come from the fish houses, where men are making new traps from oak and spruce. At the store, there is a run on bright paints. For the fisherman's colors must be freshly painted on every lobster pot buoy, marking the owner of each trap on the ocean bottom. At night, all hands, male and female are knitting twine into new potheads — a lattice of string to catch and hold the lobsters inside the traps.

A few days are specially set aside in the late Fall for "rocking." Every lobster trap must be weighted down with flat rocks.

But rocky and cliff-edged as Monhegan is, there are few flat rocks on the island of the right size for weighting down traps. Therefore fishermen take their boats to the mainland for a day or two of "rocking."

By the last weeks of December, traps — as many as 400 to a fisherman — are piled around village homes. Then, starting a week before Trap Day they begin transfering them to the docks.

On New Year's Eve, the trap traffic is tremendous. Traps are piled high as a man can reach; and piled so deep, only a narrow path remains for walking along the normally wide dock.

Fishermen bring their boats alongside the dock while helpers pass down traps enough and other gear to weight the vessel down sharply in the stern. Until dark is thick, the work goes on, piling pots, warp, rocks, bait barrels aboard.

After supper on New Year's Eve on Monhegan, there is no energy for parties. All lights on the island are out before ten o'clock. Many last prayers are said that no storm will blow up in the night-time to spoil Trap Day.

Trap Day, New Year's morn, comes up across the Atlantic. The old sounds of early morning come back, sounds forgotten since last June. First, the stomping and shouts of men on the dock. Then the soft plopping sound of the dinghies being cast off, and oars dipping into water as the fishermen row out to their boats. The cough and splutters of engines starting up and finally the blue-white smoke from their exhaust stacks smudges the New Year Day.

Lobster boats purr out of harbor. Now comes the sight and sound of the first traps being nudged over gunwales, the warp slithering out and then the bright painted buoys are bobbing on the icy sea.

Despite the rugged competition of Trap Day, there is a rare and wonderful gentleness among the Monhegan lobstermen.

If one of them is sick, unable to set his traps on Trap Day, everyone will wait until he is better and well enough to have an equal chance to reach the fishing grounds.

When one fisherman's wife lay near death in Damariscotta hospital, all fishermen waited for her to get better or to die. For almost three weeks they waited.

One bitter cold day near the end of January, the lady died. So cold was it that the hearse, carrying her from Damariscotta back to the coast, froze up. Her body was transferred to a truck in Bristol Mills. Finally the pick up truck brought her to the water's edge near New Harbor. A boat carried her back to Monhegan. The other Monhegan fishermen stood with her husband in the small church there for the funeral services.

Then, only then, did they and he go down to the harbor and race out on their postponed Trap Day.

Sometimes the tragedy is smaller. An engine "acts up"; a bad leg is not yet mended. One man, for some reason, is handicapped. So all men wait. Trap Day is postponed until chances are equal for all.

The high and the mighty of the world might well look to the men of Monhegan. There, with no PhD's preaching sociology, men are big enough to treat each other as brothers.

KENT ISLAND—WHERE BIRDS LIVE UNDERGROUND

JONESPORT — Kent Island is owned by Bowdoin College, according to legal papers. But the gulls and the petrels know better. Kent Island belongs to them.

More than 30,000 pairs of birds own the island in the spring and summer. Muskrats own it the rest of the year. And in between times some scientists and bird watchers from Bowdoin are tolerated on the 200-acre island that lies 15 miles out from Cutler, and 25 sea miles from Jonesport.

But the eeriest inhabitants of Kent Island are the petrels. Thousands of them live underground.

These little, bat-like creatures, called Leach's sea petrels, are about the size of a catbird. During the day they ride the waves, far out to sea. At night they come winging back to the island, after the gulls are at rest and sleeping. As many as 15,000 pairs of petrels fly in after dark.

They live in holes, burrowed into the ground like a mole's hole. About an arm's length down, the female lays a single white egg. One parent always is down there in the dark burrow, sitting on the single egg, while the other is out at sea, foraging for food. The forager flies home early in the night. Then its mate takes off under cover of darkness, safe from attack by the sleeping gulls.

I've been reading a bit about the birds on Kent Island in a book called "Gulls." It is beautifully written by Frank Graham Jr., who gull-watches from his home in Milbridge; and it is beautifully illustrated with fantastic bird pictures by Christopher Ayers, who lives at Freeport. This makes for a superb Maine combination. Remember the book "Gulls" when it gets nearer to Christmas, and give it to your very best friends.

Graham writes beautifully of his first nighttime encounter with a flight of thousands of returning petrels.

"The moonlight fell on the forest . . . spruce trees basked in radiance. As we pushed through the glinting branches, I half expected to hear the popping of tiny light bulbs. But the moonshafts simply dropped through the fleeting openings to strike fire from a lower level.

"The air around us was in a flutter, alive with shadowy winged things silhouetted against the radiance. Petrels were coming in from the sea, threading their ways through the trees to their burrows. In flight, they uttered a sweet twitter, a thin burst of sound spiraling down to silence . . . . From the porous floor of the island forest came a sound few human beings have heard. It was the melodious purring, pulsing yet sustained, a song crooned in the subterranean blackness by petrels to their mates during those intervals when both were on the nest."

These little, gentle, night-living petrels last a long lifetime. Dr. Charles E. Huntington who bands them, finds that some petrels live to be at least 25 years old. One that he banded as a baby in 1963 came back to burrow a hole as an adult in 1967 only four feet from where he had been born.

Some petrels banded on Kent Island have been found as far away as Spain and Africa—a flight of thousands of miles performed by a bird no bigger than a catbird.

There is an awesome mystery about the life, the flight, the subterranean burrows of Leach's petrels. Man may never understand the mysteries that lie under his feet on Kent Island, 15 miles to sea out of Cutler.

THE DUCHESS OF DIX

ABOARD 'STEER CLEAR' — We could feel ghosts surrounding us through the night. Yet we were at sea in a small boat, safely anchored between the little, uninhabited islands of Dix, High and Birch, a few miles out of Rockland Harbor.

Until now, we had thought ghosts only haunted houses and grave-yards on land. But that night in a little boat on a deserted sea, tucked away between empty islands, we could feel the ghosts of a thousand stoneworkers around us. And on our ears, out of the empty, silent night, fell the ghostly blasts of dynamite, the crash of falling rock, even the yells of pain from men crushed by the granite they were quarrying. We could almost smell the cordite and rock dust swirling at our nostrils.

Deserted now, these little islands just off the Muscle Ridge Chanel, were boom towns 100 years ago — as teeming with money, muscle and brawls as a gold rush town in the West.

We had explored Dix, High and Birch islands in daylight. In grass and wildflowers waist high, in meadows where larks still played, we had to search to uncover traces of "Shamrock" and "Aberdeen". These were the names of two huge boarding houses, big enough to house more than 1,000 stoneworkers and quarry men from Ireland and Scotland, over 100 years ago.

These tough, brawling men, who were paid $2.50 to $5.10 for a 10 hour day, cut the granite from seven quarries on Dix Island to build the New York and Philadelphia Post Offices, the United States Treasury in Washington, and dozens of massive offices in the building boom following the Civil War. In all, 150 buildings, plus giant cranes, overhead railways, enormous wharves and stonesheds once crowded this little island. A total of 2,000 men, women and children once lived here. Now it is practically deserted and barely a trace remains.

On a high point on the northwest of Dix, we looked hard to find a remnant or two of the elaborate mansion presided over in the

1870's by a lady destined to become the Duchess of Tomaro, in Portugal.

The lady was a vivacious beauty, four times married, and one of her husbands was a New York millionaire named Horace Beals, who in 1850 had accepted Dix Island reluctantly as payment for a bad debt. "It would be a good place to commit suicide" he said. But thanks to some dubious contracts Beals finagled with contractors who needed granite to build huge government offices in New York, Charlestown, Philadelphia, Washington and elsewhere, the granite in Dix Island made a rich Horace Beals even richer.

Beals plowed some of the profits back into Maine — and lost them. Hoping to create another Saratoga spa, Beals built a grandiose hotel on the banks of the Kennebec. It flopped. And the huge hotel was turned into a National Soldiers Home, called Togus — and it is around Togus that Maine's Veterans Hospital was built.

But in the boom years of Dix Island, Horace Beals built a magnificent mansion on the island to persuade his beauteous wife to live on Dix. The 26 room house had marble fireplaces, carved ceilings and an Italian walled garden. Nevertheless, the lady left Dix and left Horace and later married the Duke of Tomaro.

The boom lasted only during the 1870's and 1880's; and collapsed as swiftly as it had developed. In time all 150 buildings on Dix Island fell to disrepair, and some were destroyed.

After the beauteous Duchess-to-be abandoned her sumptuous mansion, a herd of sheep found shelter in the drawing rooms, and it was not long before cows and geese and hens were bedding down near the marble fireplaces. We looked hard but found only part of a cellar hole where the mansion had stood.

The now empty island once was a hub of politics and union activity. A Great Hall seating 500, the biggest hall in Knox County, was built on Dix. Theatrical stars from New York entertained packed houses of granite workers. Thompson H. Murch, a granite worker himself, was elected to Congress. And James G. Blaine brought Washington politicians to Dix aboard a company yacht, when Blaine was Speaker of the House and was seeking government contracts for his home state.

When the boom burst, the bars and sporting houses of nearby Rockland had to shut their doors. They had catered well to the 1,485 men working in the quarries, who together drew the biggest payroll Rockland had ever enjoyed. Then, suddenly it all stopped. A brief flare-up of prosperity came to High Island, 300 yards across the channel, in the early 1900's, thanks to a $3 million contract for granite to build the new John Wanamaker store in Philadelphia. And then one day that suddenly ended.

All one recent afternoon, we walked where thousands had quarried granite. Barely a trace of the buildings or great cranes or railways are left. But the quarry holes are there. Enormous bolts and hawsers which once held cranes in place are rusted to a pile of filings. The wharves on High Island stand strong, high, immovable, built of tons upon tons of granite. Three schooners, each 100 feet long, could be loaded simultaneously there. Now only abandoned lobster traps rot in the weather.

Trees and brambles grow through the walls of granite, where thousands of men once drilled and dynamited. As we walked through the eerie remains of the quarries, a sudden loud whirring noise frightened us. Then we saw a big flock of Canada geese rising in noisy panic as they heard us approaching the brackish pond.

When the geese had flown, silence returned again to the abandoned quarry. We looked in awe at huge slabs, perfectly cut, each weighing several tons, standing ready for shipment. How did men move those tremendous weights 100 years ago on this island? We saw thousands of paving blocks, perfectly shaped which were never shipped.

There were fights and murders and terrible accidents and gruesome deaths here once, cheek by jowl with fortunes made. Today, except for a few lobstermen and an occasional cruising boat like ours, the islands are deserted. The quarries are quiet as tombs.

Yet anchor off them at night, and the ghosts come out.

Breaking the ice in winter

ABOARD COAST GUARD CUTTER — Ice big enough to hinder boats forms on Maine rivers about Dec. 7 most years. Soon after that, Coast Guard ice breakers begin their winter's work from their stations spotted along Maine's coast. The steel-hulled, slow, powerful icebreakers must keep open the big rivers on which oil and other essentials are carried to upriver towns and cities.

The fishing harbors begin to freeze after the rivers do. And the icebreakers must keep at least the channels open so the fishing boats can come and go in the subfreezing cold.

First, the fresh-water ponds freeze. Fresh water freezes at 32 degrees Fahrenheit.

Next the rivers. The flow of the tides and the tang of the salt sea fights freeze-up. Salt water won't freeze until 29 degrees; and the tides' movement breaks up minor freezes. (For the hoarders of odd facts, the average salinity of sea water off Maine is 35 parts of salt to each thousand parts of water.) Finally the harbors freeze.

Experts can look at the salt water and tell if it is on the way to freezing. The surface gets an oily look, caused by the formation of tiny ice spicules. This is a fancy word for very thin ice crystals only a third of an inch across.

Second stage of sea ice is soupy slush. Although it's not hard, when it gets 12 inches thick it's enough to stop a boat.

Third stage is the formation of an ice crust. This is not yet hard and brittle. It is rubbery, and stays rubbery until the temperature drops and stays down to 16 degrees.

Then comes the fourth stage, when prolonged cold weather, below 16F, makes sea ice hard and brittle. Then it gets to be between two and eight inches thick. This is called "young ice." When it has lasted a season in cold regions it becomes "winter ice." In the polar regions ice more than one year old quickly gets to be 12 feet thick.

The final stage is "rotten ice." This is when "young ice" becomes soft, gets holes in it and begins to disintegrate.

Several Coast Guard cutters along the Maine coast keep the rivers and harbors open.

The Coast Guard cutter Swivel can break any ice in Maine, says her 36-year-old skipper Chief Ray O'Neal. "Last year in Swivel we cleared slush ice 18 inches thick so the state ferries could get into Rockland harbor from Vinalhaven and North Haven. Back in the deep freeze of 1968 we broke young ice up to 24 inches thick on the Kennebec River. Ice jams were causing floods in Augusta.

"The Swivel is a steel-hulled, 65-foot Coast Guard cutter powered by a strong Caterpillar diesel.

"She is a slow boat to China, but she is strong. But we take no chances. We come at dead slow, then stop and just nudge into the ice. We inspect it.

"Sometimes a huge oil drum is locked into the center — and if we hit that hard, it would hurt. So we nudge and look. Then we put the power to her, more, more and more. If that doesn't break up the ice, then we back off five boat lengths and come hard at the ice at full ahead.

"Another trick in breaking ice is to turn. We turn full left rudder. Then full right rudder. Back and forth. Soon we are rolling side to side as well as slowly ahead. And that does it to most ice."

Maine fishing boats will ice up at sea this winter, as always. And, as always, this is dangerous. Icing up begins when spray is flying and the air temperature is 20 degrees Fahrenheit or less, the sea water is about 30 degrees — and the wind blowing the spray is Force 4 or more.

If enough ice forms on one side it will capsize the boat.

So when the wind blows Force 4 and the thermometer reads 20°F and you can draw a chair closer to the fire — stop to pray that the ships at sea are not icing up.

STEAMBOATS: LOVELY LADIES OF YESTERYEAR

ROCKLAND — Wouldn't it be a nicer world if summer visitors still came to Maine by steamboat?

I bet thousands would prefer to come by the old night boats from Boston and New York than to ride the turnpikes.

Steamboats fill my mind today because I've been rereading that lovely nostalgic book, "Steamboat Lore of the Penobscot" by John M. Richardson, onetime editor of the Rockland Courier-Gazette.

His book begins with a newspaper story from the Dec. 28, 1935, issue of his paper. Here are the first two paragraphs which ran that historic day in Maine:

"The aching tragedy of this thing called progress was summed up last night by three long, deep, melodious blasts from the great whistle of the steamship 'Belfast.'

"As the last musical note echoed over the windswept harbor and city, it spoke the final farewell to the waters of the Penobscot of a century old service of steam-propelled vessels to Boston, the last and saddest sailing of one of the great white fliers."

For a moment, let's cry in our beer over the passing of the steamboats and recall a few of those lovely ladies of the Maine Coast.

Begin with the "Bangor," the first steamer on the Boston-Bangor division. She was a 400-ton sidewheeler, fore and aft rigged, with a crosshead engine and a 10-knot speed. She came out in 1834 to begin the service. She burned wood, a whopping 25 cords of wood per trip.

They sold her to the Turks in 1842 and she carried pilgrims to Mecca. But the pilgrims would not board her when she first arrived painted white. For white is the color of mourning among Moslems. Not a mussulman would cross the gangplank till she was repainted black. She ended her days in the Turkish navy.

"Bangor II" was an iron ship, 131 feet long, built on the lines of a smart yacht and was launched in 1845. But she came to grief on her second trip, catching fire off Dark Harbor and being beached at Isleboro. The owners abandoned her and the underwriters had her rebuilt at Bath, after which the U.S. government bought her and renamed her "USS Scourge."

The "Boston" was a 630-ton beauty, 225 feet long, built in New York in 1850 and finished with utmost elegance. The Mariners Museum of Newport News, Va., describes her accommodations as follows:

"In the Gentlemen's Cabin she has 157 berths, which look the very pattern of neatness. The Ladies' Cabin has 42 berths fitted up in splendid style, with a dressing room and mirrors and special arrangements for washing et cetera. All upon the most improved plans. Besides the above, there are 20 staterooms, including two 'bridal staterooms', well lighted and ventilated, with an air of comfort sufficient to quiet all forebodings of that pest of steamboat-traveling to the fair sex — seasickness."

The "Boston," God rest her frames, came to her end in the Civil War. She was burned off Hilton Head in May 1864 to prevent her falling into Confederate hands.

Steamboats by the hundreds sailed the Maine coast every day for a hundred years. Up until the 1920's more than 30 passenger steamers arrived and left in a day from Tillson's Wharf in Rockland. Reading Richardson's book, with its old pictures of hundreds of these steamships, it is astonishing how so many perished in fires, explosions and groundings. Insurance sometimes may have influenced fate.

The greatest steamship disaster in the maritime history of New England was the loss of the 2,283-ton "Portland" in the wicked hurricane of November 26-27, 1898. The vessel was lost on her run from Boston to Portland, and all 176 persons aboard went down with her.

Weirdly, 50 years after the "Portland" went down with all hands, a scalloper dragged up from the bottom a stewpan, a glass doorknob, dinner plates with the Portland engravings on them and half a dozen bottles of champagne, labeled for her dining room.

KEEPERS OF THE PORTLAND LIGHTS

PORTLAND — Joshua Strout and then his son, Joseph, were keepers of the Portland Head Light for more than half a century. How many ships were guided to safe passage between 1869 and 1929, the 60 years when father-and-son Strout manned the Portland Light? Probably more than 60,000. Think of the cargoes out of China, the Indies and Europe. Think of the sailors. Think of the schooners and steamships which sailed past Portland Head in the 60 years that the Strouts kept her burning.

But the Annie C. Maguire, a three-masted bark, was one of the ships that never made it. On Christmas Eve, 1886, just before midnight, she piled hard aground onto the ledges only a stone's throw from where Joshua Strout manned the light. Working by the lighthouse beam, Strout roped ashore the 15-man crew, including Capt. O'Neil, his wife and two children.

It was a strange wreck. For on that Christmas Eve, Portland basked in balmy weather — temperature 46 degrees, breeze southerly, visibility clear. The tale that a blizzard was howling is only a tale. The Annie C. Maguire, a 34-year-old vessel, departed in debt out of Buenos Aires about three weeks earlier, and in Portland the sheriff was waiting to attach her on behalf of Kidder, Peabody, Boston bankers. All they got was a wreck.

Her punctured hull was worthless. At an auction on Dec. 29, the Annie C. fetched a mere $177.50. Yet Mrs. O'Neil may have salvaged a little fortune. The story goes that she got to the captain's sea chest before the sheriff, took out a big roll of bills and hid them in her bandbox, which went ashore with her on the rope ladder to safety. And she sat on the bandbox in Joshua Strout's lighthouse until the sheriff left.

Three tremendous gales in recent times have assaulted Portland Head Light. The great Cape Elizabeth Gale of March 3, 1947 tore a 2,000-pound fog bell from its steel moorings. Monstrous waves in a December 1962 storm cracked three walls of the engine house, tore loose a bulkhead and ripped off much of the roof. Then on April 3, 1975, a day and night of tremendous seas demolished the whistle house, knocked out the foghorn, tossed the bell aside like matchwood and extinguished Portland Head Light. Nothing worse can happen to a light.

Eleven miles out from Portland flashes Halfway Rock Light, halfway between Cape Elizabeth and Small Point, the western and eastern arms, which shelter Casco Bay. Sail by and even on a calm day, Halfway Rock's treacherous, deadly ledges and boiling sea are a spine-chilling sight. A sailor's imagination can picture the crash, then that awful terrifying smashing sound of a ship's hull hitting hard again and again on a dark and stormy night. Hundreds have. Scores of crewmen have drowned off these cruel, hidden ledges. All that was left to identify one big wreck in February 1861 was the single word "Bodicea," burned on a washed-up medicine chest. Not one of her drowned crew ever washed up on Jewell or Inner Green, where spars and flotsam washed ashore. She was a British bark, bound for Glasgow on a return voyage from New Orleans. The Bath brig "Samuel" died earlier on Halfway Rock; the schooner "Lydia" in 1869, tore a vast hole in her hull, lost her rudder, boats, chains, anchors, boom and mainsail but somehow made it into Mackerel Cove on Bailey Island, with a hull completely filled with water.

Finally the light was built. On the night of Aug. 15, 1871, a beam first flashed from Halfway Rock Light, shining from a granite tower 76 feet above the cruel sea. But that cruel, powerful sea swept away parts of the light station, year after stormy year. It was built and rebuilt, stronger and stronger.

Wild sea marooned lightkeepers out there, far from land and supplies, for months. Even launching a dory or sailing skiff into those tumultuous seas was perilous. Once launched, 11 miles of open water lay between the keeper, with his oars, and Portland. Now, Halfway Rock has a helicopter pad, telephones, power boat. But the crash of the surf on the lurking ledges on a black blowy night makes a sailor shudder and quickly turn his helm and head his boat to open sea.

How Darrell Lamb harpoons Tuna

BAILEY ISLAND — "W-O-W that's a fish?" gasps a six year old tow-head. Blue eyes bug out of his freckled face as he gapes at a 710 pound tuna on Merrill's Wharf.

Each night of the Bailey Island tuna tournament held in late July, hundreds of summer visitors throng to this wharf on Mackerel Cove to gape in astonishment at the giant fish men bring in from the sea.

First day of a recent tournament 40 boats brought in 24 tuna; second day 31; fog was so thick the third day was declared a "no fish day."

Gone are the boats in the million dollar fleet which gathered here. But the fish boated, fish harpooned, fish which struck rod and reel, fish sighted, fish chased, fish which got away, will all live long in the memories of the fortunate people who have been out chasing the giant fish in a Bailey Island tournament.

One local hero is Darrell Lamb, the brown eyed, reddish haired Brunswick man in his forties, who is the ace with a harpoon. Lamb ironed and boated four fish the first day, seven the second day — close to 7,000 pounds of fish in all.

Darrell Lamb is persnickety about his harpoons.

"I make my own poles. Use ash," he says, "cut to 12½ foot lengths."

Darrell says he kept throwing from his boat in harbor, experimenting with different length poles until he found "12½ feet balanced out just right for me."

Tied to the dart or barb (a standard commercial sword fish dart) Darrell has 50 feet of heavy nylon rope, followed up by 65 fathoms (390 feet) of heavy manila on his harpoon. For "flags" Darrell has 15 foot bamboo poles with four styrofoam lobster buoys as floatation.

Darrell holds his pole at the very end, firing it off with just one finger on the back. "In throwing a dart, it is the follow-through that

How Darrell Lamb Harpoons Tuna / 205

counts, just like in golf. If your throwing arm follows through right on course to the fish, the dart will get him. But if your body or throwing arm goes askew, then the barb will go askew."

After years of practice, Darrell can iron a fish swimming 12 feet below the surface, instinctively making the necessary adjustments for water deflection, speed of the fish and boat in relation to each other.

"In coming up on a school of tuna, the secret is to make any changes in your speed very gradually. Just ease the throttle very gradually open or gradually shut. You can go 2,000 rpm or 1,000 rpm, to keep pace with the fish. That speed doesn't bother them. But any sudden change in engine sound will scare them off."

The tuna around Casco Bay, says Darrell Lamb, are in here only in a migration pattern, heading toward Nova Scotia. They are not in here to feed, though the feed here is good. They are not in here to stay for the summer. They are on their way somewhere, passing through. One day the bay can be alive with tuna. Next day, they are gone.

Ten miles out to sea from the wharf, competing boats begin the tuna hunt soon after 7 a.m. and keep at it till 5 p.m., when all lines must be up, all harpoons sheathed.

To catch tuna, you first must spot the fish.

"Spotting fish" is the job of everyone on board, but most especially the two look-outs in the tuna tower, one facing forward, the other watching aft.

The tower is about 20 feet above sea level. There is barely room to stand comfortably on it, and every sway and every roll and every pitch of the boat is magnified hugely. The tower is not the spot for anyone with a queasy tummy.

You spot a tuna in these ways: First—and most often—by seeing the tell-tale wake which a swimming school of tuna leave behind them on the surface. It is nothing but a ripple of slightly swirling water, or a trail of small white foam. It is hard to spot. It's deceptive. It takes practice to differentiate between the aftermath of a boat wake, a school of small mackerel, a shark and a tuna.

Second, you can spot tuna as they leap, making a giant and exciting splash. But that splash lasts only a split second.

Third, as the tuna swims close to the surface (which again may be only briefly) a tail and dorsal fin will show a few inches above the surface.

From a high tower, the spotter can, in a calm and glassy sea, see below the ocean surface for a few feet and spot tuna which have no fin showing, are not leaving much wake.

"Fish to port eleven o'clock, quarter mile away!" yells the spotter.

A shudder of excitement goes through the boat. The helmsman cracks the throttles ahead, gently. A sudden change in engine revolutions may scare the fish. Tuna are frightened by sudden noise. But the steady throb of a boat seems to mesmerize them. When hunting tuna, you travel mostly at trolling speed.

The "ironer" moves into the stand. This is the tuna pulpit, a narrow plank surrounded by guard rails at the prow of the boat.

Harpoon up, at the ready, the boat moves forward, a hair faster than the fish are swimming, gaining, gaining, gaining on them.

If the fish turn, the boat follows.

But fish can turn quicker and faster than any boat.

Now, the moment of truth is at hand. The harpoon arm goes up to position.

The fish are within a dozen or so feet now!

"THROW!"

There is one split second, only that, to find whether you have missed or hit.

If you've missed, the pole and harpoon float miserably by the boat, and you give full rudder to recover them, dejectedly.

If you've hit, a few hundred feet of heavy line go streaming out, red hot.

The barb is in. The fish is plunging deep, racing away.

Overboard now goes the "flag." This is a long bamboo pole, attached to the tail end of the line. It is about 15 feet long, with a flag at the top, and is kept buoyant in the water by long splices of cork or styrofoam.

Wherever the fish goes, he tows the flag. The fish is separated from the boat now.

Fish and flag may go zipping off full tilt, hell bent for freedom.

Or the fish may plunge downward, submerging the pole and flag with him.

Or the fish may have been hit a mortal blow, and die immediately. Then the flag will be almost motionless. Sometimes the whole gear will disappear, never to be found again. The fish is then lost.

Most often, the boat will circle for 20 minutes or so, keeping the flag always in sight. Then the boat comes alongside and recovers the flag, and the fish at the end of 65 fathoms of line.

Now begins the hard, hand over hand task of hauling in a hundred yards of line with perhaps 800 or so pounds of reluctant tuna.

That tuna may want to go in the opposite direction. But even dead 800 pounds is a lot of fish for a 180 pound man to haul in.

But the hauling work is delicate too, calling for more than brute strength. The small harpoon head—the dart—can pull loose if you pull the wrong way as the fish angles. Then the fish is gone, lost. And there is a knot of sour disappointment in the stomach of everyone aboard.

The dart is strong and sharp, but it is small, measuring only about three inches across, six inches long, shaped like an arrow head.

To harpoon a tuna, you aim just behind its eyes. Then the combined speeds of boat and fish will work so the dart sinks where it will hold in the flesh near the dorsal fin and backbone, or heart.

Finally, when the fish is alongside, a winch may be used to haul him aboard. Some "plush" boats have a hatch through which the giants may be easily slid into the hold. Others haul them over the freeboard. Others tie them on the outside of the boat.

If you are trying the great sport of rod and reel fishing for a blue fin, your lines are trailing 50 to 75 feet behind the boat, swinging from the outriggers.

On one line are three large mackerel, their back bone removed and a big hook sewn into place with neatness a surgeon could not better. These bait fish must swim so realistically that they will tempt tuna to bite. These baits may skip on the surface.

The second rod and reel line may be a foot or so below the surface. Sometimes squid is used instead of mackerel to bait it.

How Darrell Lamb Harpoons Tuna / 209

If there is a strike, the huge rods burn as the heavy 130 pound test line whirls out.

The massive reels can cost up to $500 each. The test line alone can cost $35. A rod may cost $150. Elaborate outriggers can cost $1,000. When a tuna strikes, he strikes with 200 times the force of a big salmon hitting a fly. The fight between man and fish may last over five hours.

By dark all boats are in. The huge fish are weighed — 600, 700, 800, even 900 pounds each. The parties and the fish stories begin and both go on and on, in a carnival atmosphere. But eight hours of tuna hunting take their toll. And to some, sleep comes soon and deep. The boat lights wink out. The boats rock.

And out at sea, those giant tuna swim. They swim fast, covering 100 miles in a day, 5,000 miles in 50 days. Where will they be tomorrow?

A new federal law limits the catch to one fish per boat per day. It's hurting Maine tuna fishermen.

Blue Blood and Old money, 15 miles to sea

NORTH HAVEN — Here, 15 miles out to sea from Rockland, are clans of Cabots, tribes of Lamonts, hordes of Saltonstalls and Gastons, roomfuls of Rockefellers, Reynolds and Rhinelanders, IBM Watsons, Standard Oil Jennings, plus coveys of college presidents, eminent surgeons, judges and lawyers enough to pack Supreme Courts, theologians enough to talk you into heaven.

Here from July until September, senators in shorts sail dinghies older than they are; here ambassadors in sweat shirts play chef at cook-outs; here learned judges lick ice-cream cones while their wives buy groceries; here college deans in torn-off denims clean fish; bankers and brokers from Wall Street and Back Bay borrow nickels from paper-boys; blue-rinsed dowagers go raspberrying and dish up beans; presidents and even kings shop at Waterman's general store; and

Episcopal bishops swear like troopers when their outboards refuse to start.

North Haven and Vinalhaven are summertime havens for blood that is very blue and money which is very old and deep.

No one knows even the approximate total of all the wealth and power represented here. But the 'old money' must surely run into hundreds of millions of dollars; and the power of the families controlling that wealth must reach into most fountainheads of American life, and far beyond our shores.

But wealth and its trappings do not impress the island people. One reason is many island families are the First Families of America; they have been landowners here for more than 200 years. Another reason, is competence. Competence in the cycle of seasonal chores — making a boat, fixing the plumbing, getting in wood, setting and hauling traps, skinning a deer, digging a mess of clams, turning out a tasty covered dish or baking a flaky squash pie for a supper, in being a reliable, good neighbor and a trusted, respected parent. City trappings count for little on these islands where there are no headwaiters, no doormen, no porters to tip, no exclusive clubs, no hoity-hairdressers, no couturieres, no charity balls or Opening Nights.

Summer people blend amazingly well with island people on North Haven and Vinalhaven.

The credit for that must go largely to the summer people. They bend with the island ways.

A summer person gets a bigger sense of success when the island people on the wharf or the ferry slip or the store call him or her by his or her first name than they do if the broker rings up to say their stock has jumped 10 points. They want to be accepted here most of all places. For local acceptance hinges wholly on their qualities as a person, and not on their bank account or family name. Not every summer person is given it, by a long shot.

Summer people first began coming to the Fox Thorofare about 100 years ago. Then Dr. Weld, of Boston, dropped anchor here one night while cruising the Maine coast with friends. They rowed ashore and were so captivated by the coves and islands and the beauty of North Haven that they promptly bought land. They ended that cruise right here and spent the following days drawing plans for summer cottages and contracting with local craftsmen to build them for use the following year.

Dr. Weld's imprint is still strong on the Thorofare. His daughter, Mrs. Mary Pingree, has long summered in the big, handsome house at Iron Point, with its commanding view of the Thorofare.

Today, North Haven youngsters still sail the famed North Haven dinghies first built for Dr. Weld by J. O. Brown back in 1880. North Haven may be the most enthusiastic, competitive sailing center on the coast, thanks to the tradition Dr. Weld began.

On race days in summer, up to 50 of the 70 or so North Haven dinghies compete with each other in coves along the Thorofare. These 15 foot, four inch racing dinghies have been unchanged in design for almost 100 years, except for a modification in the twenties, when 300 pounds of inside ballast and flotation gear was added to prevent them from capsizing easily and sinking, as well as throwing the crew into the chilly sea.

Dinghies stay in the families becoming heirlooms, outlasting the generations who once sailed them. Some youngsters on North Haven today proudly sail the same dinghies which their fathers and grandfathers sailed. And when new North Haven dinghies are built, it is most often J. O. Brown who builds them.

The fourth generation of Browns now works at J. O. Brown's wharf and boatyard, started on the Thorofare in 1888. When Brown's built the original North Haven dinghies for Dr. Weld, they cost a few hundred dollars. Today's version costs $2,500 fitted out, ready to race.

Fewer than 100 families — 350 people — live year round on North Haven. Most of these families trace their ancestry back to the first settlers who came here 230 years ago.

Island people today own only about 25 per cent of North Haven, while 75 per cent of the island is owned by summer folk. The summer folk now own close to 100 per cent of the shoreline.

Three miles across the island lies Pulpit Harbor and Minister's Cove. These are perfect and beautiful harbors. There are no stores,

no supplies, but they are ideal for visiting boatmen. The view of the Camden Hills, with towering Mount Battie, 800 feet high, Mount Megunticook, 1,138 feet, and Bald Rock, 1,100 feet, against a brilliant sunset across Penobscot Bay is a sight of such moving and idyllic beauty that once seen it is never forgotten.

At the harbor entrance, famed Pulpit Rock juts up rugged from the sea, topped by an osprey nest which was home to fish hawks for 300 years and was mentioned as a landmark in earliest colonial records.

Here, on the west of the Pulpit Rock is Cabotsville — a colony of unpretentious cottages where the Cabot clan gathers in full force each summer.

Directly across Pulpit Harbor from the Cabots are finely restored, red-painted farm dwellings. One belongs to Garrison and Kim Norton. A Norton sister, Lucy, married Garrison Valentine — and the Valentines own and occupy the adjacent property. That is the way it goes on North Haven estates. To protect the neighborhood, make sure the family next door is your own.

High on the cliffs, back from the Norton properties, stands the huge yellow house which is a landmark from the water. This magnificent property, commanding views across Penobscot Bay and the in-between islands, looks out across to the rolling Camden Hills. It belongs to Mrs. Eleanor Lamont, widow of Thomas Lamont, the famed banking partner in J. P. Morgan. Here again, in North Haven tradition, the big, family homestead is flanked, surrounded and protected by smaller homes for other members of the family.

All the immaculate cottages nearby, along the road leading to the Lamont mansion, are summer homes for other members of the large Lamont family. Dr. Austin Lamont, the famed doctor who administered anesthesia in the world's first open heart surgery, occupied one of these homes until his recent death. Nearby is the cottage of Corliss Lamont, the likeable, literary 'black-sheep' socialist in this wealthy family. His son, Hays Lamont, summers on North Haven too. Ellie Lamont, Tom Lamont's sister, married a Cunningham — and now of course, Cunninghams own summer property here in Lamont-land on North Haven.

Down the winding road a piece, close to the Mill Stream, John Rockefeller summers in a traditional, modest sized but immaculately maintained white farmhouse.

Nearby is the most lavish estate on North Haven. It belongs to Thomas J. Watson, chief of International Business Machines. Watson's long, rambling white home fits well into its landscape, unlike some of the ostentatious summer excrescences near Bar Harbor, but has wings and suites and outbuildings of simple, elegant luxury to house his guests. It has its own private airfield, nearly a mile long to accommodate Watson's two private jet planes, plus a smaller plane for local flights and a seaplane for island-hopping.

The most unusual house, architecturally, on North Haven is the vast Norwegian Cottage, built for Ambassador Strong, who once represented the United States in Norway. This rare and handsome example of native architecture was erected by Norwegians sent here for this specific job. The roof of the house is covered with half a foot of sod, with green grass and lovely wildflowers growing out of it. In Norway, a goat usually is tethered on such roofs to munch the grass down to manageable length. A roof like this provides ideal insulation. Outside and inside the Norwegian cottage is handsomely hand-carved, beautifully hand-painted and has huge stone chimneys. A Norwegian sauna bath house stands nearby, complete with a huge bell atop of it for summoning people outside.

The estate belonging to Anne Morrow Lindbergh is nearby. The big open meadow running down to the sea was once the landing field for Charles Lindbergh. It is overgrown now.

Close to the Morrow place is the lovely, peaceful home which belonged to Ambassador Chester Bowles. One wall of this one-time farm has been made over so it is almost all glass, giving magnificent views across Penobscot Bay to the Camden Hills. Chester Bowles sold this home to Judge Gerhard Gessel — the Federal Judge who ruled in favor of the Washington Post in the Pentagon Papers case.

Actor Robert Montgomery, who starred in innumerable films and television plays and later coached President Eisenhower in television techniques, has long summered on North Haven. Grandchildren crowd his home now too, in the pattern of North Haven and Vinalhaven summer homes which act as magnets for pulling in all the family clans. Actor Montgomery's mark of acceptance by island people is the fact he was guest speaker one year at the alumni banquet of North Haven High.

Speaking of theater, Claire Booth Luce, once a Congresswoman from Connecticut, once Ambassadress to Rome, and wife of Time-Life publisher Henry Luce, wrote her famous play "The Women" on nearby Crotch Island.

John Barrymore came there. And Barrymore's wife at the time — Michael Strange — painted murals in the ladies room. The Lunts came out to Crotch Island.

On the Vinalhaven side of the Fox Thorofare, is another Gold Coast of large summer cottages belonging to the Rhinelanders and the Reynolds and the Saltonstalls and Lewises and the Brewster Jennings of Standard Oil.

Isador Gordon of Rockland once owned over 1,500 precious acres of Vinalhaven and he speaks of the property market there in the late 1930's and early 1940's.

"They couldn't give island property away then," he says. "I didn't get much when I sold.

"In those depression days, you could have bought the whole of Vinalhaven island, people included, for $10,000 . . . If I could sing, I could have bought it all for a song."

Gordon, in a telephone interview, recalls "Back in 1929, they wanted to sell me a summer estate out there. I said I didn't want it at any price. But they got me out to take a look. A beautiful waterfront estate it was, the best, — about 45 or 50 acres. Fine home too. Finally I said I would pay last year's taxes. So I got the estate . . . for about $700."

Land values have soared since the days when Boston Brahmins bought in here at bargain prices.

Even the prices of village homes have boomed beyond all expectations. One modest village home changed hands for the fifth time since World War II. In 1945, the house sold for $600. In 1953 15,000. And in 1971 it sold for $25,000. In 1977, it would fetch $55,000.

Now that all the waterfront is taken, the lovely inland parts of the islands, rich in wildflowers, quiet meadows, small streams or tidal estuaries are beginning to be developed.

No spot on the islands is more than a mile from the sea.

One child was born, there were two weddings, nine deaths and 67 dog licenses were issued in a recent year on North Haven.

But whatever the statistics show, the islands are a special kind of paradise to those lucky enough to be born there, or rich enough and sensible enough to summer there.

VI /

Maine Personalities

*T*HERE ARE TOO MANY MYTHS *about Maine. One is the myth about "Downeast characters". Another is the myth that Maine people are of few words. Another is that they are insular, intolerant of outside ways or people. Another is that they are pinch pennies. Another is that they are standoffish.*

Most of these myths are sold to the tourists by Maine people. They are kind of a folk-lore to sell to suckers from away. These myths are kissing cousins to the myth that Maine battens down from Labor Day till Memorial Day, and that the months from September till June are frigid.

Truth is that from after Labor Day till deer hunting in November is about the loveliest time in Maine for weather. Truth is that the February sun in Maine is brilliant, and bright and warm on crystal clear days. Truth is that Maine people can be the most talkative tellers of tales, relayers of news and gossip and many will argue off your ear about politics, crops, religion, weather or coon dogs. As for being standoffish, as soon as they know your first name, they will never again bother using your last name.

Far from being pinch pennies, Maine people are open handed on major matters or for friends and family needs or for town schools or for a man whose house burned or whose boat was lost. Maine people are often "snug" when it comes to not wasting money on things they do not need or on buying to impress. The man who wears green work shirt and pants and lace up boots and has Tom stitched over his workshirt pocket may be banking more money than you do.

In reporting from all over Maine for a dozen years, I am convinced the ratio of more interesting people in Maine is higher than in Washington, New York, London or Boston. Why? Perhaps because they do not bother with a shell of outer conformity. They know who they are, what they are and to hell with pretending. This lack of false shell is what makes Maine people more interesting.

They are tolerant too. I recall my first summer seeing a far out painter in New Harbor. His feet were bare, his hair was to his shoulders and more, his beard was long. This was in the days before hippies made such traits common. He stood out, believe me how he stood out on the wharf in New Harbor. Did the fishermen say much about how he looked? No. Six out of eight in the wharf office talked about the man's painting.

If oddities do not turn Maine people off, celebrities do not turn them on. We've got corporation presidents, college presidents, bishops, famous surgeons, millionaires galore, authors, poets, pols, big shot generals—you name them, we've got 'em in Maine—with summer houses and often year round.

Nobody gives a damn. The trappings, titles, bank accounts are best if they are never visible. If flaunted, they become jokes.

But if the millionaire or the ambassador or the famous painter is a nice guy, a decent fellow, he is accepted and called by his first name, and forgiven all the fame and money.

Variety. That is the spice of covering Maine. You don't need to dig far anywhere in Maine. The man or woman coming into the post office has done something interesting, something remarkable. If not, wait a few minutes and they will be along.

MAINE'S MOST FAMOUS BIRD WATCHER:
ROGER TORY PETERSON

WISCASSET — Clarence Allen slit open the yellow telegram and read the message — a message which eventually altered the lives of a million bird watchers.

"If you want your camp naturalist, send me $39.50 for rail fare. I'm broke" . . . signed Roger Tory Peterson.

The time was May, 1928; the place Camp Chewonki, on the banks of the Sheepscot River at Wiscasset, Maine.

"I sent the money, but reluctantly" says Clarence E. Allen, founder of Camp Chewonki. "Forty bucks was a pile of dough back in 1928. And I'd never clapped eyes on the sender. But I desperately needed a nature counsellor and someone had recommended a guy called Roger Tory Peterson."

Two weeks later Roger Tory Peterson, aged 19, walked into camp, lugging two suitcases and caked with dust.

"Peterson was flat broke, without a nickel to telephone me he was at Wiscasset station. So he walked the six miles into Camp. He was a pale, sickly specimen for a nature counsellor. Then I found out he was suffering from poison by illuminating gas, contracted while he was painting chairs in a hallway tenement."

And that is how Camp Chewonki, Maine, helped launch the career of Roger Tory Peterson, who became the world's best-known author, painter, photographer and lecturer on bird life.

Peterson's "Field Guides" have sold over a million copies. His books and his illustrations are bird watchers' bibles all around the world. But only a few Maine people know that Peterson's career as a naturalist really began here in Wiscasset thanks to the $39.50 sent by Clarence Allen.

"I remember Peterson's first night at Chewonki", says Allen. "Roger displayed his well-known skill at imitating bird-calls by sounding off like a Whip-poor-will. Quickly, all the Whip-poor-wills around Wiscasset responded, and we were duly impressed. But at midnight the Whip-poor-wills were still at it and whatever popularity our new nature counsellor had developed was lost."

That summer of 1928, before Peterson was 20, he proved himself a pied piper. Boys gladly plugged after him through swamps and thickets, up hills, down gullies, swimming swamps, climbing trees. Suddenly, to win merits in nature study under Peterson became as respectable as winning the camp tennis championship.

Camp Director Allen was soon besieged by young campers showing off their new nature knowledge "Do you know how to spot the male Monarch butterfly?" "Do you know that goldfinches nest latest of all our summer birds because they wait for the milkweed seeds to use in their nests?"

But at summer's end, Peterson was still a young man without a job, nearly broke and with nowhere to go.

"I was headmaster of the Rivers School in Boston," says Allen "so I offered bed and board to young Roger Tory Peterson if he would help out in the Science Department."

Peterson shared a room over Allen's office with Alexander Maley and there it was that the Peterson "Field Guides" and the Peterson system of bird identification were born.

"There were long night sessions of drawing and painting and writing, which resulted in yawns in the classroom next day. Peterson would finish teaching, then dash off to the museums and laboratories around Boston, comparing bird skins and skeletons so he could pin point the one field-mark of a bird which made it instantly recognizable — the "Peterson System" of identification."

For five years Peterson worked with Allen, as a counsellor at camp at Wiscasset in summer, and the Rivers School in Boston in winter. In both places work on the Field Guide progressed.

"Finally" recalls Allen, "my secretary, Phyllis Bergen, typed the manuscript, and the day arrived when the text and the pictures were loaded into the old Essex and Al Maley drove Roger to the Park Street offices of Houghton and Mifflin in Boston.

Five publishers had turned down Peterson's "Field Guide". But this day Peterson was lucky. The editor who saw his work was Francis Allen, an enthusiastic bird-watcher and a director of the

Massachusetts Audubon Society. "Houghton and Mifflin will publish the book for you, Mr. Peterson," said the editor "But we can't pay you any royalties until we have sold 3500 copies and covered our costs."

The book has sold over 1½ million copies, has been reprinted 40 times, translated into many languages.

Next time you open your copy of "Field Guide to the Birds" note that the book is dedicated to Clarence E. Allen of Camp Chewonki, Maine.

Today this Chewonki camp counsellor, stands showered with international honors. The kid who wired for $39.50 so he'd have train fare to Maine, has been deluged with innumerable honorary degrees, countless medals and awards. Peterson who lacked a nickel for a phone call from Wiscasset Station, has led naturalist expeditions into every corner of the globe. He has searched for bird life high in the Andes of Chile and Bolivia, he has led expeditions into both Antarctica and the Arctic, into Africa, to the Galapagos Islands, to Patagonia, the Straits of Magellan, to Japan and the remotest Pacific Islands.

He has written a dozen books on birds himself, co-authored half a dozen more, painted thousands of matchless illustrations, delivered lectures, broadcasts, telecasts throughout the world. And all of it began with him imitating a Whip-poor-will on the banks of Wiscasset's Sheepscot River.

CLARENCE ALLEN:
GRAND OLD MAN OF CHEWONKI

CAMDEN — Why am I sitting on the living room sofa at 69 Chestnut Street, Camden talking to 84 year old Clarence E. Allen about boys and birds?

Because 11,842 miles away in Bangkok a Thai prince and a Thai ambassador came striding across a verandah to me and said "We hear you are from Damariscotta. We went to Camp Chewonki, Wiscasset. So when you get back to Maine, please go and see our old camp director, Clarence Allen!"

I live 12 miles from Chewonki. A thousand times I have driven past the Chewonki sign — now near Maine Yankee Atomic Power plant. But it took a Thai on the other side of the world to tell me what a story was right under my nose back home. That is the way it is in Maine — our men, our institutions exert huge influence, are given recognition and honor far beyond our boundaries. But too often we pay them no heed here, where they are rooted. It is the old, old story of the prophet without honor in his own backyard.

If I'd been in Venezuela, Antarctica or in Turkey or Kuwait, some other famous 'old Chewonki boy' might have come striding across some other room and said the very same sentence. For the Chewonki network reaches to every continent and all 50 States.

Play "Chewonki in Politics" . . . sons of three Maine governors camped at Chewonki. .two grandsons of Woodrow Wilson went there. .And if you wonder why Eleanor Roosevelt and FDR Jr. prowled Wiscasset, it was because they were visiting FDR's grandson at Chewonki.

Play "Chewonki in Education". .Kingman Brewster, president of Yale, says "my two years at Chewonki were the most influential of my life."

The Headmasters of prep. schools like Phillips Exeter in New Hampshire, Noble and Greenough in Dedham, Mass., the Park school in Buffalo, the Holton Arms School in Bethesda, Applewild in Fitchburg, and hundreds of teachers and principals across 50 states are old Chewonki campers.

Play "Chewonki in Government" — and you'll find the stem-winders in scores of state and federal departments concerned with environment, wildlife, conservation, spent their summers as boys at Chewonki. Or if churchmanship is your field, the Dean of the Washington Cathedral, Francis B. Sayre, was a Chewonki boy . . . in movies and theater, stars such as Jack Lemmon and the president of the Center for Performing Arts in New York City . . . in aviation, boys of the Charles Lindbergh clan . . . in writing, Rachel Carson's adopted son and Roger Tory Peterson.

For more than 56 years, this boy's camp on the banks of the Sheepscot River at Wiscasset has been a fountainhead for the environmental and conservation movement now flowering across America.

Clarence Allen, the son of a Bath candy store owner, founded Camp Chewonki 56 years ago.

"It began," says Allen, "in February 1915. When my father sent me an advertisement from the Bath Times offering for sale cheap an old sheep farm. I came home from my teaching job at Country Day in Newton, Mass. and snow-shoed out to see the land. When I told the owner I was thinking of starting a boy's camp there on the banks of the Sheepscot, he said "Well, if my land was good for a sheep ranch, it should be right for a boy ranch."

That summer of 1915 Chewonki started with 15 boys. By 1918, there were 48 boys. Soon thereafter, over 100. And for 52 years Clarence Allen personally ran Camp Chewonki each summer. "Close to 3000 boys in all came to Chewonki in my time" says Allen, wistfully. "Four years ago, when I was 80, I turned the camp over to young Tim Ellis of Wiscasset, a Chewonki boy, like his father before him." Ellis first came to Chewonki in a bassinet. His father used to be Head Counsellor for 25 years.

In his living room at Camden, the very spry Mr. Allen showed me his gorgeous collection of original bird-paintings by his camp counsellor Roger Tory Peterson. He pulls down books on birds and nature by other campers, and copies of conservation laws passed in many states by other Chewonki boys.

Then he brings out what may be his most treasured document of all — the Teacher's Certificate issued to him in Marshfield, Vermont back in 1904. It is small, browned with age, but lovingly framed.

"When I was 17, cigarettes were a nickel a pack . . . at my father's candy stores in Bath and Brunswick. And I almost ruined my health by smoking too much. So, to clean out my lungs, I got a job teaching in a one-room school at Marshfield near New Discovery mountain in Vermont.

"I taught there one winter. I was 17. Some kids I taught were older than I was. Others were aged five. Some days I'd have 22 pupils. Other stormy days we were down to two. My pay was $6 a week. And at the end of the winter I was due an extra six bucks for cutting firewood."

The experience made Allen decide on teaching as a career, and he went to Dartmouth College (1906-10). On graduation he got a teaching job at Country Day School, Newton, Mass. There he taught for almost 20 years until 1929.

By 1930 Allen became headmaster at Rivers School, a position he held for a quarter century. Later he became Director of Development for the Washington Cathedral, finally retiring to Camden. .

How many lives has Allen touched and changed?

I drive past the sign to Chewonki, through Wiscasset, through Bath. And relish the knowledge that the son of the candy store owner, has influenced so much. Our whole land must be glad Clarence Allen turned a sheep ranch into a boy ranch. The reach of Maine is long — and good.

E. B. WHITE

Photographer Don Johnson and I did a lot of features together and had a fine time. This interview with E. B. White took place late in August 1971. Don Johnson and I worked for five days in one small part of the Maine coast. In those five days we interviewed and photographed E. B. White, Walter Lippman, Nelson Rockefeller and Russell Wiggins, former editor of the Washington Post, ambassador to the United Nations and now editor to the Ellsworth American.

Lippmen lived at Seal Harbor. The postmistress gave us directions to "Walter's place". He was about 80 then, but came out to meet us in the driveway as we drove up. He was a handsome man, bigger in the shoulders, stronger, taller than I had expected, and immaculately dressed in resort type summer clothes. He showed us through the gardens and pointed out the views with loving pride. He and Mrs. Lippman fed us an elegant lunch. Then in his small study we talked. It was marvelous listening.

E. B. White had just turned 70 when he met us in the dooryard of his farm. White was disturbed at the start, following a long telephone consultation with doctors about his wife's illness. White is a very private person who does not enjoy interviews, but when he took us walking around his farm, he was kind, charming, warm hearted.

Russ Wiggins lives on the banks of the Benjamin River, just off the Eggemoggin Reach and near to E. B. White. He too has a lovely old farm, rich with fruit trees, hens, geese, dogs and sheep. There is a very special old world courtliness and scholarship with humor about Russ Wiggins and his wife Mabel. Frequently we visit them by boat—a wonderful way to go calling. Wiggins has made his weekly newspaper, The Ellsworth American, into a star in Maine journalism.

Rockefeller was born in Maine and his clan keep many homes, islands and boats here still.

During that five day jaunt, the Maine coast was at its loveliest. And the company—Lippman, White, Rockefeller, Wiggins was another nice part of Maine.

I have chosen to run a shortened version of the talk with E. B. White as we walked the fields around his 185 year old farm.

BROOKLIN — The man who writes the clearest, loveliest prose in the American language is E. B. White of Brooklin, Maine.

We began talking about his home and his roots in Maine.

Q. Have you had this farm quite a while?

White: I bought this place long ago, I think it was 1931. But I got my first smell of Maine back in 1904. My father had a camp in Belgrade Lakes. We had a big family, and all of us used to go up each summer into this little bit of shack in Belgrade. That was my introduction to Maine.

Q. How did you find Brooklin?

White: We found Brooklin after I was married. My wife had friends here and we were looking for a place to spend the summer. We went to Blue Hill and spent two happy summers there. I was scooting around in a boat. I like to sail. One day I noticed this place, and admired it. Next time we drove down this road, darned if there wasn't a "For Sale" sign on the lawn. We bought it on the spot, from a musician named George Wedge. That was in 1931.

Q. Were you living in New York City, at Turtle Bay then?

White: We were in New York, but down on East 8th Street in the Village. We came here summers. Then in 1938 we moved here, added to the house and lived year round for a great many years. I left my regular job with the New Yorker when we came here. I needed a new job, and Harper's gave me one. I wrote "One Man's Meat" for Harper's after we came here.

Q. This is your home during the winters too?

White: Oh, yes. We're here year round — except for my wife's illness. We have no place in New York.

Q. Are you sailing still?

White: I still sail some — I've got a sloop. To me it's the most fun there is.

Q. How do you feel about the dilemma that Maine is beginning to face now — industrialization and oil coming in? Do you think we can learn enough from other people to get these things in here without despoiling Maine?

White: I doubt it. We never seem to learn anything from other people. I'm not talking about Maine — I'm talking about the human race. There's always a fight between those who want to keep it for rusticators and those who want to develop it. You can see that in a small place like Blue Hill. There are those who want to make Blue Hill into a little Toledo, Ohio, and those who want to keep it the way it is. This battle is going to go on, and of course it will become more tense. It's a matter of priority obviously. When the population is increasing, when more and more people are coming in, you

do develop and land does get taken up. But I think pollution and environment are certainly the number one priorities. If you don't have air to breathe and the sea to wash your feet, you haven't got much. The rest is just window-dressing.

Q. Do you feel that this is really the number one problem facing not only the nation, but pretty much of the world?

White: I sure do. I believe that streams, rivers, lakes, estuaries and of course the sea itself belong to everybody. The rugged, early American idea that a man need only own a mill site and the stream was his, is no longer any good. There are still plenty of industrialists who see a river as nothing but a very handy way of getting rid of waste products; they believe in the divine right of discharge. It should be apparent to everyone that those days are over.

And it's not just industry; quite a bit of raw sewage finds its way into the harbor of this small town, the clam flats are closed, and the way to correct this is not to decontaminate the clams but to stop the flow.

It's amazing that people defile their nests the way they do. You watch a bird's nest, like a Cedar Waxwing nest with four or five young ones in there. You'll find it's immaculate. There is not a dropping in there. The parent bird lugs it away. And that's the only way they can survive it. If the excretions stayed in there, the young ones couldn't live. We are in the same fix, really. We are just excreting ourselves out of the picture. So we should model ourselves after the Cedar Waxwing.

Q. As a farmer, how do you feel about the problems created by pesticides?

White: When I first came here to live, there was always a fish hawk poised above the cove. He is long gone, and so are the sculpins and flounders that he used to catch. It has been pretty well established that hawk eggs and eagle eggs are not hatching these days, because they contain minute quantities of long-lived pesticides, notably DDT. Yesterday I read that the eggs of haddock are not hatching, and for the same reason.

Q. Do you use pesticides on the farm here?

White: No, not now. But for years the Agriculture Department kept sending me bulletins saying "Pour it on." Whether you were raising sheep or growing vegetables or fruit or anything, bulletins came in every mail about how you could kill this or that. This was the USDA speaking.

Finally — my wife showed me a clipping last night — the Department of Agriculture banned 10 very offensive pesticides, starting with DDT and on to Endrin and Eldrin and so forth. This is late in the day. Rachel Carson was right, years ago.

Q. If you have been on the receiving end of these USDA bulletins over the years, have you been pretty actively farming?

White: I don't know what you call "active." I have a fellow working for me year round here — I am old. But we grow a lot of stuff. I'm sort of a subsistence farmer, by nature. I like to grow what we need. I have sheep — but that is just because I happen to like working with sheep. I have had sheep off and on for 30 years.

Because of my wife's illness, I have had to cut things down. We have tremendous expenses now for nursing and care. But I like birds — I like to raise hens. I start with day old chicks in the spring. We have broilers and roasters and fryers. And then I have a laying flock . . . Look over there, and you can see the replacements. Those pullets are young females and they will go into the laying house next winter.

I grow all the eggs we eat, and more besides. I take some to the store and give others to my friends and children. I like to keep the fields up, and I've got good pasture down there, with cattle in it. This is really just a sort of high-class zoo.

Q. Will you show us your zoo? Could you take us around?

White: Yes, love to. This is the biggest pear tree in the county, as far as I can see. The pears are not very good eating, but they're awfully good for canning — we use them for spiced pears.

My principal year round crop is barn swallows. This place, the barn, hatches an incredible number of barn swallows. They're all gone now. At the end of August, they all pull out. This is the cellar down here, and it's great in the winter because it's warm. I keep sheep down here all winter long. That's a yearling there — she never had a lamb. The last one on the right is another yearling . . . This is a three year old. I started with just three ewes, way back. Then I got a purebred North Country Cheviot ram — I sold him just the other day.

I've been away during the lambing season for the last three years, but I have a lot of fun out of my sheep — I love lambs. I had triplets once. Don't like triplets, I'd rather have a good pair of twins.

(Pointing to a timber) . . . See this hackmatack knee? That's what they used to use in the stern of a boat. But the farmer who built this barn was a smart carpenter. He put the knee in here instead of an upright post so he could get in to handle the manure from the cow ties easily.

(Pointing to a barn swallow's nest jutting out from a post). This nest was active. That's another thing about the fouling business, where birds are way ahead of people. The young birds for some instinctive reason always turn and put their tail out over the edge of the nest . . . These eaves swallows nests are an amazing piece of architecture. Sometimes they'll start them on a nail, then build straight out.

(Moving across the barn) . . . My lambs are out in the pasture now, not here in the sheep pen. I weaned them recently. They are almost as big as the sheep now.

Over here I've got a hen pen. They are awful looking now, all shed out . . . And down here is where the farmer had his blacksmith's shop. I made all the hinges, you see.

(Opening a door to a two holer) . . . And this is a very lucky room for me. This is where I first saw Charlotte. Watched a spider spinning her web in here one day. You know my book "Charlotte's Web"?

(Moving outside) . . . Here come my geese. A goose seems a very strange animal to me. But they are good watchdogs. Thanks largely to them perhaps, I've never lost any hens . . . Here are my birds. In all the years I raised birds here — I cross my fingers — I never lost one to a dog or a fox, or a mink or anything else. I shut 'em up, of course. When it gets dark, I come out and close that little door every night. After dark, nothing can get in. And before dark, nothing comes around here very much. I get these birds from Connecticut, as day old chicks. They're a cross between a Rhode Island Red and a White Plymouth Rock . . . Let's walk across here and take a look at my pond.

Dammed up my brook a couple of years ago and made this little pond out of it. I've got some trout in here now . . . There! See them rise? They're too small still but later I'll be able to fish. I come out here at night and throw stale bread or trout chow. And the place just boils with them.

This whole house and farm and pond is fed by a spring across the road. It's been terrific as far as a good supply. Most of the time, there is a good flow into the pond. (Throwing a stick into the pond for his dog) Here Jones! Go swim for it . . . He loves the water and he's a fine swimmer.

He's a Norwich terrier. They used to be called Jones terriers, and that's how he got his name. He's very shy. I think he got badly scared when they flew him over from England. He's coming out of it now, though.

Come over here and see this plant . . . This little plant which now looks ordinary to you maybe, is a very rare plant indeed . . . My wife writes a garden column for the New Yorker and in one column she mentioned a Japanese single white iris that she had seen pictures of in the Dupont gardens at Winterthur outside Wilmington. Well, she got a lot of mail from all over the country, indeed the world, and finally a fellow down there at Winterthur sent her this plant. It's one of those rare single white iris, and we are nursing it along here, hoping it will flourish.

Let's walk on down to the water now. I'll show you the dock and the boathouse — fishhouse — I've got for writing in. I keep my typewriter down here, by the water.

Q: You don't work up at the house?

White: Well, I've got a machine up there too. My normal routine is to come down here in the morning so I can get away from all the mess up at the house. Right now I'm finishing a book. I've not done much work in recent years, because I've been so disturbed about my wife. She's got a very rare skin disease and the usual way to control it would be with a sulfa derivative drug. But she can't take that because she's allergic to it. So she has to take cortisone — a derivative. She's been doing that for 6 or 7 years, and it's got to her. It's breaking her bones down, and she's now a semi-invalid because of osteoporosis, which is softening of the bones.

(White points across the pastures, from the water up to the barn) This gives you a pretty good look at the barn, from here. I put that cupola on. Actually it was a better looking barn before I did that. But I wanted to put a weathervane up there, so I stuck that on.

. . . I'll unlock the fish house, so we can take a look inside . . . I've just had its face lifted, got the place fixed up a bit. I used to lug my typewriter all the way down from the house, now I just leave it here and lock the door. I put in this big window, which lifts up by a pulley and weight, like this . . . And over there I've got a schoolhouse stove hooked up, so I can get heat.

Q. This is a great place to work, I'm astonished at how sparse and neat everything is. Have you got a phobia about not having any clutter around?

White: I guess I am a neat sort of person, but I don't need a lot of stuff around when I am writing here. I just bring down what I need that day. All I need really is typewriter and paper. I write by the window, at this table. I sit on the bench with my back to the wall.

Q. That narrow bench? No cushion, no chair?

White: For years I just stuck my back in against the wall, and I wondered why my back seemed sore. I discovered after working here about six years the reason I was so uncomfortable. The nails came right through the shingle boards at shoulder height. So finally I decided to give myself a little comfort, and I put in this piece of plasterboard as a back rest.

Q. What's that other narrow bench, in the middle of the room?

White: That's my bed. I lie on the bench and stick a pillow under my head. It makes a good bed . . . My bed, my desk, my stove, that's all I need.

Q. Do you keep your sloop out here, off the dock?

White: Not now. It's handier over at my son's boatyard in Center Harbor on Eggemoggin Reach. I enjoy sailing there more, because there are more boats around, more activity. I love to sail the Reach.

Q. How long has your son Joel had the boatyard there?

White: Well, he started just as a hand working for Arnold Day. Then he and Arnold went into business together. That lasted a couple of years, until Arnold got tired of the headaches and pulled out. It was a shoestring operation from the beginning. Joe has put up a lot of buildings and made quite a thing out of it now.

Q. You are writing your new book down here now, in this boat-house?

White: That's right. It's a storybook for children.

Q: I had a wonderful time reading "Stuart Little" and "Charlotte's Web." But how did you get started writing children's books?

White: Well, I spent most of my life doing journalism and editorial work and writing essays. But I got into writing for children by a complete accident. Little children visiting always wanted me to tell them stories, and I wasn't able to tell them a good story, so I decided to arm myself with material. And I wrote a couple of chapters of "Stuart Little." Stuart Little was a bit of a fluke, but it was a successful book financially and spiritually. Then "Charlotte's Web" was a deliberate attempt to write something for children. And "Charlotte" has kept me alive, been my bread and butter. It's now used in schools a great deal. They read it to children in the third and fourth grades, and it's one of the children's best sellers in the country right now even though it was published back in 1954.

I like to write children's books. It's very rewarding. The letters I get are fabulous. Thousands from children, and every once in a while I hear from teachers and librarians about the impact of the book. I had a perfectly marvelous letter a week or so ago, about "Charlotte's Web" from a mother down in Greenville, S. C. telling me about what it had done. She has a defective child. Experts gave up on the child. But the mother and the family stuck with the little girl and somehow or other she learned to read — and Charlotte's Web was instrumental in the therapy. When you get a letter like that, it makes a difference.

E. B. White / 237

MR. CHIEF JUSTICE: ROBERT B. WILLIAMSON

AUGUSTA — It was snowing heavily in Augusta when hundreds gathered at the South Parish Congregational Church Dec. 29, 1976 to say goodbye to Robert B. Williamson, for 14 years Chief Justice of the Supreme Judicial Court of Maine.

The snowfall gentled all the sounds, so there was no unnecessary noise when the Chief Justice left us.

And that was in keeping. There was never unnecessary noise around Bob Williamson.

Gentleness: Quietness: Graciousness: Humility: Old world courtesy and courtliness. These were the hallmarks of Robert Williamson, a very gentle gentleman. These qualities made the Chief Justice more than a great judge; he was a much loved man, a warm and compassionate human being, even to the accused standing before his bench.

Edith Hary, State Law Librarian, had been getting reference books for Williamson for over a quarter century. "We knew his voice over the phone, of course. And as Chief Justice, we'd jump to satisfy his every wish. But when he wanted a book, he'd phone himself. And that voice we knew instantly would always begin by saying simply 'This is Robert Williamson . . . ' He was a modest man."

A shipping clerk, Norman Pierce, used to bring reference books from the Law Library to the office of the Chief Justice. When Norman Pierce died, the Chief Justice sent to his widow a moving, sincere, hand written note saying how much he had enjoyed knowing Norman Pierce.

There are envelopes upon envelopes of news clippings about Williamson in the Telegram's library. Each is an imprint upon the state left by one of Maine's finest sons.

The smallest is a yellowed little clipping datelined Augusta, Sept. 2, 1923. It begins "A popular Augusta young man, Robert Byron Williamson, recently took the examination for admittance to the

Maine bar and came through with flying colors. Mr. Williamson will soon enter into partnership with Lewis A. Burleigh. Their fathers were also partners in an earlier Williamson and Burleigh firm."

Maybe one reason Robert Williamson carried his high judicial honors with so much grace and modesty, was because he was the fourth in a line of five generations of Williamson lawyers, who began practising here four years before Maine became a state. His great-grandfather, Joseph Williamson began his law career in Belfast in 1816.

Williamson's mother was the daughter of Maine Governor Edwin C. Burleigh.

The clippings tell the march of 24 year old lawyer Williamson up the ladders of Maine. The first appointment, three years after Harvard Law School, came in 1926. He was named the U.S. Commissioner for Kennebec County. He resigned in December 1928, after being elected to his first and only term as a Republican representative in the State Legislature. There is a clipping of his marriage June 2, 1925 to Miss Grace Warren Whitney. Grace, his wife for 52 years, went to Cony High, as did her husband and she went to Wellesley College, while he went to Harvard. For a half a century and more, tiny Grace, just topping five feet, stood by his side, the strong dependable support of her long, lanky, topping six feet husband.

At 46, Williamson was named justice of the Maine Superior Court by Governor Horace A. Hildreth, on Aug. 15, 1945. Within four years, Williamson was elevated to become justice of the Supreme Court, named by Gov. Frederick G. Payne on April 28, 1949.

Six years later, on Oct. 4, 1956, Gov. Edmund E. Muskie gave Williamson the oath of office when he became Chief Justice of the Maine Supreme Court. And seven years later, in Sept. 1963, Gov. John Reed named Williamson to his second seven year term as Chief Justice of Maine.

In August 1970, Williamson reached mandatory retirement age. He had served 25 years on the Maine bench, 14 as Chief Justice. But in retirement, his service continued without let up. He served on many nationwide and statewide commissions and panels.

"He was in the Law Library on the Tuesday before he died on Monday, Dec. 26," Edith Hary said.

Edith Hary considers the Law Library kind of a special monument to Williamson. "He helped us beyond measure. When we opened as a special law library in 1970, I asked him to let us hang his portrait here."

This is the portrait by Waldo Pierce. "I like it. It has his special boyishness. Even at 77, Judge Williamson never lost that boyishness . . . He was up beat, enthusiastic. We'd sit through long, dull meetings. But he would come out saying 'Don't you agree So-and-So spoke very well?' and 'So-and-So made severel excellent points.' "

Lawyers and judges know best what great improvements were made in the whole fabric of Maine's judicial systems during the 14 important years Williamson was Chief Justice.

"He made few waves himself. But he had a quality of a special kind which made everyone around him do better work, and more of it, than they ever dreamed they could," says Edith Hary.

To members of the press, Judge Williamson was always helpful.

"I like newspapering," he said. "I worked once for the Kennebec Journal. And at Harvard, I was an editor of The Crimson. There have been many times I'd rather have been a newspaperman than a jurist."

Ten years ago, Williamson as Chief Justice, wrote two major articles for the Maine Sunday Telegram on the future of the courts in Maine. A seeming conservative, Judge Williamson broke totally with the tradition that a presiding Chief Justice of the Supreme Court should not speak out publicly about Court reform.

But he was indeed a rebel, the quiet, the gentle, the modest rebel. A colleague has said that one reason such enormous changes occurred under Williamson, was because of "his gentle, conservative way of doing things." Few realized how much he changed the courts, or they might have opposed him.

Seldom has Maine justice been so well personified as it was by Robert B. Williamson. In him, knowledge and compassion, rectitude and humility, authority and humanity, majesty and modesty commingled into the epitome of a Chief Justice of Maine.

Duane Doolittle:
Mr. Down East Magazine

CAMDEN — You've heard the dream. Heard it from a hundred, maybe a thousand people.

"If only I had the courage to chuck the city ratrace" they dream, "I'd start my own business on the coast of Maine! What a glorious life that would be!"

This is the case history of how one dreamer made his dream come true.

He is Duane Doolittle. This quiet spoken, small boned, brown eyed man at age 42 chucked his job as a university professor of Marketing and Statistics, came home to Maine and sank his life-time savings into starting Down East, The Magazine of Maine.

This year Down East Enterprise Inc. will print over 100 million magazine pages, calendars, posters, art reproductions, books and greeting cards — all featuring the beauties of Maine.

The magazine was born in Camden in August 1954, a scrawny infant, underfinanced, just 32 pages big. Its first issue of 5000 copies priced at 25 cents each. There was not a single subscriber.

"We lost $10,000 that first year. It took three more years of struggle before we broke even" says its founder, Duane Doolittle.

Today Down East is one of the handsomest, most successful regional magazines in America. And Doolittle has pyramided its success as a magazine into a dozen profitable sidelines of Down East calendars, Down East posters, Down East notepaper, Down East Christmas cards, Down East color prints of Maine.

It all began on the kitchen table of a farmhouse at nearby Lincolnville, in 1954, the dream of a college professor and his wife.

Doolittle's wife, Katherin E. Perot on the masthead, is Secretary-Treasurer. This husband and wife team own 99 per cent of the stock, and the remaining one percent is held by a Doolittle son.

A neighbor, Marge Hanna of Rockport, designed the logo for the title Down East, which has run unchanged since the first issue.

Another neighbor, Margaret Shea was first managing editor. The first issues were pasted together in her living room.

A third neighbor, Lew Dietz of Rockport, who still writes regularly for the magazine, described what the title meant in the first issue.

"Cleared away and sailing a northeasterly course out of Boston, the first landfall is the dark and jagged coast of Maine. That's where Downeast begins.

"In the great heyday of sail, windjammers took advantage of the prevailing westerlies on the run to Maine and the Maritimes. They sailed down-wind with canvas bellied taut and shrouds singing. Down-wind to Maine became a manner of speaking, slipping with time into the salty brevity of the term, downeast. The word has a lilt and it has a sure meaning.

"Language is a repository of history. Windjammers have vanished into the past; but downeast is still downwind from Boston."

Contradicting Lew Dietz's spelling of downeast as one word, the title on the magazine cover became two words. Publisher Doolittle explains why; "Down East just looked better to the eye in the lettering designed by Marge Hanna. So we kept it two words."

If you read Down East, it is only natural that you should picture the man who founded it as a nostalgic man, a sentimental man yearning to re-live the 'good old days when Maine was really Maine' . . .

Now, meet the Publisher and prepare for a shock!

Shock number one is that Duane Doolittle is not "from away." He is a Maine-born boy, raised in Boothbay Harbor. He is the adopted son of Harry Smith, once superintendent of Boothbay schools.

Shock number two is that Doolittle is no nostalgic sentimentalist. He is a hard-nosed graduate of the Harvard Business School and used to be a professor of Marketing and Statistics at Syracuse University.

Shock number three is that Doolittle is not, by training, a publisher, a writer, a photographer, an advertising salesman or a circulation manager. Until he was 40 years old, Doolittle was a teacher, who'd never come closer to printer's ink than a school year-book.

Today Professor Doolittle is the owner-publisher of one of the most handsome and financially successful regional magazines in America, and heads a publishing and direct mail business whose retail cash flow tops the half million-dollar-a-year mark.

Looking back at the first issue of Down East, August 1954, you'll find this sign of how times and prices have changed . . . "A beautiful Cape Codder on 35 acres . . . eight rooms, full bath, stunning living room with exposed beams and fireplace. Cabinet Kitchen, hot air heat, electricity, telephone. Three miles from Belfast. Price $8,500."

"Maybe the reason Down East is a success with readers" says Doolittle, "is that the magazine is about Maine as Maine was — and as people wish it always would be. They read Down East for escape if you will. So they can feel the world can still be a wonderful place . . . Readers get their fill of war and crime and city problems and ghetto strife from all the other news media. When their copy of Down East comes in, they can depend upon getting pleasant, relaxing reading all through its pages."

The formula has spelt success. "We change," says Doolittle "but we change as imperceptibly as possible. I saw what happened to the Saturday Evening Post when they embraced change."

I look out of Doolittle's office to the idyllic loveliness of Camden harbor, and the Camden hills running down to the sea. I look at the next, handsome, profitable issue of Down East, grown from nothing to a half million dollar business. To produce a magazine of Maine in surroundings like this, it is a dream come true. Then I look at Doolittle's boat, in which he seldom cruises; at his Lime Island, where he never lives, and the six day week he still works. "It doesn't come easy anywhere — even in Maine." But in Doolittle's magazine of Maine the sweat doesn't show.

* * *

In 1977 Duane Doolittle retired as Editor of Down East, and has been succeeded by Davis Thomas.

ADELAIDE BYERS AND THE SEEING EYE DOG

The Seeing Eye dog program is known and admired across the nation. A Maine woman, Mrs. Adelaide Byers of Newcastle, brought the first Seeing Eye dogs to the United States from Switzerland. She was the first trainer of Seeing Eye dogs in this country.

NEWCASTLE — Adelaide Warren Clifford Byers sits in her elegant living room overlooking her ancestral acres running down to the Damariscotta river and happily puffs on her pipe.

"A pipe tastes better, smells better and is better for me than smoking cigarettes. So I smoke a pipe" she forthrightly explains, while elegantly scraping the bowl with an antique silver letter-opener and re-filling her pipe from a transparent, lucite tobacco pouch.

Adelaide Byers is a grandmother now. But she still retains all the defiance of conventions which set her apart from the crop of debutantes with whom she made her bow to New York and Boston society in 1928.

On Dec. 12, 1929, when that year's debs were primping for the Cotillion, the New York Times carried pictures of Adelaide Clifford, 19, walking down the gangplank of the Leviathan in New York harbor. She was leading ashore three German Shepherds — the first Seeing Eye dogs to be brought to America to guide American blind.

Since that day when Adelaide Byers led those first three Seeing Eye dogs ashore, over 10,000 dogs have been trained in their guide-dog footsteps at The Seeing Eye in Morristown, N.J.

"My mother and I had traveled to Switzerland for my brother's wedding there. I stayed on with a family friend, Dorothy Eustis of Philadelphia at her home near Vevey. She had for several years been interested in the way the Swiss Army and Police trained German Shepherd dogs to work for them. Soon we became fired up over the idea of training the shepherd dogs to work with and for blind people. It was not a new idea.

"In nearby Germany, after World War I, the German government had supplied thousands of war-blinded soldiers with trained guide dogs.

"In fact" says Mrs. Byers, "you can see blind men being led by dogs in paintings made way back in the 16th century."

Adelaide Byers spent over a year working hard in Switzerland, learning how to train German Shepherds into becoming guide dogs for the blind. In Dec. 1929, she and her friend and financial backer, Dorothy Eustis brought three trained dogs to New York.

"One of the three Seeing Eye dogs we brought back to New York died of distemper in my apartment. Soon I went from New York to Nashville, Tennessee, where we established the first Seeing Eye school for a brief period, before settling in the Morristown, N.J. area. And Seeing Eye has been in that part of New Jersey from 1930 on till today."

One of Adelaide Byers' earliest 'pupils' in New York was 34 year old Herman N. Immeln, an official of the New York Association of the Blind.

"I worked with him and his 22 month old dog Bella for weeks" recalls Adelaide Byers. "Then on March 29, we were ready to show New York dramatic proof of how reliable a well-trained Seeing Eye dog could perform in the worst city traffic."

Reporters, Grover Whalen and officials of the city watched the demonstration. Next day the New York Herald Tribune ran a major picture story. Its story said that "At high noon, the blind Immeln and his shepherd dog Bella crossed and recrossed Fifth Avenue at 42nd Street with the ease and confidence of those who have perfect sight."

To educate her dogs to lead the blind, Adelaide Byers had to educate herself to blindness.

"I would walk the streets of Morristown blindfolded, with a dog to lead me. Strangely, this is more dangerous for a sighted person than for a blind person. Because we have sight, our other faculties, such as hearing are far less acute. So when a sighted person is blind-

folded and must walk across a busy intersection, he is more likely to make dangerous, even fatal, mistakes than a blind person would."

"If my dog failed to make me stop at a curb, I would have to correct him. The way I did this was to fall down on him. When I 'fell', I would slap the pavement hard and loud. And almost simultaneously I would slap the dog under the chin. To the dog this meant that when he failed to stop at the curb, the street came up and hit him.

"The same treatment was used if my dog took me too near to a wall or a store or a lamp post. I would use the two almost simultaneous slaps again . . . so the dog learned that if he came too close to an obstacle it would reach out and slap him.

"Dogs, we feel sure, are color blind. So when a dog stops his master at a curb, the dog cannot see whether a traffic light is red or green. The blind master must know through his ears how traffic is moving. And when it stops in one direction, he must instruct the dog to move by the command 'Forward'. If after man and dog are out in the street, a car suddenly threatens them, then the dog takes over and pulls the master out of danger."

It takes about 60 days of intensive work to educate a highly intelligent shepherd dog.

Final job of a trainer is to match the right dog to the right blind master, and then weld them into a team.

"One hard part for the trainer is your sudden, but essential, total separation from your dogs" says Mrs. Byers.

"A dog I have trained and fed and watered and petted and loved for months must be given up totally as soon as the new master arrives. From then on, it is the new master's prerogative to feed, to pet, to comb, to work with that dog. When the dog comes near to me, looking for a pat, I must ignore it. I must never again pay the slightest heed to it.

Seeing Eye dogs perform almost uncanny miracles every day, only a few of which come to public knowledge

For example "Buddy", the pioneer Seeing Eye dog in the United States saved his master, Morris Frank from almost certain death in a Dayton hotel.

Morris Frank had rung for the elevator on the 14th floor. When

Frank heard the elevator door open, the dog refused to obey Frank's command of "forward." Frank then did what no Seeing Eye owner should ever do — he dropped the harness and started forward alone toward the elevator doors.

"Buddy immediately threw herself across my feet, pushing so hard against me I could not move forward" wrote Frank. "At that moment a maid coming out of one of the rooms let out a terrified shriek.

"Don't move!" she shouted. "The elevator door is open, but the elevator's not there! There's only a hole!"

Dorothy Eustis, the founder of Seeing Eye, issues a few important "Do Nots" for people who marvel at Seeing Eye dogs they encounter.

"Remember" she warns, "the leading dog is the eyes of the blind man first, and a dog second.

"Therefore do not speak to the dog and under no circumstances call the name of the dog. Do not whistle or in any way divert the dog's attention. If you do, you take away the blind man's eyes.

"Never touch the blind man unless you speak to him first. The dog can only protect his master and himself by a growl and a baring of his teeth.

"I wouldn't know Seeing Eye today" says Mrs. Byers from her home on the Damariscotta River. "It has hundreds of dogs, elaborate kennels, beautiful facilities. With an endowment of $20 millions. It is a far, far cry from the days 43 years ago, when as a girl of 20, I was Chief Trainer of the first few Seeing Eye dogs in America."

"Those were great years!" she says puffing happily on her pipe.

New Duke of Windsor: Earl R. Hayes

WINDSOR FAIR — A new Duke of Windsor is alive and well in Maine, at age 84.

His name is Earl R. Hayes and he rules over the Windsor Fair. The fair has been going without missing a year since 1853.

Hayes was secretary (which means general manager without salary) for 42 years. Now he is president.

A big man with a big cigar and royal manner, his castle on the fair grounds is an old wooden office building held together by 1,372 yellowed newspaper clippings, old programs and political posters. Thumbtacks by the thousands reinforce the crossbeams and support a nostalgic history of Maine.

Horses and politicians have always gone together, one way or another. This year's candidates have booths in the Exhibition Hall, among the prize corn, the pumpkins and the crabapples. And campaigns of the past are evoked by the old political posters.

There is one of Carl Milliken, running for Governor, and others of Fred Payne, John Reed, Lewis Barrows, Stan Tupper, and LeRoy Hussey. They look very much at home, hanging among faded blue ribbons for categories of prize bulls.

Probably 150,000 people will visit the fair. Frank Siegers, 43, who will be taking over from Hayes expects 30,000 for Labor Day at the Windsor Fairgrounds, a traditional way to end summer.

More than 300 horses will have run in 72 races, 150 pulling horses and 20 pair of oxen will have strained to haul weights of up to 3,600 pounds and maybe a million dollars will have changed hands at the parimutuel windows.

In that connection, I must report on an amazing little device in daily use at the Windsor Fair.

The rules of horseracing in Maine require that every winning animal be examined through saliva and urine tests to make sure it has not been drugged.

The saliva test is fairly simple: State vet Dr. Colburn DeGoosh just takes a wad of cotton in a pair of tongs, opens up the horse's mouth and rubs the cotton all around its tongue. The resultant saliva is decanted into a dish and then into a small bottle.

But even people cannot always produce urine specimens on demand. So what do you do with horses?

Stanley Bubier, who performs this chore at Windsor and many other fairs, confided his secret. "For horses we whistle. A little whistling of the right sort usually gets results," he says.

Doesn't all this whistling make him, er, rather hoarse?

Well, there's another little trick to overcome that problem, he says, leading the way to a special stall where the horses are invited to do their stuff.

"We lead the horse in here, then I press this button on a recorder. We have on tape some of the best and most effective whistling around and these sound effects produce the desired result almost every time."

Another insight which I obtained into harness racing, thanks to the "Duke" of Windsor and his chief steward, was a chance to ride in the starter's car.

The Windsor car is a yellow Cadillac with the license plate of MCGEE, named for Arthur B. McGee, a veteran horse owner and track operator in Maine and now an associate judge of the Windsor fair.

Inside, there are the usual two front bucket seats. But a third bucket seat is in the back, built on a platform which lifts it about level with the heads of front seat riders. Up here sits the starter. John Nichols. A special glass blister added to the Cadillac roof enables him to look out at the line up of the horses.

Nichols opens and folds the starting gate and controls the accelerator. He also has a mike and loudspeaker so that he can talk to the drivers of the harness horses. The driver of the car simply steers until the starting gate is folded up and the race is under way. Then he goes like the wind for the nearest exit, horses thundering down the track behind him.

The wings of the starting gate are scissored in on each side of the Cadillac and when we are ready to call the horses up, Nichols pushes a button which extends them out for a total 58 feet in all. The horses coming up to the gate trot (or pace) until their muzzles are firm against it or just an inch or so away. As this happens, Nichols keeps increasing the speed of the car by his hand throttle and the horses also increase their speed.

The horses come into the gate at speeds of about 12 miles an hour. As they do so, Nichols increases the speed as he moves toward the start until at the start itself he is doing at least 22 miles an hour and up to 30. Immediately the eight horses are off to a fair start. Nichols presses the button which folds back the wings hydraulically, a process which takes three seconds. Then young McGee, still in first gear, gets back control of the entire car and gives it the gas so he can get away and off as the horses tear by.

Back in the stands I relay to my wife Barbara these new sights and sounds just witnessed.

"I wonder what it would be like," she says, "if horses sat in the grandstands and bet on people racing around the track."

The Maine start of Weight Watchers: Marie Ludwick

NORTH EDGECOMB — More than 10,000 fat Maine men and women have lost over 305,000 pounds of fat in the first three years since Marie Ludwick came back to Maine and started her first Weight Watchers here. On opening night of October 8, 1968 five fat people showed up at Marie Ludwick's first weight watcher class in Westbrook. Two and a half years later, 10,300 Maine Weight Watchers had shed more than 150 tons of unwanted flesh.

Marie, 48, mother of three sits trim, slim and pant-suited (size 12, weight 138 pounds, height 5 feet six inches) in her glass-walled canti-levered living room on the river at North Edgecomb and tells me how she got started in Weight Watchers herself, and later brought the program to Maine.

"At age 43 I weighed 190 pounds. I wore size 38 dresses, was a compulsive eater and getting fatter. To top it off, I was pregnant" she says. "If looking at me now you don't believe it, here is a picture of me at 185 pounds in a swim suit. And one of me in a size 38 dress. I carry them in my purse, as my own personal warning in case I feel a compulsion to eat like a glutton coming on."

When she weighed 185 to 190 pounds, Marie Ludwick was a housewife at Grandview-on-Hudson, some 25 miles upstream from New York City. Her husband, Walter, ran automobile and electrical repair businesses.

"He hated me being so fat. I hated myself. I was sick of hiding my fat inside raincoats on sweltering summer days . . . Sure, I went on starvation diets to lose weight. I would agonize fasting on black coffee and cigarettes and swelter in steam cabinets. Starved off 20 pounds or so. But it didn't last. One day I would nibble; then I'd get a compulsion to eat and gluttonize. And the fat cycle would start up all over again."

The calm voice of this trim, size 12, composed woman suddenly turns bitter . . . "The world thinks fat people are happy! The truth is most of us were miserable, ashamed and guilt-ridden. How I hated wearing muu-muus that hung over me like tents. I hated shopping at Lane Bryants, buying pregnancy clothes when I wasn't pregnant.

"Marie", I asked, "what triggered you at age 43 to get into Weight Watchers, to lose 40 pounds and to stay thin? You'd been fat a long while. Did something happen to make you change?"

There is a long silence in this lovely room which juts out over the Sheepscot River.

"You've hit a tender spot" Marie finally says. "Yes, there was an incident that triggered me . . . It was around New Year, 1967. My husband and I had been out for the evening. When we got back, he drove the baby-sitter home. And I was alone in the house, except for the sleeping children. I went to the refrigerator. And there sat a huge strawberry shortcake, untouched. I had made it for the baby-sitter, as a special compensation for sitting over New Year. And that bean-pole, rake-thin girl had sat in my house all night, knowing that luscious cake was there at hand. And she hadn't even touched it!

Marie Ludwick / 253

I was furious—idiotically furious . . . I wolfed down the whole cake, using my bare hands to eat with. That way I avoided any incriminating evidence of a fork and plate . . . Then when my husband got back I told him "You know what that pig of a baby-sitter did? She ate that whole strawberry shortcake by herself!"

Marie stops talking. Shakes her head in puzzlement. And asks "Can you understand how a 43 year old woman feels about herself when she does something like that? Then lies about it to her husband? And shifts the blame to a baby-sitter?

"That was the episode which sent me to Weight Watchers, seeking help."

The day Marie Ludwick first went to Weight Watchers sticks in her mind still. "It was January 11, 1967 . . . At last, I had learned to eat properly. I thought differently about food. At age 43 I learned to regard food as fuel . . . until then I had looked on food as a reward for being good or successful ("Let's celebrate with a bang-up dinner!")

"Lots of mothers — mine included" says Marie "create that kind of attitude in their children toward food. . . If you fall down and hurt yourself, as a child, Mother picks you up, cleans the cut knee, gives you a big kiss and then says 'Now . . . have a glass of milk and some cookies!' . . . And as a grown woman, I was using food still to comfort my hurts . . . Or as a kid, Mother rewarded my high marks at school with a big roast for dinner . . . But if I had left my room in a mess, or disobeyed my Mother, I was punished. 'No dessert for you tonight! You leave the table NOW, while we have ice cream and cake!' "

"Oh, those strange, tribal attitudes toward food as reward, as punishment, a big family reunion meal with all the trimmings . . . these things can get really into the brain of someone who has a food compulsion."

Walter Ludwick, entranced by his newly slim wife, urged her to stick close to the program and become a lecturer for Weight Watchers classes near home in Grandview. Walter stayed home, baby-sitting with three boys — Paul, one year, Walter Jr. 5, and Mark, 8.

"One night at the end of that year, 1967, I came home from

lecturing. And Walter said 'Marie, why don't we apply for a Weight Watchers franchise? We are both fed up with New York. With luck, we might get Maine!' "

The start-up of Weight Watchers in Maine was hard. "We were short of money. Our house in New York didn't sell. We were beginning a new business in a new state. Nobody here had heard of Weight Watchers (the national organization was not five years old then). We had our kids to get ready for Maine schools and their first Maine winter. The first printer I saw predicted we'd flop and demanded payment in advance. The next printer, picked out of the Yellow Pages, turned out to be one of the fattest men I ever saw — over 300 pounds, and he thought that his wife had put Weight Watchers onto him . . . Then when we held our very first class in Westbrook only five people came. The third night in South Portland, we got only 11."

Within 30 months, enrollment topped the 10,000 mark and classes were being held weekly in 56 Maine towns and cities.

Weight Watchers began in 1962 with just six women meeting with one other fat New York girl called Jean Nidetch. Today over millions have attended Weight Watchers classes. The organization became a public stock company in September 1968, with an offering of a million shares. Shares were $11.25 each then, rose to $67 and split. A Weight Watchers cookbook is in its 30th printing. Weight Watcher scales are ordered in lots of 500,000. There is a Weight Watchers Magazine, and a Weight Watchers line of frozen foods. There is even a special Weight Watchers Camp for fat girls at West Copake, N.Y., where 146 girls lost a total of 3,091½ pounds.

"I've bared my soul and talked two hours" says Maine's chief Weight Watcher Marie Ludwick. "Now, would you like something to eat?"

Weight Watchers in Maine have grown from the original five at the first meeting to over 6,000 people a week attending 93 classes. Among them, they have lost 1,166,925 pounds. Marie Ludwick has expanded her operation to Canada where she oversees 380 classes with 18,000 Weight Watchers.

Marie Ludwick / 255

VII /
Seasons

I WAKE UP and I go to sleep with an eye on the weather downriver. Our bedroom faces southwest, looks downriver toward Ram Island Light for half a dozen miles. Our windows are 20 feet high and 30 feet wide. There are no curtains. At night we sleep with the moon shining on the pillow and a thousand stars overhead. At dawn, we see the first sunrays kiss the trees on the westward bank of the Damariscotta river. We lie abed, drinking coffee, watching the dawning day wake up the water and the fields, hearing gulls cry for breakfast and watching diggers fork the mud in the clam flats.

The weather out there changes every day. And every day I enjoy it more. If you like weather, you love Maine. In one day Maine can get up to five kinds of weather. In one year, we get 10 seasons.

The wind at dawn along the coast is often dead calm, especially from May till October. An hour after sunup, the breeze begins and she breezes up a bit in the morning. After dinner, at 2 p.m. the wind shifts. An hour after sundown most summer evenings she drops and the night is apt to be still by the time moon is up.

Go to a store such as L. L. Bean and see what peacocks the seasons make of people in Maine. Yellow slickers, blaze orange for *hunting season. Lumberjackets, red and black, green and black, black and white. High boots for the woods. Low boots for mud season. Fly dope for blackfly season. Mosquito oil for mosquito season. Lures for when the bluefish come. Beautiful colorful flies for the salmon and the trout. Snowshoes, cross country skis, downhill boots. Boat shoes and submariner's low boots for washing down decks. Rubber boots tied above the thigh for clamming, walking in the herring dory or a fish stream. Swimsuits, and wetsuits for diving. Snowmobile suits for locking out that icy wind. A "red-hot" seat for keeping your bottom warm in a cold duck blind. Decoys and whistles for calling the geese.*

Seasons make us garden slaves. Seeds for the garden, wire to keep raccoons, deer and rabbits from eating it before you do. The tempting galaxy of bulbs. See the seed packages and you can taste the first peas. Maine foods in their seasons flash across your palate. The first clams dug after ice is out. Spring and the first trout. The first fiddleheads. Salmon. Lobsters, when the price drops. Then shedders in July boiled up on an island shore. Berries—blackberries, blueberries, raspberries picked wild and all eaten till your face and hands are colored, your shirt stained and your tummy full. Venison steaks. Fresh fish chowder with big chunks of haddock and hake. Native corn roasted in the husk. MacIntosh apples in the Fall. Cider pressed fresh at a friend's farm. Sauerkraut made the Waldoboro way.

Seasons mean chores. Wet cellars and floods to pump out when the big snow melts come February-March. Mud season. Potholes to fill. Spring means scraping the boat's bottom, getting her over. Spring means turning over the asparagus bed, painting porch furniture, taking storm windows down, putting screens up. Then vice-versa. In November Fall means splitting wood on the woodpile. Cutting wood in the woodlot in winter. To list the chores makes them seem backbreakers, but one-by-one, they are mostly enjoyable.

Seasons spell sports. From Christmas to St. Patrick's Day, skis and snowshoes and snowmobiles. Ice fishing. Smelting time, then oiling up the rods for spring trout. Getting the mackerel rig ready for the runs where you get five at a time. Tuna rods for the salt water boat; and clamming on the islands. The long distance sail races—Halifax, Monhegan, Gulf of Maine; the Friendship sloops homecoming in July. In early fall, walking up birds in the woods; going for deer in November.

Seasons mean work, changes in jobs. Into the woods to cut trees in winter, getting the trees out over the snow and before the mud season softens the ground. Moving lobster traps from the shallow close-in water out to deeper water offshore. Changing the nets on draggers. From fin fish to shrimp and then back again with scallops in between for a bit. Mechanics make their switch to repair snowmobiles instead of outboards, chainsaws and snowblowers instead of tractors and lawnmowers.

I don't think I could again get through a year happily where the weather isn't changing, where the seasons are not on each other's heels, where the world outside isn't switching colors.

Weather affects the mind too. Seeing and being excited, invigorated by all these changing seasons, I recall an episode from days covering NATO. The suicide rate among young American soldiers in northern Europe used to hit an appallingly high percentage around March. Medical researchers linked it to their depression over the endless damp, grey, chilling days of Fall, Winter and Spring, the endless weeks of rainy sameness outside.

In Maine, look at the obits in the paper today. See how many are three score and ten, four score, with some into their nineties who "died unexpectedly after a brief illness." Having 10 seasons in 12 months keeps Maine people alive and lively a long time.

JOYS OF A WINTER DAY IN MAINE

DAMARISCOTTA — I stand by the high windows of our bedroom looking south down river and marvel at the swift death of night, and the spectacular birth of a new winter day in Maine.

I swig from the hot mug of black coffee clutched in my hands for warmth. And swear there is no moment of the day and no place in the world and no season of the year more beautiful than this. Dawn. In Maine. In cold white winter.

The sun peeks over the rim of the world, seeming to chin itself on the wooded hill behind Alvin Piper's huge, hipped barn. Now its first rays show up before the sun itself comes over the ridge. The rays illuminate the white smoke from chimneys. The smoke hangs heavy white and barely drifting this minus-ten morning. Now the white turns iridescent, a pale and beautiful plume of orange, pink and gold.

That moment of glory passes fast. Now the climbing sun paints parts of the western shore of the Damariscotta River a faint rose and salmon pink. Hues so delicate upon the hard cold trunks and snow covered limbs of tough old pines.

This magic too is short-lived, seen by few, gone in less than five minutes. But replaced by a bigger spectacle — the whole frozen river is suffused with the pale golden light of the first full sun-up.

In midstream, where the cold winds blow, the ice surface is clear of snow and is a mirror reflecting and magnifying the birth of day. The ice reflects the shoreline too. The angle of reflection puzzles me this morning, as always. Far out in the river, you see the pines on the ridges reflected in the ice, though they are more than a quarter mile away.

Closer, just across the snow meadow, in the old brickyard cove, a dusting of snow masks the ice, impairing any reflections. The color is different here. First sunlight on this sheltered cove is a mauve, a faint purple on the snow, darker than the sunlight on the river.

Suddenly the angle of the sunrays changes and the effect is an extravaganza of glitter. The sun strikes the upthrust, jagged edges of salt ice floes in the cove. The rims glint brilliantly, like the peaks of miniature Alps, and the cove, a muted blue-grey a moment ago, sparkles with a million pinnacles of gold and blue.

A wet cold nose thrust into the pocket of my bathrobe puts a stop to this admiration of sunup. My dog thinks there is a biscuit left in the pocket, and biscuits take precedence over everything. There is no biscuit. But she snatches out a Kleenex. To this Dalmatian, ripping up a Kleenex is almost as good as eating a dog biscuit.

I watch the new day coming to life. The sight is still a kind of wonderful, surprising shock.

For my first 35 years I hated the very idea of waking early. Bed was the place, sleeping late the luxury. The late hours of the late nights were the hours of enchantment.

Now my clock has reversed.

Midnight is the back of beyond, when once it was the very hub, the pivot point of a busy night. Now dawn has become the delight.

This break of day, this first light, this dawn, this sunup — call it what you will — this is the mainspring, the coil out of which today springs to life.

Maine gave me this gift of daybreak and its progenitor, nightend. That end of night is another special winter marvel. The blackness draining out one end as first thin light creeps in at the other side of heaven, and the last stars go out.

Tracks I see across the snow-deep meadow bring back the blackness and the starlight of last night.

We made them, my Dalmatian dog and I.

Last night, half an hour before bed, I bundled up, strapped on snowshoes and called my sleeping dog away from her fireside dreams. We went out into the night. It was brittle cold, dead still, completely silent. So cold the brilliant stars seemed to crackle in the crowded sky, and hung down close to earth.

Underfoot, the snow squeaked as if in pain. As I glided on snowshoes past the trunks of 120 year old trees, I could sometimes hear a kind of groan, then a cracking expulsion of sound, as the

ancients shuddered from cold that had sunk into them like a blade. "We've endured worse! We'll endure tonight," the great trees seemed to mutter.

The amount of light in a winter night is a surprise. Stars above are extra bright and the snowfields reflect and multiply the light. Man may sleep and shut his eyes in blackness. But in the world, there is always light, always wakefulness.

Now sun rays glint on the tracks the dog and I made last night across the meadow, through the pines down to the old brickyard cove. We left our mark on the world, at least overnight. I put the big fieldglasses on fresh tracks. Something had walked there after we had gone. Snow rabbits? Old coons, ambling down to get a drink where the stream runs still in a trickle, despite the ice and snow?

I swing the glasses down along the river, close to shore, among the thin and weirdly shaped ice floes.

Have you ever seen ice floes, those weird sculptures made where salt tidal water freezes over the clam flats?

They are, I think, one of the most extraordinary and beautiful dividends of winter in Maine.

They can be treacherous too. The salt ice, with the tides flowing and ebbing under it, can give way without warning.

The bonds which bind a man to Maine woods and rivers, to Maine harbors and coves, seem stronger and tighter in winter than do the bonds of summer.

Lovely as summer is, it is a carnival, a time of pleasure and play, of gaudy spinnakers that fill like circus tents, a time of picnics on the rocks, of fast skinny-dipping and moonlight sails. Autumn, mature and belly-filled with harvest, is golden hued, wise and contented. Spring is a frolic, a skittish, changeable, chameleon half season here in Maine, a time to open up the garden, to put away storm windows, to copperbottom the boat and to curse the lawnmower into its first start.

But winter in Maine is the greatest season of them all. No beauty matches the beauty of white snowfields, deep green pines, white capped with fresh snow, of ice floes in the water and the clear cold-blue heavens of a brilliant Maine winter day.

These days spell work. What work is finer than swinging a sharp axe well, splitting wood, good heavy Maine trees felled from your land? What clothes are better than the winter work clothes, heavy insulated boots, the great thick red stockings, the tough breeches, the home knit sweaters and thick lumberjack shirts? Unless, maybe it is the winter playclothes. Good as girls look in summer bikinis, there is no sight lovelier than a lovely girl in tight and brilliant ski clothes with frosty snow from the slopes clinging to her hair. What drink is better than cream topped, thick hot chocolate when you come inside from nighttime sledding? What dawn of day is lovelier than a winter sunrise after a soft snowfall in the night has whitened the green pines and cleaned the whole world white. Thank God for winters in Maine!

Joys of A Winters Day / 265

MOONBEAMS ON MUDFLATS AT EASTER

DAMARISCOTTA — Thank God for being able to see the moon shining on Maine mudflats, for the lowest tide of the year, and for the wet rock ledge lying all exposed.

When a man can see these, he can better endure the world's woe. I get out of bed at 4 a.m. to enjoy it more.

Stark limbs of trees, black and barren now, are backlighted by the moon, a full yellow moon coming down across a blue velvet sky, jeweled bright with myriad stars.

Frost is back this night. The cold upper air makes the stars glitter and sparkle in Maine heavens. In bare feet I walk out onto the upper deck to sniff, then swallow drafts of the cold clean night air. Down inside the lungs, it washes, freshens, rinses off the linings coated from legislative hearings in Augusta yesterday.

A twelve foot tide this night is at dead low, lowest of the year, exposing places hidden almost always by cold salt water. This moonlight on the mudflats is more beautiful even than moonlight on the ocean or a snowfield. Down in the mucky mud where clams hide and down in the troughs dug by clamdiggers, the black stickyness holds moonbeams, magically.

It is cold. And the cold cuts through pajamas and the soles of bare feet and I go back inside. From my window, I watch the black, bare branches wave in the cold wind. So bright is the moon that tree shadows dart eerily across the moonbeams' path in the mud. Mudflats, scarred from clam digging, look wrinkled, like the hide of an elephant. Further out in the path of the moon the wet black ledge lies exposed to its roots by this neap tide.

Down drops the moon, going down fast now, dropping toward the high ridge on the western side of the water. At intervals this night, I've watched this moon traverse my slice of sky from East to West. Before bed, the same moon shone bright on the big barn and the frozen meadows to the east. By the small hours of the night the moon had risen high, so it shone straight through my curtainless windows onto my pillow. And its light on my eyelids woke me.

It is strange and wonderful to be wakened by moonlight in your eyes. I got up then and went to the windows and watched the moon and watched the stars, the heaven, and watched the moonbeams sticking in the mudflats and shining on the wet rock ledges. And felt brimming with gladness to be standing alone in the night, a witness to the moonlit world.

Alone? I guess not. Millions around the world were probably seeing this same moon. I hope so. I think a half heathen prayer — wishing all men and women who were hurt or bereft yesterday could stand here in the balm of this moonlight.

Memory flashes back to a night I watched Vietnamese planting rice in their paddies by the light of a full moon. I think of bombers' moons. Then of the refugees, streaming in fear and panic out of Hué, racing to the beaches, to be lifted in a cargo net and dropped to sanctuary of a ship's hold. I think of a man I saw in court yesterday, being tried, sitting alone in the accused's chair, wearing a face that seemed a mask. I think of the Maine people who recently lost their jobs, or whose payments have run out. It wouldn't help. But I wish they could stand here.

The moon. The mud. The wet rock ledge. These three have been through nights like this, maybe for half a million years. In them lies order. There lies permanence. There lies beauty. For a hundred generations of men's up and downs, they endure.

The big moon drops fast now, as morning nears. There are no moonbeams left on the mudflats and the ledge. They are back to nothingness, in the dark. The moon drops so it touches the high ridge line. Across the river, tips of trees begin to cover the edge of the moon. The color of the moon changes as it comes to earth. The clear yellow takes on a tinge of orange, of flesh. It sinks, so only its trailing edge shows above the hill. Then, that is gone.

Down to the kitchen, to make coffee and cut up morning fruit. The radio clicks on automatically. And there sounds the herald of the day — your morning newscaster . . . "The Israelis mobilize at borders . . . Million refugees head to sea . . . Unemployment up."

I look out the kitchen window to the east. There, by the big barn where first I saw the moon rise last night, comes a faint glow. Pale rose . . . and above it very light washed-out blue. The rim of the eastern sky lights up, herald of the fresh day. The moon is down. The sun is coming. Thank God I'm here to see them both, here in Maine at Easter.

RITES OF SPRING: STRIP AND SCRAPE

BOOTHBAY HARBOR — A special magic flows over Maine some Saturday in Spring. When it strikes, thousands of Maine men and women decide to strip and scrape.

You can see them stripping all along the coast, and inland by the lakes. Some do it in their own backyards. In front of God and the neighbors, this fever drives respectable Maine men and women to a frenzy. With frantic fingers they untie restraining knots and joyously throw off whatever covers their hulls and their transoms and their poop decks.

Naked to the Springtime, they happily expose their sterns, their bowsprits and their binnacles. Without a twinge of shame, they reveal all in this lovely rite of Spring in Maine . . . Strip down time.

Uncovering is a sport to be played together by men and women from miles around. It is a time for making new friends.

As soon as you and your wife have stripped down, it is time for visits from other strippers. That prim couple on the ketch strolling over to see how your hull survived winter. People you only nod to in the supermarket walk over. Smiling, they inspect and appraise your bottom and then turn and say; "My, your seams are beautifully tight. We are all apart at our seams. We need a good caulking!"

That lady with the handsome grey eyes who sits across the church most Sundays, strolls across the boatyard and speaks to you for the very first time. "What perfect planking you've got!" she says with frank admiration. "You should see mine! I'm so checkered that I'll have to be scraped down and sanded before I'll be fit for summer!"

Before the Saturday sun is over the yardarm, Maine boatyards are infected with a happy, pagan, carefree feeling this strip-down day. Soon a couple of dozen boats are stripped, admirers stand around eyeing each new hull as it is bared.

It is a moment that calls for celebration. Stripping is thirst-making work and soon there is the sweet small sound of cold beer foaming. With a cold one in your fist, a smile on your lips and a glint in your eyes, you stroll on an inspection tour. After a buttoned-down tarpaulin winter, you now feast your eyes upon one lovely bowsprit after another, admire and compare the flare of shapely hulls. As you pass by, your affectionate hand reaches out to pat the nice way a quarter rail turns. Ah! Spring in a Maine boatyard!

Stripping down is exciting. But the fun is short-lived. By midday everyone who is going to strip today has done it. The admiring glances and sudden camaraderie are over. Now comes the work, and the blisters and the dust and the dirt and the cuts and the stretched muscles.

Time to start scraping. The lovely shapes of hull and bowsprit admired so much this morning are just so many square feet to be scraped, sanded, scrubbed, puttied, filled, undercoated and painted. The curves which made your heart sing this morning now spell "c-h-o-r-e-s."

Today and on weekends ahead, 100,000 boat slaves and their wives, kids, girl friends will be at work performing their annual devotions of love and care.

Picture in your mind's eye, 23,623 assorted bottoms of all shapes and sizes being coppered red or blue or green.

Before this bottom-painting rite begins, picture the scene in thousands of homes, workshops and basements, where shelves and cupboards are ransacked for re-usable brushes, and scrapers. Hear the blue language as 17,327 paint-hardened brushes are cursed and hurled in disgust into garbage pails. Then hear the cash registers ring up the sales of new brushes and gallons of copper paint.

Yesterday, we guess, $21,943 were spent buying new brushes. And $117,294 were spent this week buying enough copper bottom paint to safeguard 9,378 bottoms of assorted sizes from 10 to 126 feet.

How many tons of sandpaper? How many cans of varnish, seam compound, paint thinner, epoxy have been bought? How many thousand of stainless steel and chrome screws?

Most Maine boats are small. Over 57 per cent of them are under 16 feet in length. The Watercraft Bureau says there were 28,766 boats of 16 feet or less, equipped with motors of 10 horsepower or more last year.

At the big end of the boat scale, there were a mere 238 boats between 41 and 65 feet and only 10 over 65 feet.

Maine is a small-boat country despite 2,000 miles of seacoast. A whopping 92 per cent of all Maine registered boats were under 25 feet long. Less than half of one per cent were 41 feet and more.

Reason is that most Maine boats are used on lakes, ponds, rivers. And very few are commercial boats. Over 85 per cent are for pleasure.

Strippers and scrapers may be a disappearing breed. Along with other honored traditions, painting your bottom with copper may be a vanishing delight.

For I regret to report that wooden bottoms are vanishing in Maine. Maine boatowners won't willingly admit to it — but 20,688 have plastic bottoms. There are, alas, only 16,470 wooden bottoms left in Maine.

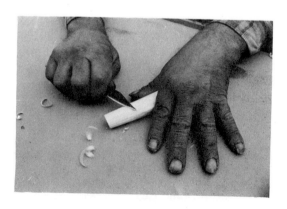

SUGARING TIME: SWEETNESS OF THE TREES

MOOSEHEAD — April is "sugaring time". The sweet sap flows in the maple trees when nights are frosty and the sunny days of spring warm our world up to 50 degrees.

Out of the 10 kinds of maples in Canada and 13 in the United States, only two give sap sweet enough to make syrup — the sugar maple and the black maple.

How did it all begin? There is a story that many hundreds of years ago an Indian watched a red squirrel bite with its sharp teeth into a maple tree and then suck, and then lick its chops and suck again. So the Indian took his knife and cut a V into the maple and when the sap ran out he sucked it and he, too, liked its sweet taste.

The story continues that the early Indians found that eating and drinking the sweet sap drove off the "spring sickness". After a long winter diet of dried meats and no vegetables or berries, Indians suffered from scurvy. The maple sap with its high sugar content proved a preventative.

Before long, the Indians turned the sap into more concentrated syrup by dropping red hot stones into a batch of sap and thereby boiling off the water content.

Finally when the white men from Europe arrived and felt starved for sweets and sugar, the Indians traded with them in maple syrup. The Algonquin word for maple sugar was "Sinzibuckwud"; the Ojibways called it "sheesheegummawis" (sap flows fast). Sugar became a prime ingredient in most Indian foods.

"Sugaring" is a springtime rite all over Maine. Up to 10,000 gallons of syrup may be made from about 440,000 gallons of sap collected this spring. But the most intensive "sugaring" is in Maine's north woods near the Canadian border.

Each year hundreds of French-Canadian families — men, women, children, grandparents — cross the border and head for their old time "sugaring camps" deep in the woods. Mostly these are old log cabins rented for a modest fee from paper companies at a price based on the number of trees tapped. There are about 40 such camps. In the average operation, about 5,000 buckets are hung from 3,000 or so maple trees. The maple sap gathered over several weeks may amount to 35,000 gallons. But after it is boiled and the water is evaporated there may be only 800 gallons of syrup. And that is one reason a gallon of maple syrup costs so much in stores.

The new-fangled way to tap is to use plastic tubing running from tree to tree, with the sap being drained into central collection tubs. But in the north woods most of the "sirop d'erable" is harvested in the old fashioned way. Snow is deep in the woods there in the spring, so the families go on snowshoes. Their 400-gallon containers, into which they pour the sap collected from each tree, are drawn by horses pulling a big sled.

Back at camp the womenfolk tend the big fires over which the sap is boiled hours on end. (Sap is 97 per cent water and only three per cent sweet minerals. That's why it takes so much to make one gallon of pure syrup.) The syrup must have a density of 65 per cent, and it must be so thick that it weighs 11 pounds to the gallon. It must be strained so it is clear and all the "sugar sand" is removed. This is a fine kind of sand which the roots sucked up out of the soil and carried through the tree in the sap which ran through limbs and branches.

Even in the north woods, maple syrup production is waning. Ten years ago about 50,000 gallons were produced. This year it may be only 20,000. To the families who come to the sugar camps year after year, generation after generation, "sugaring" can be a kind of special holiday, which also helps sweeten the cash flow when lumbering is over.

When the "crop" is fully harvested, the camps put on a gala "sugaring-off" party. The wilderness rings through the night with the joyous noises of feasting and drinking, dancing and music and much singing.

A good way to enjoy maple syrup on the spot is to pour it fresh and hot over clean cold snow. It hardens into a taffy. Grab it, chew and relish a treat.

Or pour hot syrup over baked beans after a morning of work among the trees.

Or take the syrup home and make pralines. Use two cups of maple syrup and half a cup of the meat of pecans or walnuts. Cook the syrup until it forms a soft ball in cold water (240 F). Remove immediately from heat and let stand for one minute. Pour syrup into a lightly buttered dish. Sprinkle nuts over the top. Serve cold by the spoonful. Give to highly favored friends — if you have any left.

SUMMER SADNESS:
LAST ENTRIES IN PENOBSCOT LOG

ABOARD "STEER CLEAR" — The Penobscot Bay cruise is over. And the end is bitter-sweet.

It is sweet to round the final buoy back into your home harbor; to thread your familiar way among fishing boats whose hulls and names and owners are all friendly landmarks; and finally to tie up, back on your own mooring which you left so long ago, it seems.

You are home. The boat is fine. All aboard are fine. And that is sweet. But there is bitter with it.

It is bitter to know this is the end. The last stop. The cruise is over. You are back in the world.

It is bitter to know that tonight you will sleep landlocked in your own bed, ashore in your own home. Tonight you will not be at sea, watching the sun set, feeling the wind drop, marvelling at how the choppy waters smooth out to glass. Tonight you will not see the big moon rise up out of the Atlantic and shine down in serene tranquillity on a pine-crested island where no people live and no lights burn. Tonight after supper you will not douse the fry-pan off the stern and your heart will not leap in joy at the magic phosphorescence in the sea around it. Tonight you will not hear a wild loon cry to starbright heavens nor watch for shooting stars to fall into the ocean. Tonight you will be back in the world; and your mundane company will be telephones and television and sheets on the bed. And tomorrow's work will begin with a shoe-clad foot pressing down on a car's accelerator pedal instead of bare hands hauling up a ship's anchor.

And this prospect is bitter.

So you postpone it. You stretch out the business of closing up the boat, hating to say goodbye. You pack your gear — slowly. You tidy up — immaculately. You swab down — scrubbing every plank. Then you re-tidy; and swab down again. Then you coil lines, meticulously, so each is in perfect symmetry. Finally you decide this is the time to clean the dinghy, which has bounced behind in your wake so faithfully for so many miles.

Instead of growling at the chore, you get sentimental as you scrub her down, wallowing in suds from bilge cleaner.

"How many buckets of mussels and clams for dinner have we loaded into you? How many rocky beaches have we scraped your tender bottom on? How many little plants and tiny trees have we hauled in you from loved islands to plant as memories in our garden ashore?"

You clean the fool dinghy like it has never been cleaned before. And enjoy doing it. It is far far better than going ashore.

Then suddenly there is no more work to do. But still you hate to face the ending; hate to go ashore, as you must, to climb into a car, as you must, and drive home as you must.

So now you take refuge in the writer's excuse. You drag out your typewriter, set up a table in the stern and tell yourself "This is the place to write the finale, here on the boat!" And you smile happily at the new reprieve you've handed yourself.

In "Steer Clear" this little secondhand 30 foot boat, we had found heaven on earth, just off the coast of Maine. For 10 days we cruised where whimsy took us; dropped anchor where we felt like stopping; dug clams, gathered mussels, picked raspberries, swam in silent coves, sunbathed on lonely granite rocks, watched sunsets and sunrises and the moon come up and the stars come out. Listened to wild birds sing; watched terns dart and soar; heard fish plop in the stillness of the night; climbed high hills and beachcombed uninhabited islands; marvelled at discovering a garden of Indian Pipes, a meadow of wild orchids, a blazing assemblage of glorious wild roses; and gazed in amazement at the revelations of life in tiny tidal pools into which, perhaps, man had never looked before.

"This beats any jet plane holiday to any plush resort," said Barbara one night off Saint Helena Island. "And, Big Spender, it cost you $7.85 today for ice and supplies!"

The days and the nights, the sea passages and the quiet coves, the islands we loved and explored come wafting back as I sit at the typewriter, back in home harbor, hating to admit the cruise is over.

Duck Harbor, on the western shore of Isle au Haut, was where we spent the first night. We came in avoiding The Brandies (how did ledges get that name?) and were lucky to find the little harbor empty and so laid on the single mooring. It is said Indians used to drive ducks up into the narrow head of this harbor and kill them by the hundreds in the molting season, and then smoke them for winter provisions.

Tide was ebbing fast, exposing mussel shoals to us for our dinner. We used the dinghy to gather a bucketful. Then went ashore to climb Duck Mountain. But we never reached the top. For at every turn through the woods, Barbara would stop to marvel at the clusters of white Indian Pipes and the lushness of lichens and the colors of gray-green and silver mosses. And our appetite for the mussels grew sharp. So we went back aboard and she cut up celery and onions and threw these along with oregano and garlic and cups of white wine over the mussels which I had scrubbed and washed and we set them to boil.

While the mussels boiled and opened and made a delicious smelling broth, we made garlic French bread in a makeshift oven, by turning a pot upside down over a flame controller on the alcohol stove. Then as we watched the sun go down over Vinalhaven in the Western Penobscot Bay, we dined like epicures. The bucket of fat mussels finished, we ate freshly picked wild raspberries from the shore for dessert and watched "Flying Feather," a catamaran from Larchmont, N.Y., and "Quadrille," a schooner from Marblehead, and "Tart," from Manchester, come in, drop sail and anchor. To see the moonrise, we rowed ashore again and climbed the high granite bluff at Duck Harbor entrance and, standing atop, looked out across the islands of Penobscot Bay seeing the moon's track light up the combers breaking out on Saddleback Ledge. Night birds cried out as we tramped back, down through the woods and over the rocks to our dinghy and rowed out to the shipboard bunks, where sleep is sweetest.

Saint Helena, that blessed island lying between Merchant Row and Deer Isle, is unforgettable and unforgotten. Anchored in its lee, below its one simple, lovely house, we spent a heavenly day and night there, wholly alone. In the bright clear morning we climbed atop the mammoth granite rock which crowns the island and looked out on an indescribable paradise of blue ocean water, small islands, green pines, white sails. We swam in the fresh water of an old quarry and sun-dried on sun-baked beds of moss. We spent that hot afternoon watching birds arch and sail against an azure sky, we explored animal paths, gorging lush ripe raspberries as we walked. Then as the evening tide came in, we went down to the granite ledges which run out to sea and swam in the clear, cold salt water as the tide crept up over the hot, hot stone. That moonlight night we enjoyed a serenade. On a sailboat anchored off an island a mile away, someone played a guitar well and sang softly some folk ballads, and the tunes came deliciously downwind to us.

In all the world I have seen — and I have circled it a dozen times — no part of this planet excels the beauty of a slow passage on a brilliant August day among the blessed islands off Stonington, across Jericho Bay to Swan's Island and into Burnt Coat Harbor. We dallied in delight among Bare Island, Spruce Island, Devil Island, Saddleback, McGlathery, past Whaleback Ledge, Halibut Rocks and among the ledges and islands with wonderful names such as Irish Point, High Sheriff, Ringtown, Brimstone and Toothacher Cove. Names are a part of the special loveliness of Penobscot Bay. In one day's cruising, you can pass the Popplestones, Shabby Island, Sunken Egg, Ship and Barges Ledge, Colby Pup, Great Gott and Little Gott, Sally Prude Ledge, The Drums, Gooseberry Point, Smutty Nose and Goose Pond Mountain.

So the magic days and nights went by. Dallying in loveliness to Surry and along Newbury Neck, up into Morgan's Bay; then the heaven of Blue Hill Harbor, with its hospitable club and assemblage of lovely yachts and lovely homes with lovely gardens.

Still another day and night among the beauties of the Eggemoggin Reach, the Benjamin River, sailing unnder the great arch of the Deer Isle suspension bridge into the lovely horseshoe shelter of Bucks Harbor. Going by boat to visit Russell Wiggins, editor of the Ellsworth American now, and former editor of the Washington Post.

Near to the last, the choicest of them all; the great beaches and woods and hills of uninhabited Butter Island. There we lolled and roamed and swam and sunned in bliss for yet another epic day of idyllic idleness. In late afternoon the winds blew up strongly and we relished a wet, salt-soaked run into the teeth of the breeze down into Pulpit Harbor. There we spent the final night of an interlude of heaven upon earth, known as cruising the Maine Coast.

Rites of Fall: Stern medicine

NEW HARBOR — About the nastiest way a man can say goodbye to a lady he loves is to take a wire brush, dip it in acid and scrub her bottom with it.

But that is what I just did, when I hauled out my boat for winter. And I feel like a heel.

"All men are ungrateful beasts, but sailors are the worst."

From Portland Light to the Philippines that is what many ladies who are close to sailors say.

This morning, I agree. This Sunday morning you may feel good, sweetened by an after-churchly glow. But I feel like a heel, sour with remorse and ingratitude.

From May until November, that boat had given me the best months of her year. She had served me well and faithfully. She gave me comfort, gave me pleasure, gave me happiness.

And what is her reward?

Now the best days are over, she is tossed aside, hauled up on the bank, put on the shelf.

"All men are ungrateful, but sailors are the worst".

Now summer is over, something new and different catches a man's roving eye. Now November is here and a man's fancy turns from the water to the woods. He casts aside the lovely hull he dallied with all summer long; with barely a word of farewell, he walks away from his summer love and starts out on a new fall flirtation.

Deer. Guns. The woods. Hunting.

When a sailor wakes in the morning now, and brews his coffee and snaps on the radio for news, even the little things are different. No longer is his ear tuned to marine weather forecasts. What attracts him now are reports of frost, or snowfall in the woods.

When the summer sailor looks up from work and gazes out the window these November days, he is no longer interested in wind and sea conditions. No longer are his daydreams focussed on the enticing wench bobbing at her mooring in the harbor, waiting for his love and attention.

No. That ungrateful man's daydreaming eye is now filled with a different love. He now has thoughts only for a white-tailed deer. Gone are the summer thoughts of an island cove. He now sees only a crook in a tree, where he will sit remote in the silent woods, basking in the pale November sun, waiting eagerly for the sight of his white tailed deer.

At night now, when the summer sailor comes home from work, he walks right by the trappings of his summer love, heartless. Gear from his boat lies stacked in the cellar, ignored, while he makes a beeline for his guns. The hands which so recently and so lovingly spliced docking lines and varnished the brightwork of his summer love now caress the stock of an over-and-under, or fondle the barrel of a Winchester.

In the one closet of the house he can call his own, his hands rudely exile to the far, dark corner the yellow oilskins which saved his skin from a salt water soaking. Instead his eyes light up now as he pulls on that blaze orange cap and snuggles his shoulders into the warmth of that heavy lumberjack shirt, and fits his feet into lace-up boots.

I have hauled my boat and I feel like a heel, looking back on this day's work.

First work I did, on my last visit to my summer love, was to strip her of all the gifts that I had bought for her in the halcyon days of summer. Snatched up and packed into cartons were all those lovingly bought presents — the new oil lamp in the galley, the new pennant on her bow, the expensive new cushions for her day cabin, the gleaming new spotlight which guided us to our moorings after dark.

Then like a callous lover leaving, I retrieved all my personal belongings. The shirts and sweaters, the pajamas and toothbrush, the bedside books, the pipes and tobacco pouches — all the evidence I had lived here with her from May to November. — I bundled into a seabag and rowed ashore.

Then, the final brutality. A harsh steel hawser is snubbed around her bow chocks . . . the very chocks where on summer nights I had snubbed the anchor line before lying down to sleep in secure happiness.

A truck on shore winches up the hawser and drags my summer love yard by reluctant yard out of the sea, onto the alien land.

How does a summer sailor say goodbye to the lady who has shared her life with him, day and night, from May to November?

Brutally.

I fill great buckets with diluted acid. I get a long-handled rough wire brush and dip it in the acid. Then I scrub her bottom.

When that brutal deed is done and she sits ugly on her cradle ashore, I fetch grey tarpaulins. I hide my summer love in burial shrouds, and lash this ugliness all about her beauty. And walk away.

This is a sailor's gratitude to his summer love.

NOW COMES THE BEST OF ALL—OCTOBER

BRUNSWICK — A stretch of the road on my way to work is blazing red and gold today.

The sight makes my heart jump with admiration; and then the sight fills me with sadness at the end of summer.

In Maine, there are more beginnings and more endings. And that is one reason there is more to enjoy in a Maine year than in a year anywhere else.

Love it or hate it — there is a feeling roused in you by the first snow. And another feeling by the first day of hunting or the last day of fishing. There is a special feeling the smell of the first fire in the fireplace brings. And another special feeling the smell of the first burning leaves of fall brings. (Can they legislate away that smell, when the no-burning law is enforced? Can they take away that special pleasure?)

Count the changes we feel in Maine. Ice out. The mud season. The day in spring the boat goes overboard. And the sad day you haul her out. The day you close up camp, and the surge of sudden tenderness that sticks in your throat when you drain the water pipes and board up the big windows. Who ever admits that a grown man gets tears in his eyes when he performs that final chore of draining the pipes?

Never mind, it has been a good summer, even as you close up the place, you think that maybe you will sneak down here again when the snow is deep, and bring a lantern and a sleeping bag and to hell with water and toilets.

The color in the trees is the beginning, not the end.

Men and women of forethought will be down in the cellar soon, checking the gear they will need to go into the woods after deer.

Some who hate hunting can console themselves by trying to find last year's ski wax and by soaping the hint of mold off the ski boots. Sure, snow is a long way off. But in your mind's eye, behind the golden leaves, you can see the sight of a white mountain trail, and hear the squeak of packed snow under your heel.

Enough of all the lovely thoughts. The reality is the big oil truck, on its first trip to unload its liquid gold into your hungry tank. That is another joy of Maine . . . the highest priced fuel oil that any American can buy!

The sight of the oil truck pumping, and clocking up the dollars, sends you to hunt for the axe. You rub a thumb along the edge, blunt after a summer of idleness. And you promise that soon you will discover where you left the sharpening stone last March; and then you will hone a new edge on your oil-saving axe, and go to work on the wood pile.

Early this morning, I saw deer in my meadow. In less than a month, they will know November is coming and they will take to the deeper woods — I hope. I want them back, with offspring, next year.

But there is a special blessing still in store. In September, Mainers got the best of summer. Now in October come the most wonderful days of all — the sweet last taste of our Indian summer and the first spicy nip of clean white frost.

WINTER—TALKING LIKE A WOOD SNOB

PORTLAND — A new topic when men talk together is wood-burning stoves.

"Can your fire make it through the night?" This is the acid test.

When you climb out of a warm bed and head down those chilly stairs, will there be red embers glowing — or only grey ash, dreary, dead and cold?

The kind of greeting a fellow gets from his fire at six o'clock of a winter morning colors his whole day.

In the fight to keep fires going through the night, in the battle to spend less on high priced oil, I admit to a bit of treachery.

I took out a Maine-built Franklin stove and replaced it with a Norwegian wood burner. To be exact, I took out a 100-year-old Wood, Bishop No. 1, made in Bangor and put in a Jotul made in Skiensfjord, Norway.

Fires in the Maine stove had lots of eye appeal. With doors open I could see the wood flame and glow. The Norwegian stove is airtight, its door must be shut. I can see no heartwarming fire. But the rest of me is warmer. It throws more heat with less wood for a longer time. And it should. It cost a lot more to buy. These Jotuls cost from $300 to $800, complete.

But I am glad that a Maine lady named Eva Norton is the importer of the Jotul stoves, and that it is making her very rich. Eva Norton, born in Norway, married to an oceanographer, was raising three children in a cold rundown farmhouse in Andover, Maine. Her Franklin stoves were not efficient. So from her parents in Norway, she got a small Jotul, to heat three upstairs rooms. Then Sverre Gahr, president of Jotul, sent her a large Jotul out of respect for her father, who was an anti-Nazi activist in the Norwegian underground. Soon she imported 500 Jotuls to sell, going into business at age 40 for the first time. That was four years ago. In 1977 Eva Norton will sell 20,000 Jotuls. She has the franchise for all the United States and Alaska. She has 370 dealers. Dollar volume runs into millions.

But I am convinced that in Norway they know something about wood and stoves that I do not know. Or else they are kidding us.

They tell me that in northern Norway they keep Jotul stoves burning 300 days a year, stoke them with new wood only twice a day, and they say that two sticks of wood put on a properly drafted fire at bedtime will still be burning when you get up next morning.

That happened to me once. I went to bed at 2 a.m., and got up at 5 a.m. I'm lucky to find an ember glowing.

Until now, I have endured my share of wine snobs, cigar snobs, foreign car snobs. Now I am meeting wood snobs. Where wine snobs judge by bouquet and color, wood snobs judge by BTUs and hardness.

I used to love burning applewood because it smelled so good. But that means nothing to a wood snob. He praises applewood because it generates 23,877,000 BTUs per cord. And that is the heat equivalent of burning 244 gallons of No. 2 heating oil.

For my nice amateur friends BTUs stands for British Thermal Units and not — as I thought — for Bean's Thermal Underwear.

You too can learn how to talk like a wood snob. Here is the jargon with which you can shame your neighbors . . . . A cord of beech generates 21.8 million BTUs, is equivalent of 222 gallons of heating oil. Elm is right up there with apple. If you see white birch, wrinkle your nose — it is down to 18.9 million BTU rating, a mere 193 gallons of oil equivalent.

If you want to go slumming, visit a slob who burns fir, spruce or basswood. The nasty stuff burns fast, spoils the chimney, is full of creosote, and its BTU rating is down around 11 million.

For heaven's sake do not mix with the crowd that burns young, green wood. It's slow. It's smoky. It's as bad as new jeans. Don't let wood in your house unless it has been cut two or three years. Be snobbish about your wood. And if you must burn oil, be sure it is imported — aged in the desert.

VIII /

One Man's Family

My wife Barbara recovering from a skiing accident.

Our son John and his wife Cheryl their baby girl Chiloe.

"H OW DID YOU *come to Maine?"*

That is a question asked alike by people born in Maine and by those from away, who think they'd like to move to Maine.

Our kids did the deciding for us. They, at age 14 and 15, were responsible for getting us out of New York City and into Damariscotta.

It happened one evening in late August on the porch of a rented summer cottage which overlooked John's Bay and Pemaquid. We had been together for our first summer vacation on the Maine coast. After lunch, John and Susan had gone out together in the skiff and in mid-afternoon had come to me and said very seriously "We want to talk to you after supper."

They said it straight: "We don't want to go back to New York City, ever. We want to stay here in Maine. We want to go to school at Lincoln Academy."

That night, Barbara and I sat on the porch looking and thinking and talking. We listened to soft still noises of a summer night. We watched the night turn the ocean purple, then black. We watched a tiny mast light bobbing on a little boat, night fishing. And we knew the kids were right. All of us ought to move to Maine. We talked, as if we were sensibly weighing the pros and cons, drawing up some sort of balance sheet on whether to stay in Manhattan or move to Maine. But that was surface talk. In our bones, we knew that coming to Maine was inevitable.

The only way to do a move like that is just to do it. If you think about it too long, or plan the move too carefully, you never make it. So I went quickly back to New York to close up shop there. That was right after Labor Day.

Barbara and the kids stayed. Susan and John enrolled at Lincoln Academy, founded 1806, high on Academy Hill, Newcastle. Barbara found a house in Damariscotta within walking distance to school. And she found a part time job.

By Christmas, four months after that announcement by the kids, I was free of New York City and moved into the rented house in Damariscotta, and at age 46 was about to look for a job.

That answers the question "How did you come to Maine?" Then the next question is usually: "Once you moved here, how did you make a living?"

I don't want to sideslip into an autobiography here, but it is a fair question and should be answered by a reporter who has been asking other people all kinds of personal questions, and publishing their answers.

I job-hunted hard for 10 weeks. Then I found a job selling advertising for a small, new weekly newspaper in South Portland. The round trip from Damariscotta to South Portland was 120 miles a day. The pay was $120.00 a week. I recite the figures because they show quickly the deep-sea changes in values you face in leaving Manhattan and moving to Maine. My pay in Manhattan in 1964 had been $25,000 plus liberal expenses and a lavish office a few blocks from our apartment. In Maine, I was travelling 120 miles to earn less money at age 46 than I had made at age 26. My wife Barbara was out bread winning too. She had been a star performer at a New York advertising agency handling time and talent in radio and TV before we were married. Now 22 years later she went to work again. The pay was a lot less but so was the rent. Our rent for a ship captain's house of 10 rooms on a tree lined street was $85 a *month in that January of 1965. The rent for our penthouse in Manhattan had been $600 a month, plus $80 for garaging a little imported car, plus tips for doormen, etc. But that first winter we found out that it cost more to heat that ship captain's house than to rent it. (Prices have changed. By 1977 the combined rent of two apartments in that same ship-captain's house was $400 monthly.)*

What about John and Susan? At 14 and 15, they seemed to love the change to Lincoln Academy from the schools they'd been to in New York and before that in England. Even our dog—a beagle then, named Bugle — relished the scents and smells of Maine after the sidewalks of New York.

That first year in Maine was probably the biggest change we had ever gone through — and we'd gone through many. For the record, Barbara and I began married life living and working in New York City; then five years and two babies later we made our first move; to Irvington-on-Hudson, a Westchester suburb of Manhattan. I worked for Time-Life, then for Fawcett Publications, now a part of CBS. In 1953 we moved again, to Washington, D.C. I had worked for the election of Eisenhower and took a leave of absence from my job to travel the country for him. After his election, I was appointed Director of Public Reports. I was 33, and the job was a grade 18, highest in civil service. The job was in the Foreign Operations Administration — the agency which was spending six billion dollars a year for military, economic and technical assistance in 60 nations.

We grew to love Washington and spent 7 years there although I had joined the Administration planning to spend only one or at most two years in government. The work was fascinating, if frustrating. The travel was tremendous and frequent, to many of the 60 nations where FOA operated.

But seven years of government was enough. We quit, went back to publishing and newspapers and the next move was to London for four years. The kids had their schooling at those strange but wonderful English preparatory schools and saw a bit of Europe. The fifth move was back to New York City — a far, far different place in the 1960's than we had loved years before in the 1940's.

How Did You Come to Maine? / 291

And then came Maine. Thank heavens.

Maine has been good to us. Every year has been good and the year after it has been better. The columns in this section are milestones in Maine for this man and his family.

OUR DOG, THE FRISBEE PLAYER

DAMARISCOTTA — This Sunday morning God smiles at my place by the river.

My boat is in the water.

My asparagus is in its bed.

And my Dalmatian dog is shaping up as a great frisbee player.

It is my wife's birthday. Happy day!

How much more can a fellow in Maine want by May 9?

The very best job after a bout of political conventioneering, is to dig your asparagus bed.

Gardening books tell you that if there is one thing asparagus beds like, it is manure. Good, rich, aged manure. And lots of it. So since I dug my asparagus bed fresh from the State political conventions, I am looking ahead to a rich harvest.

This is our first year at raising asparagus. We bought three-year-old plants at the bargain price of eight cents each. So we bought plenty. Who can ever have too much asparagus?

As I planted them in the deep rich loam of political dirt, I marvelled at how these little roots with white tendrils running out 24 inches, would ever turn into those gorgeous green stalks smothered with hot butter and lemon juice.

And as I ladled the compost and manure into the furrow, I wondered which would change most as time went by — the politicians' planks or these plants?

There is no doubt, however, about which will change for the better.

About the time I had put in 20 or so plants, my Dalmatian came bounding into the bed at full speed. She landed with a thud and instantly the roots attracted her full attention. Down went her white nose into the black dirt and the burrowing began.

I went to the encyclopedia before I started on this ambitious asparagus bed.

The Greeks and the Romans grew it 2,000 years ago in the Mediterranean climate. Same stuff as I am planting by the banks of the Damariscotta river. They used it for medicine as well as food.

The fern which florists put into flower arrangements, and which also is called asparagus, is sissy stuff. It must live in greenhouses, because frost kills it. It originated below the equator in South Africa. We have no truck with that in Maine soil. But the eating of asparagus was a joy to the early settlers. Those smart fellows believed in a touch of luxury in their New World so they brought asparagus roots with them, and began planting it here in the early 1600's.

However, if the Dalmatian is so wild about the roots, I shall never harvest the spears.

Here is where the frisbee comes in.

I spot a green frisbee in the wheelbarrow, among the hoes and rakes and forks I brought to this task — heaven alone knows how it got there. I lunge for it, call "Piper! Piper!" and hurl the frisbee high into the air, sailing it far from the asparagus bed.

She bounds away, chasing that elusive disc as it floats, drops, turns and finally falls. She grabs it in her teeth and prances with triumph at having caught this strange new beast of the field. She bounds back, coming across the field in leaps 10 feet long, two feet high. I accept the frisbee from her and hurl it off again. Off she goes; back she bounds, frisbee clenched in her teeth. Again. Again.

Are we headed for some new entry in the Guiness Book of World Records? In Portland, frisbee players last summer kept a frisbee flying for over 16 days. That was with all human teams. Has anyone tried the man-dog combination?

Piper makes three more recoveries from my next three throws. I worry lest the rains come and night falls before the rest of the asparagus is planted. But better to throw the frisbee than to have the dog dig up the plants. Once started, these asparagus beds yield for 15 to 25 years.

On the next return, Piper keeps the frisbee clenched in those strong white teeth. I pull, she growls. I pull harder; she digs her toes in and growls louder. I tug harder, and — split! The frisbee tears. I am left with about 70 per cent of it: Piper has the rest. I throw my part. It will not fly. She savages it to shreds. Her attention is wholly diverted. Probably for the first time in American history, the frisbee has saved the life of an asparagus bed.

As for Dalmatian frisbee players, I would not wish this on anybody else. I think that idiot dog has begun to read over my shoulder. Seven times since I typed out the sentences about Piper and her frisbee, she has come, frisbee in mouth, to make me throw it for her. Yes, she has some new frisbees; she picked them out at the hardware store herself.

She is my wife's dog. And for my wife's birthday today, I am going to give her back this frisbee-crazy Dalmatian.

Your new Home is Finished!

DAMARISCOTTA — Our new home, begun on Independence Day is going to be finished. I never thought it would. Now we have a positive reply to all the inquiries "When will you move in?" The answer is "Ground Hog Day."

I can't wait for it to arrive. The final brush of paint and last slap of plaster and ultimate piece of plumbing cannot come soon enough — we've had 180 days and nights of waiting.

But secretly I dread the coming of that Completion Day.

The thought of it brings the same feeling in the bottom of my stomach I used to suffer when I glimpsed land toward the last day of an ocean voyage. To see the destination is a thrill. Exciting new faces and customs, new languages, new money, new foods are waiting there to be discovered.

Yet there is a fearful sadness as the voyage is over. Tomorrow the people with whom you have lived so closely, eaten meals with, clocked miles around the deck with, lost to at bridge, beaten at shuffleboard, stood by the rail and watched the ocean with — they will all be gone tomorrow.

Tomorrow will be the commotion of baggage littering passage-ways; porters giving a shrug as you wince at the way they heave your personal cargoes. Tomorrow will be the stamping of papers, passports, landing cards, citizenship statements — documents which in effect tag you with a number, and mark "end" to one page and "begin" to another.

The new house is elegant. The design we planned so long has come off splendidly, though we have broken most rules in the architect's bibles. Each room will be a joy. The colors on the beams are right. The grasscloth on the walls, made in Japanese hill villages, looks perfect by the banks of the Damariscotta river. There are now, at last in my life, acres of shelves for my accumulated books—which in desperation I had been giving away. There is a wing for the teenagers, separate and sound proof; and their own vast recreation room, remote and insulated from my study. Quiet! after all the noisy years! And probably I will go looking for the noise I will miss — only to find the children are grown up now and flown the coop.

Each day before going to work for 180 days I have driven to the new house. On the bend of the driveway I have seen the green convertible which meant Ervin the master carpenter was on the job; Cliff Grindal's battered wagon, which meant painting was going on; a truck which signified the Dry-Wall crew; another which meant Harold Achorn was laying tile in the bathrooms or Pat Boise was doing weird and wonderful things with electricity; or the hen brown wagon which meant contractor George Sheloske was making "bossing" rounds; or Kelsey's pickup which showed Norman was laying more lovely old brick for the fireplaces.

Goose pimples and icy chills have run up and down my spine each morning as I have seen money running out while I counted trucks and cars lined up. And I will miss that reckless feeling of future bankruptcy. It won't be future any more.

After supper each night for the past month, my wife and I have prowled like robbers through the empty, half finished rooms. Barbara walking like the Lady of the Lamp, with a great naked bulb in an outsretched arm; and me dragging yards of cable behind me like Marley's ghost until the blasted plug pulls out far down in the basement. Then I stumble over workmen's debris, and trip back down the unfamiliar stairs in blackness to fumble the disconnected plug back into its cantankerous socket.

Room by room we have peered at the day's work. Sometimes we couldn't find a visible result, search as we would. Other nights we'd laugh with excited joy at the miracle of a sink in place — just where we wanted it! Or a layer of paint, exactly the shade we had dreamed of — as though it were a miracle of creation instead of pigment from a can. We'd stand in the cold night on a porch, watching the moon shine on "our" snow and hear the cold creak in the trunks and branches of "our" trees.

Then we would drive home to the "old" house. There, among mountains of home-building and decorating magazines, we knew a king-size bed was hidden. And we'd crawl into it. And surround ourselves with blueprints, pencils to change them and home magazines (the new ones out this week) and swatches arrived from the decorators and wallpaper sample books.

Then I'd fall off to sleep for an hour; only to waken from the rustle of House Beautiful at my feet and an 18 pound weight of Schumacher's wallpaper book across my manly chest.

Oh! how I will miss all the agony and ecstasy of building a home when they hand me the keys on Ground Hog Day and say those frightening sweet-sharp words . . . "It is finished!"

MAIL FROM VIETNAM

DAMARISCOTTA. No stamp. The naked-looking envelope with "Free" scrawled in the upper right jumps out from the pile of flyers, bills, other mail and leaps into your anxious heart.

The leap is like that magic moment when your waiting eager eyes scan a sea of faces outpouring from a plane, bus or train — and suddenly spot that familiar, missed face you long to see. Instantly, an invisible lasso of shared love links two people separated by space.

This morning our letter from Vietnam came in. Standing by the worn shelf table in the post office, we quickly ripped it open. "Dear Mum and Dad . . . We are on the gun line now . . . We are firing shells day and night into the coastline of Vietnam, four miles off our beam . . . Ten more days of this and we head for R&R in Subic Bay and repairs . . . ."

Together we race through the seven pages. The thin-stroked scrawl is achingly familiar. The news it tells is partly of war in the Tonkin Gulf; of bombardment, fiery nights, missiles, shell loading, six hour shifts on and off duty, battle stations, hard high speed turns; an achingly strange kind of news from his young, familiar handwriting.

Around us, neighborly faces come to and go from their mail boxes, all exchanging 'hellos!' "Let's take it to the car and read it alone, slowly" says my wife. At the opposite shelf table in the post office we spot another lady, devouring a similar letter from the Free Zone. The rest of her morning mail, ignored, is piled by her elbow. She has no eyes for it or the people moving around her, for anything except the mail from Vietnam.

Are there a thousand such letters from Vietnam being opened on this same morning in Maine? Two thousand? I picture Fran in Patten, Bruce in Jay, Corliss in York, Harry at Rockport, Judy and Bill on Monhegan, Bob on the Cape — scores of friends all over Maine with sons and husbands in Vietnam who may be getting their letter this morning from the Free Zone.

"Does the Vietnam mail get here in great wonderful batches on the same mornings?" I wonder to my wife. "All over Maine, right now, is there this same simultaneous link radiating out from Here to There, 10,000 miles away? Tying Maine close to Vietnam?"

Sitting in the car we pass the letter, page by page between us. One moment my mind leaps to the gun stations and below decks on the Boston, trying hard to picture precisely what my son looks like now, exactly what he may be doing now.

The next moment I imagine Judy on Monhegan, fresh from the post office, stampless envelope in hand, running down the wharf to show the letter to her husband. Or Fran, driving back from Patten and shouting across the field and over the noise of the tractor to Chubb "A letter! A letter! A letter from him!" And I see Chubb switch off his motor, climb down and come jogging over up onto the porch. I see them together reading their stampless letter, trying to picture through the ink how their son looks as he gets ready for a helicopter take-off.

We drive back to the house, hurrying to read the letter all over again. "It is different, reading it with all his things all around me" says my wife. And she is right. We read it over again, sitting in our son's room, with his belongings around us.

"Tonight we are still shooting" he writes. "We stay in one place, shoot a while and then pull a high speed turn. 'Hit and git' — away fast. So far today we've damaged two or three tank convoys. Tonight it is mostly just harassment firing . . . ."

Inside her head and inside mine, our separate pictures form. What she is imagining, I cannot tell. She like most women, has never fired nor been shot at in anger. Yet my own memories of how it was in another war don't help much to really pinpoint him, now, today.

He is not writing now about war.

"Would you mind terribly going up to school one morning, Mom? And seeing Mrs. Powell, Art teacher, about where you can get me some special pens and inks. About half a dozen fine point nibs, three wide points and one italic. As for inks, get as many colors as you can, please! And two sketch pads, and assorted size water color brushes. I might get a chance to paint, when off-watch. Here is a list for Dad, who is not going to get off easy as he hopes."

His switch-over from gun-firing rates to art supplies is hard to take.

Now there are three gaudy (and bawdy) paragraphs about his 24 hour liberty among the neon honky-tonks of the Subic Bay waterfront. His mother stumbles a trifle over these marks of manhood. Then in a quick ten word thrust the rascal's words hit home . . . "Dad probably remembers places like these from his war . . . Ask him!"

On the walls of his room here at home are school banners, mementos of basketball games, pictures of school track teams, snapshots of girls he took to proms. Hanging and waiting in their racks are rods he fished with here last spring and the peacetime gun he hunted with just last Fall.

It is a jumbled up world; the peace world here, and his war world there. But the letter bridges them both without trouble. "Please send me the Lincoln Academy Alumni News and give them a donation for me. Also ask Dad to send me a subscription to Playboy. And tell him to put some drops of oil onto my spinning reels, so the rust won't get in . . . ."

When he finished writing this letter, I think, he probably went above decks to his gun station to relieve other men on watch. And probably those kids came down to their bunks. And they wrote letters home like this one. And then side by side in a grey mail sack thousands of those letters were flown to Maine. And now in Auburn and Bangor, Portland and Searsport, all across the 31,000 square miles of Maine, how many others are reading their mail from Vietnam? I walk to the kitchen to get coffee. The news is on the radio. News of 586 more American combat deaths in Vietnam and the news of thousand more casualties this week. I turn it off.

"Let's go back downstreet" I tell my wife. "You get the art supplies for him. I'll get his Playboy."

Strange items to be sending to a war. And as I mail them, the darndest thought comes to mind. I wonder what kind of stuff a father in Hanoi may be putting into his post office for his son's mail there. Paint brushes and Playboy are going to my "imperialist Yankee warmonger"; what equivalents for a "Communist aggressor and terrorist" is he sending?

My son is now happily married, living in Vermont. And he and his wife Cheryl have given us a granddaughter, Chloe.

WEIGHT-WATCHERS IN THE HOME

DAMARISCOTTA — There is in Maine today an unsung band of undernourished heroes. They are the long-suffering men whose wives and daughters are in Weight-Watchers, but who are skinny themselves.

Take me, for example. When I climb on the scales, I can't push the needle beyond 160 pounds. But I might as well be in Weight Watchers, for my wife and daughter are. They gave up smoking, gained weight and now are ardent new members. They are the bosses of my kitchen. So what they eat, I eat. And that is why this skinny chronicler, whose ribs are so bony they rip holes in my shirt, is on a Weight-Watcher's diet.

Trouble with me is that I lose weight in odd places. My fingers mostly. Last week I lost so much weight in my fingers that my ring dropped off. It fell right off while I was watching shrimp boats come in at New Harbor. Rolled in the gap between the planks and dropped 14 feet into the water below. When the tide went out, Wayne Gilbert got out his hip boots and slithered in the mud under the pilings to rescue it. That's the kind of scrape a skinny fellow gets into when there are Weight Watchers in his family.

The joys of eating and cooking have gone out the window at my house. Preparing food is now a joyless, scientific production.

When I look into the kitchen to see how dinner is coming along, there is no sign of food. All I see are two heads bent over reference books and charts. The ladies are bickering about 'balance'. Before they can agree on what to eat they must first chart out what each of them ate during the day. Since they are 60 miles apart during the day-time meals, this is a prolonged discussion.

Some nights negotiation about the menu takes 55 minutes. The ladies get side-tracked. Each starts trying to recall how much of what each ate for lunch. This leads to a description of the good-looking suit the lady eating nearby was wearing. That leads to a dress my wife saw in the Cricket Shop. That leads to a hat my daughter saw in Porteous' window. Which finally leads back to a decision that neither has eaten liver all week. And the Weight Watchers rule book says they must eat liver at least once a week.

I hear this news and shudder. I ate liver for lunch today. But I dare not mention this or dinner will never arrive.

One funny thing about this Weight-Watcher's diet is that the meals are bigger than non-diet meals. To lose weight, they eat more. Every burner on the stove has something burbling on it. Tonight, the ladies say, we will eat three vegetables, a salad plus that liver.

Dinner time is getting close now. I can tell because the scales get put on the dining table. That is right. Scales — on the table.

That is another funny thing about Weight Watchers. They weigh themselves only once a week — at class. But they weigh every morsel they eat, three times a day.

At table now, it is my job to weigh out the liver. "Six ounces" says my daughter. Because the ladies are on a diet, I dole out a modest portion. "That is only four ounces!" says my indignant daughter. I pile and pile until it reaches six on the scale. "That is more than you ever ate before you started dieting" I say, astonished at what a big pile six ounces of liver makes.

"Now measure out four ounces of these" she orders, handing me a dish of beets. Gingerly I drop two beets into the scales. "More . . more . . more" she instructs. When I have piled six beets into the scale she cries "Stop! Cut that last one in half!"

Next I must weigh out string beans. "This is our Group B vegetable" says my wife. "We eat four cups of Group B if raw, two cups if cooked." I looked baffled, but do it. That done, I weigh out stewed tomatoes — a messy job.

Finally my Weight Watching wife and daughter have their diet dinners in front of them. Never in their dietless days were their plates so full.

A shriek comes from my daughter "Heavens! We forgot our butter!" and she rushes to the refrigerator. "Butter? For Weight Watchers?" I query in surprise. "Well, it's not really butter" she says. "It is an imitation of margarine, which is an imitation of butter."

They measure out two tablespoons each of the stuff and smear it over everything. What is left, they eat raw — ugh!

I finish my modest dinner. But my two Weight Watchers are eating and eating and eating their way to thinness. "This is thirsty work" groans my wife, reaching for a sip from my glass. "No! No! Not that!" cries my daughter. "We can't touch soda! Only tomato juice for us!"

My wife looks gloomy and full. "I don't think I can swallow tomato juice!" she moans.

"Well, it is time for you to have your slice of bread" says my daughter. "You skipped your one-ounce slice of 100 per cent whole wheat bread." My wife munches her bread, as if doing penance.

Chalk up one more penalty for the non Weight Watcher in the family. Since only I am able to move, I must clear the table nowadays. When the ladies finally stir, they make it only as far as the sofa, fit only to do light embroidery, the kind with thin wool.

I take a walk under the stars with the Dalmatian dog. It is 10 p.m. when I get back and announce "I am going up to bed to read a while."

The ladies look at me with envious eyes. "Lord, I wish we could! But we have to eat some more. Weight Watchers require we drink two glasses of skimmed milk. Now we must make milk shakes."

About 11 p.m. I hear the whirr of the Waring mixer going down in the kitchen. By midnight I hear my dieting wife pad softly into our darkened bedroom. I pretend sleep. And hear her murmuring "Past midnight and I'm too full of food to sleep!" Then, on a cheerier note, she adds "But in two weeks, I've lost eight pounds!"

Father of the Bride

DAMARISCOTTA — Susan Caldwell, my only daughter these 23 years is now Mrs. William Fagan. The transition took 23 minutes.

But a clock is a foolish way to measure lives and the old or new bonds of love. Banks may open and close by the clock; planes and ships and trains may come and go by the minute hand. But immeasurable mystery measures that immeasurable distance from little girl to radiant bride.

The life-span of a Father of the Bride, however is short and specific, by the clock that is. From the moment my daughter took my arm for the bridal march down the aisle to meet her betrothed to the moment the rice and the rose petals cascaded upon the departure of bride and groom, the clock measured only 240 minutes; a mere four hours; a meagre half of a single work day.

That was the official life-span of this Father of the Bride.

Yet into those 240 fleeting minutes are packed more happiness and more sadness, more ecstasy and more ache, more tension and more peace, more joy for a new beginning and more tears for an ending, more elation and more emptiness than this mere male could take again.

Thanks be that God in sympathy for the limits of my staying power gave me but one daughter to cherish so long and give away so fast.

Today there is a big hole in my pocket, a big hole in my household and a bigger hole in my heart. But no one of them hurts. Each is a hole filled now with pleasure and not pain.

The short-lived life of a Father of the Bride is a kaleidoscope of bright surprises, known only to him. Camouflaged beneath that ascot and stick-pin and formal morning coat of the Father of the Bride a galaxy of raw emotions are erupting and thumping; exploding in the chest behind that stiff shirt front are rockets and fireworks of feelings never experienced before in my half a century on this good earth.

How did all the world change in only 240 minutes, I wonder?

Even now some of those brief hectic 240 minutes I cannot account for . . . But these moments I shall always remember.

I'll remember first the dawn when my nervous eyes opened, fearful Maine skies would be filled again with rain, but instead saw a strange fireball rising in the east, and a canopy of unblemished blue above the sky, and trees bending to a cooling sea-breeze . . . sights which after the almost 60 days of rain and fog I could hardly recognize.

Then I recall the absolutely ridiculous yet lovely picture of the Father of the Bride and the Father of the Groom working together hanging great gay bows to the fence posts around the driveway . . .

And the mid-morning sight of bridesmaids-to-be and ushers-to-be still dressed in cut-off jeans, dashing about in cars on unknown errands . . .

And I recall with admiration Cheryl, my daughter-in-law and my son John, her husband, driving in from a dawn shopping spree at the Boston flower market with a million flowers filling the back of a station wagon. And Cheryl, a master professional flower-arranger, toiling in a cool damp garage, surrounded by brigades of buckets sprouting exotic flowers . . . and John forever carrying into every upstairs room mammoth gorgeous arrangements she had made.

I recall John suddenly appearing immaculate and bossy in his full regalia as usher, taking final charge of the intricate time tables of events. John, my harum-scarum, long-haired, bearded son, looking dignified as an archbishop and commanding as a grand marshal, bossing luscious looking bridesmaids into line . . . signalling to the piper to start his bagpipes . . . and precisely on the dot escorting his mother to her Mother of the Bride seat. And his mother looking young and pretty as she did on her wedding day almost 30 years ago.

I remember lines of cars bringing guests, and the meadow where the altar stood and Father Henderson finely read an outdoor marriage service and Doris Marble played the organ, while the Damariscotta river in reflected happiness shone like a bed of diamonds in the sun.

Yes, I even recall every step of that long, long heartrending, heart filling walk with my daughter on my arm. Never had I seen a bride more beautiful and radiant. Never had a Father felt more proud to give away a prize he loved so much.

I hear clearly still the skirl of the bagpipes as piper Bill Bears from Gardiner plays 250 guests through the reception line, while I tried to call my daughter "Mrs. Fagan" once in a while for practice . . . I remember the little explosions of champagne corks popping . . . I remember the boys from Leavitt and Parris erecting those huge canopies and tents, decorative insurance against rain.

I hear the magnificent playing of Ed Petra's band from Waterville, and the sudden rush to dance. Then, suddenly I remember Susan on the balcony throwing her bridal bouquet to the single girls and her garter to the single boys . . . and moments later, I recall she and Bill Fagan dressed to sail to Nova Scotia . . . Rice and rose petals flew. They were gone.

The life of the Father of the Bride is short; 240 minutes from start to finish. But the memory will last forever.

SORE THROAT

MAINE MEDICAL CENTER — This is a funny spot to write a Thanksgiving column — sitting in a corridor outside the Radiology department, waiting my turn for the cobalt machine. But this is the right place indeed for me to write a column of thanks this Thanksgiving.

I owe thanks for a very big piece of good luck, which came right on top of some pretty bad luck.

The bad luck was this. . . For about six weeks this September and October my throat got hoarser and scratchier and I felt sure I had a prize-winning case of laryngitis. Then two weeks ago I found out it was cancer. That was the bad luck.

Now for the very good luck . . . The malignancy was found early; nipped in the bud while it was still small and young and had just begun to settle in on one of my vocal cords. Thanks to that early discovery, chances for total recovery are excellent — better than 96 per cent!

Because the doctors nailed it early, no surgery is needed in this case. Just cobalt treatments, every 48 hours for about six weeks. At the end of that time, they expect the malignancy will be stopped in its tracks completely and forever.

So I am lucky. That's why a Thanksgiving column written here outside the cobalt treatment room in Maine Medical. The key to success in this cancer business is early treatment. I got started early.

So if you know anyone whose voice has been strangely hoarse for three weeks or more, persuade that person to get a throat examination by a doctor now. The exam is easy. All you do is stick out your tongue, open wide and say "Eeeech!" a few times, and in five minutes, the exam is over.

The doctor may say it's just laryngitis, and tell you to cut out smoking or yelling at basketball games. Fine. That is cheap and good insurance.

But should there be anything else wrong, it will be spotted early.

I had never known that hoarseness is a sign of anything except laryngitis or too many cigarettes. I don't believe most lay persons regard continued hoarseness as a possible warning sign.

This may be the reason that many patients don't get to a doctor as soon as they should. For example, one of the foremost medical textbooks on throat cancer reports that a majority of patients do not begin treatment until eight months after they began suffering from hoarseness. The same report says these patients have visited their physicians before they get to a specialist and throat cancer is recognized and treatment started.

If this column is going to help anyone get an examination promptly, it will be because of specifics with which they can identify. So here are a few specifics . . . regarding my own timetable . . . and procrastination.

On Sept. 19, my diary shows, I went to bed for 24 hours with a bad cold. Then a week later, on Wednesday, Sept. 26 there is a notation . . . "My throat is sore still. Voice weak and hoarse. I have to make two speeches 48 hours hence, so I went today to see the doctor. He says stop talking, stop smoking, rest the voice and prescribes medicines."

Next diary entry about the throat is a month later, on Oct. 26. "Made a luncheon speech today, with a weak, hoarse voice. Croaked through 20 minute talk, then 40 minutes of questions. Finished the first batch of medicines and had prescriptions refilled a week ago. Still mighty hoarse. Friends tell me about colds settling in throat. Maybe. But (terrible pun) it's a pain in the neck."

A week later, on Wednesday, Oct. 31, the diary mentions the hoarseness again. "So mad at being hoarse still, I swung by the doctor's office. Had no appointment. But he squeezed me in. Told him I'd been hoarse well over a month now, Medicine had not helped . . . And voice getting worse. He took one long look. Then promptly made app't for me to see throat specialist this Friday. Maybe biopsy needed??? What's up??"

The action, slow to start, now moved very fast. Inside 48 hours the throat specialist had examined me in his office. He said candidly that he saw evidence of cancer. But it was small, early, certainly curable. He sent me immediately to hospital for blood tests and X-rays, etc., and booked me into operating room as an out-patient. Monday morning to do major examination under anesthetic and take tissue for biopsy.

I checked into hospital at 9 a.m. Monday, and out by 1 p.m. All quick and easy and reassuring.

At 4:30 p.m. Tuesday, the throat specialist phoned to tell me the biopsy confirmed a small cancer on one vocal cord. The next day he conferred with other specialists. On Friday he saw me. Told me that all doctors agreed cobalt treatments would do the job completely, thanks to early diagnosis. "I have set the first appointment for you at 10 a.m. Monday Nov. 12 in the Radiology Department at Maine Medical . . . "

So here I sit today, waiting for my seventh treatment. I am a new member of the out-patient club here. Patients who drive in for daily doses and soon become smiling, friendly acquaintances. Nurses and technicians are young, expert and pretty. Doctors are young, expert and reassuring. More on MMC's Radiology Club in which I have temporary membership in a later column.

I am very lucky. The key piece of luck was that unscheduled appointment with my doctor on Oct. 31. If he had been unable to squeeze me in, I might have gone off the next day travelling on assignment. Kept on sucking on lozenges and cursing cigarettes and being hoarse. Then when I got home again, I would not have seen the doctor until after Thanksgiving or maybe after Christmas. After all, except for a croaking voice, I was feeling fine; and who doesn't get laryngitis? But a two month's delay like that might have had nasty consequences.

It is easy to understand how it can take eight months for patients suffering from hoarseness to get to the right doctor. But that delay can be a tough penalty. So if you know anyone who has been hoarse a month — be a real friend and get them to the doctor!

I am lucky I got treatment started very early. And that is why I'm outside the cobalt room here, giving thanks this Thanksgiving, fog-horn voice and all.

CANCER CHECK-UP—ONE YEAR LATER

MAINE MEDICAL CENTER — One year ago, the cobalt treatments for cancer in my throat ended. This week I went for my big 'one-year-after' check-up, with a twinge of anxiety.

I think every former cancer patient is a bit tense, a bit worried at every checkup. The checkups are to see if there is any sign of spread or recurrence of cancer. A lot rides on these visits. Under a mound of optimism, I hide a tiny knot of fear, as each exam begins. Most of us begin with checkups every 30 days. After six months, I graduated to every 60 days.

One year after cancer was found on my vocal chords, and was treated with cobalt 60 radiation, these things have happened . . . First, I feel fine and my voice is back to normal. Second, I have gained 20 pounds — up from 140 to 160, and hope the scales stop there. The gain may be because I stopped smoking and began eating snacks. Third, where the rays were hitting no beard grows. No need to shave there. A slight swelling, a little tenderness is there. If I catch cold, it is apt to focus on this area of my throat. Those are the only aftermaths of my cancer and my cobalt treatment.

I walk out grinning with gratitude inside. Today is the brightest, sunniest, greenest, best day of the year.

Two women, one small boy, one man, waiting at a bus stop, swing their heads around, look at me, startled. Instead of walking down the city sidewalk, I'm doing a dance — hop-skip-jump-hop.

Yet I am just a beginner. This is only a first anniversary. In Maine alone, thousands of former cancer patients are celebrating a 'clean-bill of health' anniversary; their first, fifth or 15th, every such anniversary is a joyful, grateful, notch on the stock of time. Happy anniversaries — wherever you are this day!

I walk and instead of seeing stores and people on the sidewalk, I see the other patients. Was it only last December we sat near each other day after day, week after week, sitting in Maine Medical Center, waiting our turn for our radiation treatment of our cancer?

We used to nod, smile, chat a moment with each other. Then as our treatments ended we'd share a handshake of good luck.

This day I remember all your faces, men, women and little children. Our friendships were often nameless, were almost unspoken. But we felt close to each other, like people in the same lifeboat, being rescued together, who have never been introduced. Happy anniversaries to all!

Can it be only one year ago? Last year when my cancer was discovered, most people avoided saying the word 'cancer' out loud to me. In a lot of places, if you had cancer you had an unmentionable disease. Friends, when they heard the news, wrote a cancer patient off, as if their number was up, treated a cancer patient with strange solicitude.

I remember vividly the debate over whether or not I should write a series of columns in a newspaper about the discovery and the treatment of my own case of cancer. Inside my own family there was, for a while strong opposition. And that was only a year ago. Today newspapers and magazines carry articles galore, complete with illustrations, on all aspects of cancer. On TV, women demonstrate self examination of their breasts. As a result, fewer people will suffer with unvoiced fears; and more will be treated early and cured.

Two women have done this. The cancer operation on Betty Ford, wife of the President, and Happy Rockefeller, wife of the Vice President, were sad occasions. Yet they have done more good for more people than Mrs. Ford or Mrs. Rockefeller dreamed was possible in their lives. The world will never know how many lives are saved because Mrs. Ford and Mrs. Rockefeller had (perhaps endured is the better word) the discovery and treatment of their cancers in the blazing glare of the press.

In Maine, we are lucky. At the same time this new public awareness about cancer is having its impact on us, Maine gets wonderful new equipment, magnificent new facilities and expert new talents for treating cancer.

This is the new Southern Maine Radiation Therapy Institute at Maine Medical Center in Portland, serving 17 towns and cities. Several million dollars have just been expertly spent to build and equip this cancer-treatment facility. Maine now has talent as expert and equipment as sophisticated as you can find in almost any major hospital in any major city of the United States.

This Southern Radiation Therapy Institute serving most of southern Maine is a frantically busy place.

For Maine has one of the highest incidence of cancer per capita in the Union. Out of a million people in Maine, 150,000 will get some kind of cancer. And about 50 per cent of all these cancer patients need radiation therapy. And now in Maine, they can get the very best — along with chemo-therapy, surgery, nuclear medicine.

I watch the men and women and teen agers go through the hospital doors. Hundreds are heading to the new Radiation and Diagnostic facility. This year Maine men and women and youngsters will get over 90,000 exams here; they'll get over 12,000 radiation treatments here; and over 10,000 nuclear medicine procedures.

Almost certainly, among those who get treatment will be people you know; know very well; maybe one of them will be you, just as a year ago one of them was me.

SEA DOG—OR NO DOG?

ABOARD STEER CLEAR — I am trying to make a sea-dog out of Piper, my young Dalmatian. And that may be a mistake. In 18 months of living, Piper has survived strychnine poisoning and being hit by a car. But making a sea-dog out of her may be the death of both of us.

Piper is on her first short cruise with us. At dawn this morning I swore it would be her last.

Piper loves to chew soft things. Last night she did. While Barbara and I slept in the forward cabin, Piper had a party aft. During the nighttime, she climbed onto the navigator's table and helped herself to a big box of soft tissues and a big bunch of soft, lush grapes which my wife stows there for some reason unfathomable by me.

Piper demolished both in a private orgy. At dawn, the afterdeck looked like a street cleaner's nightmare. My immaculate deck was ankle deep in shredded Kleenex. A slippery mess of grape skins was glued to the woodwork. And sprinkled like pepper over it all were remnants of my softest socks, which Piper had ripped off a clothes line.

By dawn's early light, this long-suffering man went to work with broom and dustpan, bucket and mop — clean-up guy for the dog. The dog lay luxuriously on the boat cushions, tail wagging in delight at the sight. She gave small barks of encouragement at me. I snarled back at her.

That chore done, I poured a steaming cup of coffee from the galley and took it forward to the bow. In splendid isolation, I could sit there sipping coffee and watch the sun come up, burning haze off the glassy sea and lifting the fog curtain yard by lovely yard from the island shore 300 feet away. This is a boatman's treasured joy; total removal from man's world, brief and frenetic and bickering and total immersion in nature's world, everlasting, orderly and peaceful. A man can hear the music of the planets as he sips coffee alone with the sunrise over the ocean.

Sea Dog — Or No Dog? / 313

Then came the hellish havoc, the split seconds of catastrophe caused by a Dalmatian dog . . . Wet black nose suddenly is thrust under my elbow; scalding coffee is spilled over pajamaed man; man yells like a fiend; scared dog leaps backward, falls overboard from the bow, six feet down to icy ocean; and panic-struck dog seems to sink. Idiot owner impulsively dives to rescue dog.

Suddenly ocean shock submerges owner. Spluttering, shivering owner surfaces. Excited dog thinks she's discovered new game. Barks joyously, circling owner playfully. Infuriated owner reaches out to grab crazy dog. Dog swims off. Owner swims after dog. Dog accelerates. Dog paddle outdistances owner's crawl stroke.

Man's brain begins to operate. He abandons fruitless swim-chase after dog and heads for dinghy. Scrambles over gunwale, scraping belly painfully on oarlock. All frozen thumbs now, owner unties dinghy from boat and slams thumb as he puts oars into oarlocks. Noisy commotion mixed with loud blue language wakes sleeping wife. Dog swimming merrily straight out to sea, full speed ahead for Spain.

Wringing wet owner rows in hot pursuit. Finally catches up with dog. Tries hauling animal aboard. Tricky. Comes close to capsizing twice. Rescues ungrateful beast from sea. Beast proud and happy after first long swim in ocean. Owner unhappy. Heads back to boat, swearing at dog.

New noise. Noise of wife laughing heart out. Sleeping wife is now wide awake on deck, bent double with laughter at sight.

"Is Piper all right?" She asks this as her husband, gasping and blue, grabs the handrail. "I'll get a towel for Piper. Then hand her up to me. The poor dog must be half frozen."

With a snarl, I hand up the soaking wet beast. The animal safely back on board, shakes himself, wildly, drenching my new boat cushions, dripping all over my immaculate decks. Wife Barbara wraps dog lovingly in my biggest towel . . . and rubs the beast down.

Ignored after my ordeal, I clamber aboard, freezing cold and sopping wet.

"Strip right there!" orders my ever loving wife "before you mess up the boat. I'll get you a towel as soon as I have dried Piper!" Naked and alone and goose-pimpled, I stand.

"Next cruise, that dog stays on shore!" I growl.

"Never!" says Barbara, as she towels down Piper.

She wraps Piper carefully in the towel. Then slowly goes to fetch one for her husband.

I glare at the dog. The dog turns her blue eyes up to me. And wags her tail.

And — curse it — I reach down and pat her. The wet tail speeds up, thumping out a drum of joy on the deck.

HOW CAN YOU MISS A SPOTTED DOG SO MUCH?

DAMARISCOTTA — Our spotted dog, Piper the blue-eyed Dalmatian, is back home after a month at college.

Piper, despite her advanced age of two and a half years, went off to learn new tricks at Frank Hazeltine's training school for dogs at Pittsfield on the 11th of June and was fetched home on 11th July.

Price for room, board and lessons at the Hazeltine academy for hounds is $5 a day, and the dog stays 30 days.

How much did Piper learn? Was it worth the money? What's more — was it worth the separation?

Well, first let me say Frank Hazeltine is about as nice a man with dogs (and maybe people too) as you'll find in New England. And as expert a trainer of bird dogs as you'll find anywhere.

But this was the first and maybe the last time — anybody had wished a Dalmatian onto Frank.

"Frank" I said "all we want this dog to learn is to come when she's called. Come quickly. But come, for sure . . . We go island visiting on our boat," I told Frank. "And there is nothing we hate more than trying to track down Piper far out to sea on an uninhabited, rocky, forest crowned island, thick with underbrush."

Nothing makes a man feel more foolish than standing on shore, yelling at an empty island for a dog that won't come. The tide is going. The sun is going. The night is coming. But the dog isn't. When a man yells and feels foolish, that man gets angry, and still more angry.

And there is nothing more foolish than an angry man yelling his head off on an empty island far at sea for a dog nobody can see.

That's a situation not to be repeated. Ever. Even at a cost of $150.

That's why Piper went to school.

And, praise be to Frank Hazeltine, Piper comes racing when called. I am not going into Frank's tricks of the trade; or try to tell how he trains a dog to come, stay, flush birds, retrieve, wait — do a score of things on command. But he does it all without ever hurting a dog.

But once a dog is trained, only the owner can keep that dog trained. Unless the owner keeps up the training by religiously setting aside a few minutes for 'refresher training' every day, the dog will stop obeying all too quickly. And all the time and money spent on training is wasted.

These early mornings and late evenings Barbara and I and Piper go for walks along the edge of the river. The dog goes running off on a scent. Stays out of sight for quite a while. Then Barbara puts the little whistle to her lips and blows, blows again; blows once more and calls the dog. Soon we hear noise in the underbrush — and see a flash of white-with-black spots. Piper's head emerges some distance off, swings about, getting a fix on just where the sound of the whistle and the call came from. Barbara repeats them. Then in a gallop Piper arrives, and drops to the ground at Barbara's feet, waiting for a patting as her reward.

On other occasions, I do the training. But two of us never do it at the same time. A dog gets muddled when two people give commands at the same time.

"I never had a dog like this before" said Frank over the phone, soon after we'd left Piper with him. "This dog has no purpose in life," said Frank, who is used to retrievers and bird dogs only.

Frank never knew what those innocent words would trigger . . . "No purpose in life?" I yelled down the phone. "You don't know Piper . . . The moment after she wakes up each morning, she is filled with purpose . . . First purpose is to eat the cats' breakfast before the cats get there. Then to get outside for a sniff at the smells of the night animals before the sun weakens them. Next to come back inside and race to the bedroom. Filled with purpose, Piper puts her cold wet nose and her dew-damp paws onto the head of sleeping Barbara. Wakes her. Licks her morning face.

"Next purpose is to talk me into opening the box where I keep a few spare dog biscuits as a morning snack. When those half dozen purposes in life are accomplished, by 5:30 a.m., Piper's next goal in life is to wheedle her way under the covers and catch forty winks at Barbara's feet . . . By 7:30, her purpose is to chase the cats around the property . . . Then to race down to the fields and chase off the big, strutting fish crows."

Another purpose I explained to dog trainer Frank Hazeltine is that my Dalmatian sits back and howls gorgeously whenever the fire siren sounds in town. And she sings the same way even if the only siren is on Emergency Squad on TV . . . "Piper" I say "is filled with higher purposes in life than merely retrieving birds."

Frank Hazeltine taught Piper a lot, for which I am most grateful. But one thing he couldn't teach her was to stop shedding. My boat, my car, my carpets, my clothes were almost free of black and white hairs after Piper had been away for a few weeks. Now she's been back a day or two, everything is covered with her trademarks again. That dog has to eat a lot just to generate the energy to keep growing replacements for all the hair she sheds each day. Last time I counted she shed 2,678 hairs in one hour.

I'm glad she is back. I missed that dog more than I care to say.

I missed her when I drove up into the drive and no idiot dog came bouncing out to the car almost knocking me down when I got out, arms filled with stuff. (Frank taught her never to jump up — thank heaven!) . . . I missed seeing her run in wild circles flat out, belly to the ground fast and beautiful as a race horse . . . I missed her sitting out on the lawn, haughty nose in the air, surveying the world as though she owned it all . . . Oh hell, I missed the fool dog more than a man ought to miss a dog. And I am mighty glad the stupid animal is home, shedding her hairs all over me.

How Can You Miss A Spotted Dog So Much? /

How to Keep Warm Without Oil

DAMARISCOTTA — Great discoveries have often been made by mistake. And last night I made mine. It's called: "How to feel Hot without Burning any Oil." It is simple.

First, lay a fire in every fireplace and every stove in the house. At least three stoves or fireplaces are required, each needing different size kindling wood and logs, to play this game.

Now turn all thermostats way down — not just to 65, but way down, right off the dial. That brings you the first warming glow of virtue. The oil burner is off. Zero oil consumption, on a December night in Maine. I'm ready to start the game. Follow me, and see how it is played . . .

Put a match to the kindling and tiny logs just laid in the littlest Franklin of them all — an antique Wood, Bishop Number One made in Bangor generations ago. This tiny firebox wolfs down logs no more than 10 inches long. Despite the size, the little stove quickly throws off a warm and cheery glow.

Next move into the living room. Put a match to the fire laid here in the fine full sized hearth. This devours logs up to 36 inches long. Watch, half mesmerized. The flames leap and logs crackle and the big room begins to warm up without oil.

"Now, for the cold upstairs," you tell yourself. "You hauled up wood for the big Franklin in the study. So light it, and work by its warmth tonight."

In my study is a big black Good Times Franklin stove. It sits handsomely on a fine brick hearth. Putting the match to the first fire in this Franklin is a special occasion. Since the house was built, that Franklin has never worked as a fireplace.

Reason is that years ago, just before our first guests were coming to our new home, my wife walked into my messed up study. She saw copy paper, research books and folders and carbons spread everywhere and let out a shriek of horror: "This room is a pig-sty! Our first guests arrive in 30 minutes! And I want you to pour drinks in here!"

I calmed her. I blithely promised my room would be immaculate in 15 minutes. I remember gathering up all my files and reference books and photographs. I got four armloads of them. I opened the sliding cast iron doors of that fine Good Times Franklin stove. Then heaved the lot inside, slammed shut the doors. The mess was out of sight before the guests arrived, and stayed there seven years.

Last weekend, years later I took out those missing files, and the Franklin is a stove again instead of a hiding place for lost papers.

I light this third fire. With amazement, I see smoke go properly up the chimney. And I am warmed again, this time by a glow of pride in having three fires going at once.

"Bill!" my wife calls from the family room-kitchen "Our little Franklin has burnt up all its tiny logs! Bring more before the fire dies out!"

I run down two flights into the cellar. Grab my axe and start splitting big logs into tiny logs for the miniature stove. Twenty minutes later, the little Franklin is brightly burning again. A fresh pile of logs in readiness beside it. The room is hot; I sink into a chair in front of the pretty fire.

"Bill," says my wife "before you get too comfortable, check on the wood in the living room. While you were chopping I put on the last two logs."

"I'm going up to the study to write!" I call out.

It is more than warm, it is plain hot now. Is it the exercise? Or the fire? The first roaring fire in the Franklin-that-was-a-filing-cabinet demands my admiration. I sit in front of it, and admire. Put on another log. Admire more. Then go reluctantly to the typewriter.

Five paragraphs later, I shed my sweater. At the bottom of page two, I take off my wool shirt. There is no oil heat in the house; but it is too darned hot.

Suddenly I smell smoke, I rush into the living room. OK there. Then the family room, where Barbara is jiggling the damper. "Check the chimney outside" she says. I do. It looks fine. "The wood is green" I diagnose professionally. Gingerly I remove a wet smoking log, throw it out. Then disappear into the cellar. This time to haul up older, drier wood.

Fifteen minutes later, I am back at the typewriter. My study is hot as a Turkish bath now. The Good Times stove is too big for this room. It makes a fine filing cabinet. I strip to the waist as I begin on page four.

By now it is time for the 11 p.m. news, so I quit work and head for the TV and Barbara. In the living room, a huge fire blazes and the dog sleeps nearby. In the family room, a tiny fire burns and a marmalade cat sleeps nearby. But no wife, no Barbara.

"I'm out here, out on the porch!" she calls, and I find her outside breathing deep on a December night, and star gazing. "I had to come out for some cold clean air." Then she saw me — stripped to the waist — "Is it as hot as that in your study, too?"

We watched the late news in the living room, windows now wide open to cool it off. "Let's go to bed to get cool!" suggests Barbara. There is no fire in there. "It ought to be cold and lovely! Come on!"

"I can't. I gotta stay and watch these fires go out. We just can't go to bed with three fires burning in the house!"

What gets into fires after 11 p.m.? Up until then, they are always on the verge of going out. But at bed time, they change. They won't burn up the wood. I walk from room to room, trying to get three fires to quit burning so I can go to sleep. The clocks strike midnight. Still the flames flicker high.

Finally, at 1 a.m., the fires die down. Finally I escape the heat, and make it to that nice cold, fireless bedroom.

There is my discovery: To Keep Hot Without Burning Oil, just tend three different size fireplaces in three different rooms, and you'll be so busy lugging and hauling, poking and banking, that your body heat gets so high you'll end up wearing swimming trunks in December.

Shouting Thanks
into the Silent Night

I was reading old news clippings about Thanksgiving in Maine long ago, when my wife called out, "Put down those old news clips! Come help make the turkey stuffing."

Oyster dressing. Chestnuts and sausage dressing. A strange new world, peeling chestnuts, chopping nuts, slicing celery, tearing up bread, peeling onions, shucking oysters, browning sausage meat, and then anointing it all with a holy mixture of sage, thyme, parsley, cumin. "Make room!" called my wife. "Here are the cranberries to work on!"

Then came pearly onions to peel, and orange and lemon rinds to cut up. I earned promotion to some astonishing work with mincemeat for the mince pies, pouring on a bit more rum and brandy. I sat on a stool, inhaling the heady aroma, and thinking that holidays would be even better if men always had a hand in the cooking.

"Take a walk outside in the night air!" urged Barbara. "Or you'll sniff all the goodness out of that mince!"

I whistled up Piper, my Dalmatian, and went out into the night. The November sky was brilliantly alive with a million scintillating stars. Starlight shone on the river. Bare big oaks creaked in the cold. Their naked limbs stood gaunt and ageless against the sky. Silence hung everywhere, part of the cold night. And the clean cold air felt wonderful on the flesh and tasted wonderful inside as I stood filling my lungs, looking in awe at the high arc of starlit sky.

Thanksgiving. Giving thanks. Thanks for being alive in Maine. Thanks for the stars and the oaks and the river and the clean cold night. Thanks for the house behind me and all the love and the warmth of family and friends it contained. Thanks for Chiloe, the 5-month-old grandaughter coming tomorrow. Thanks for a job that lets me roam this state and talk to Maine people.

The cold gets to me and I run back to the house. Hand on the door, an impulse hits. I look up to the sky, take a deep breath and shout . . . "Thanks! Thanks! Thanks!" The shout panics Barbara at the stove. It brings the dog Piper hurtling up to see what is wrong. But shouting out "thanks" into the silent night is a good idea. Try it.

SIGN OUT

When you are doing a book about Maine, the difficulty is stopping.

Here is the stopping place for this book. But not because there is any end to "Enjoying Maine". The joys of Maine are never-ending. They change and they multiply.

These columns have barely touched on a few aspects of Maine, as enjoyed by one man's family.

Yet the final question is "How has it panned out — this move to Maine?"

Ed McHale asked us that question one recent night. Ed McHale had been our close friend since Barbara and I were married in 1944. He had known us in New York, Washington, London; working on Madison Avenue, in the State Department, and on glossy magazines. Now he sat in our Maine house, asking how the move to Maine had panned out after a dozen years.

Barbara's answer was: "The only way I'll ever leave here is in a pine box, feet first."

My answer was corny but accurate: "The best years of our lives." John and Susan, although they were 14 and 15 when they came to Maine told him: "Maine is our home. Maine is where our roots are."